Strange Facts About the Bible

Also available from Random House Value Publishing:

Asimov's Guide to the Bible

The Christian Book of Why

The Complete Bible Quiz Book

3,285 Bible Questions and Answers

Test Your Bible I.Q.

What the Bible Really Says

Strange Facts About the Bible

Over 400 fascinating facts about the Bible and its people

Webb Garrison

Testament Books
New York

This 2000 edition is published by Testament Books™, an imprint of Random House Value Publishing, Inc., 201 East 50th Street, New York, New York 10022.

Testament Books™ and design are trademarks of Random House Value Publishing, Inc.

Random House
New York • Toronto • London • Sydney • Auckland
http://www.randomhouse.com/

Printed and bound in the United States of America

A CIP catalog record for this book is available from the Library of Congress.

ISBN 0-517-20828-8

8 7 6 5 4 3 2 1

To
Cindy
and
Beth

Foreword

Because the Bible is almost universally available in the western world, we tend to look upon it as commonplace. Cataracts of familiarity dull our eyes, and we seldom see it as a key factor in the drama of developing civilization.

This volume is in no sense offered as a scholarly contribution to the understanding of the Bible, its background, and its role in human affairs. Rather, it is a popular treatment of more than four hundred topics which have in common the ingredients of human interest and "strangeness."

I hope the contents and arrangement are such that it will be useful as a reference book in public and church libraries. I am confident that teachers, speakers, and interpreters of Scripture will find here a great deal of lively material short enough to be readily useable. But I particularly hope that the general public—including both those persons who have read the Bible from childhood and great numbers of others who have never come into real encounter with it—will develop a new sense of the drama and thrill of Scripture as a result of discovering its uniqueness through the pages of this volume.

Arrangement of material into subject-matter categories is for the most part rather loose and tentative. A great deal of material on "Life in Bible Lands" can be found, for example, outside the chapter bearing that title. Use of the comprehensive index will facilitate quick identification of material bearing upon particular interests.

Spelling of names is based largely upon *The Interpreter's Dictionary of the Bible* plus *Webster's Biographical Dictionary* and *Webster's Geographical Dictionary*. Unless otherwise indicated, Scripture quotations are from the King James Version.

This volume is suggestive rather than exhaustive. That is, it clearly does not treat all the unusual aspects of the Bible and its effects upon civilization. Selection of topics to be treated has been guided by the hope that they will be particularly interesting and useful; hundreds of other strange facts about the Bible could have been included had space permitted. Volumes listed in the bibliography have been essential to the preparation of this book; many of them will be of special interest to readers. For the most part, titles indicate the general areas of emphasis.

My wife not only participated in the initial planning and the research for this volume, she also prepared the final draft of the manuscript.

I sincerely hope that as you read and use our work, you will have as much genuine pleasure as we did in preparing it.

Webb Garrison

Contents

Scripture Had It First!

Earliest "Humane Society"

According to most reference books a reform-minded American is responsible for emphasis upon kind treatment of animals. It's true that Henry Bergh, inspired by earlier work in England and Scotland, founded the world's biggest humane society in 1866. But at least three thousand years before the New York movement was chartered, every Hebrew community constituted an informal society for prevention of cruelty to animals.

Moses' Law required every man to lead a stray ox or ass back to its owner—even if that owner happened to be a personal enemy (Exod. 23:4). No matter who the animal belonged to, a person who found a donkey unable to get on its feet because of his load was required to give the beast a hand (Exod. 23:5). And in New Testament times even severe laws prohibiting all kinds of work on the sabbath were relaxed on behalf of mercy to animals. A God-fearing man could perform no sabbath labor at all on imperative personal tasks, yet if a beast was in trouble, he was not simply permitted but positively encouraged to get busy and rescue the animal (Luke 14:5). At first literally and then in figurative senses, "an ox is in the ditch" came to indicate an emergency grave enough to warrant violation of customary restrictions on work.

Mouth-to-Mouth Resuscitation by Elisha

Late in the 1950's rescue workers who had spent years teaching artificial respiration made a dramatic discovery. In lieu of attempting a clumsy and often ineffective system of alternately pressing and releasing the ribs of a stricken person they found it to be possible for one to blow his own breath into the respiratory system of a victim whose lungs aren't functioning. Such mouth-to-mouth resuscitation requires no training and little skill or physical stamina.

Hailed as a radical breakthrough in the ceaseless struggle to save lives, the new system was widely publicized. Then it came to the attention of persons intimately acquainted with the Old Testament. This product of twentieth-century ingenuity, pointed out Bible readers, probably represents a rediscovery of a method known to early Hebrews.

A detailed account of one rescue by the prophet Elisha is preserved. Confronted by a widow's grief over her son who was "dead, and laid upon his bed," Elisha took dramatic action. "He went up, and lay upon the child, and put his mouth upon his mouth, and his eyes upon his eyes, and his hands upon his hands: and he stretched himself upon the child; and the flesh of the child waxed warm" (II Kings 4:34).

Though the story includes no term equivalent to "mouth-to-mouth resuscitation," the description is so convincing that Chicago's Museum of Science and Industry put up a display crediting Elisha with being the first man known to practice this form of lifesaving.

Physical Exams for Priests

Acting to protect the good name of Jehovah, Moses established rules for the world's first physical examination.

He decreed that descendants of Aaron should form the manpower pool from which priests should be drawn. But it was not enough for an aspirant to be "of the seed of Aaron" (or, later, of Levi). In order to dramatize and symbolize the absolute purity of his God, Moses made lack of physical blemishes a condition for service at the altar. Only men who had been examined and found completely sound were permitted to approach the holy place in order to go through the ceremony of offering up bread.

Moses stipulated: "For whatsoever man he be that hath a blemish, he shall not approach: a blind man, or a lame, or he that hath a flat nose, or any thing superfluous, or a man that is brokenfooted, or brokenhanded, or crookedbacked, or a dwarf, or that hath a blemish in his eye, or be scurvy, or scabbed, or hath his stones [testicles] broken" (Lev. 21:18-20).

Anticipating by centuries the selective service system set up by modern military leaders, Moses didn't absolutely eliminate blemished men from service of the Lord; they were permitted to perform tasks that did not require them to enter the sanctuary. That is, they were drafted for duty but because of their handicaps were assigned to posts where physical standards were less rigorous.

A Document as a Reminder

Though primitive forms of writing were practiced a great deal earlier, the first recorded instance of a deliberate plan to preserve history by preparing a written record occurs in Scripture.

Under the leadership of Joshua, Israelites seeking a new home in Canaan fought a decisive battle with the forces of King Amalek on the field of Rephidim. This engagement probably took place in the thirteenth century B.C. It was so important that after Joshua had "discomfited Amalek and his people with the edge of the sword" (Exod. 17:13), a divine message came to Moses instructing him to make a lasting record of the victory: "And the Lord said unto Moses, Write this for a memorial in a book, and rehearse it in the ears of Joshua: for I will utterly put out the remembrance of Amalek from under heaven" (Exod. 17:14).

Obviously, it wasn't a book of modern form that Moses used; this now universal device wasn't invented until centuries later. In 1962 translators of a new English-language edition of the Jewish Torah (or Five Books of Moses) rendered the divine message: "Inscribe this in a document as a reminder, and read it aloud to Joshua. . . ."

If Moses' "book"—or a portion of it—has survived as a long quotation within a historical section of Scripture, it can't be positively identified. But our ignorance about what he wrote in no way reduces the significance of the fact that the record of his call to authorship still survives.

Primitive Recipe for Sacred Perfume

Most or all peoples of the ancient Near East used perfumes, unguents, and aromatic compounds in their religious rites. But directions for compounding them were closely guarded secrets, passed down orally from each generation of priests to the next. Practically all such recipes perished. Hence the earliest recorded formula for the preparation of perfume appears in Scripture where personal or secular use of it is strictly forbidden.

"And the Lord said unto Moses, Take unto thee sweet spices, stacte, and onycha, and galbanum; these sweet spices with pure frankincense: of each there shall be a like weight: And thou shalt make it a perfume, a confection after the art of the apothecary, tempered together, pure and holy: And thou shalt beat some of it very small, and put of it before the testimony [or "witness" constituted by the scroll of the Law] in the tabernacle of the congregation, where I will meet with thee: it shall be unto you most holy. And as for the perfume which thou shalt make, ye shall not make to yourselves according to the composition thereof: it shall be unto thee holy for the Lord." (Exod. 30:34-37.)

Once having taken the radical step of making public his recipe for compounding the precious stuff, Moses warned his followers and descendants of dire consequences from bootleg or black market dealings in it. Banishment—a sentence just short of execution—was the automatic punishment for offenders. "Whosoever shall make like unto that, to smell thereto, shall even be cut off from his people." (Exod. 30:38.) To this day international perfume merchants refuse to publish their formulas and treat them as closely guarded secrets.

Crude Form of "Life Insurance"

Whether they developed the institution independently or adapted it from other tribesmen is uncertain, but the Hebrews left behind the first documentary account of a primitive move toward "life insurance" designed to ease the burden of a woman who lost her husband.

Technically known as the *mohar,* a stipulated capital fund was required from every bridegroom. One of the important negotiations preliminary to arriving at a formal marriage engagement was that of agreeing upon a figure satisfactory to both the suitor and his prospective father-in-law. Payment was more likely to be reckoned in terms of oxen, goats, donkeys, labor, or agricultural products than in money. Since the dowry is specifically mentioned three times in Scripture (Gen. 34:12; Exod. 22:16; I Sam. 18:25), scholars believe it was a firmly established and generally observed institution.

In spite of the fact that the nearest English equivalent to the Hebrew term is "purchase price," this fund didn't belong to the father of the bride. He simply had the use of it during his own life if his son-in-law outlived him. Should the latter die, the father of the widow was bound by tribal law to turn her dowry over to her. Title to it automatically reverted to the child if a woman bore a son during her father's life.

Crude as it was by modern standards—and almost unbelievably complicated to administer—this ancient Hebrew custom marks the earliest known plan for providing a stipulated capital fund to a widow in her time of financial crisis after losing her husband.

Dim Beginnings of the Dairy Industry

Throughout the western world most persons consider milk and milk products to be staple items of human diet. As in the case of present-day Hindus, whose relationship with the cow is shaped by their reverence for it, many early peoples refused to touch the milk of the sacred beast. The first recorded use of cow's milk is found in Scripture.

Even the Hebrews weren't enthusiastic about it, however. Like most of their contemporaries they were fond of goat's milk plus curds and soft cheese made from it. Though individual black goats of Palestine didn't yield much milk, so many of the animals were kept that supplies of the liquid food drawn from them were usually abundant. This is clearly indicated by proverbial references such as those in Prov. 27:27 and Prov. 30:33.

A reference to "milk from the flock" (Deut. 32:14 RSV) suggests that regardless of how little enthusiasm they displayed, Hebrews were the first to record dim beginnings of the modern dairy industry. Most doubt that they drank cow's milk raw. Instead they made some ancient forerunner of cottage cheese—which they valued sufficiently to mention in a list of foods that included fine wheat, wine, and fat from animals of the herd. Not quite certain what substance was indicated by the obscure Hebrew word used in the earliest reference to dairy products, translators of the King James Version settled for "butter of kine."

Since good pastureland was scarce even during the period when Palestine was described as "flowing with milk and honey," it is unlikely that Hebrews kept herds of dairy cattle, as such. They probably reared a few animals for use as beasts of burden and took incidental advantage of milk yielded by them at the time of calving.

A Start Toward a Selective Service System

Man enjoys the doubtful distinction of being the only creature other than the rat who deliberately kills within his own ranks for reasons other than hunger. Wars were fought before the beginning of recorded history. Every culture of which we have any record has had one or a variety of ways to go about recruiting an army while striving to keep civilian patterns of life from being torn apart. Far the earliest record of anything approaching a draft law with specific standards for exemption from military service is preserved in Scripture.

Descendants of Abraham knew none of the modern distinctions between church and state. For them every war was a holy war. From childhood a boy was taught to fight fearlessly, even against apparently hopeless odds, because Jehovah marched with the troops to the field of battle and fought to deliver his chosen people.

Whether or not they were consistently observed in practice, precise regulations stipulated the conditions under which a man was expected to keep his status as a civilian even in time of national emergency. These earliest exemptions, aimed at resolving a dilemma that the most advanced nations on earth still face, are stipulated in Deut. 20:5-8.

A man who had built a house but had not dedicated it was not subject to conscription for fear that he might die in battle and leave the new dwelling place behind to be dedicated by another. One who had gone through the laborious process of setting out a vineyard but who had not yet gathered grapes from it was likewise exempt. Finally, in a provision still reflected in modern draft laws of many lands, an engaged man whose marriage had not been consummated was not expected to fight for his country, the period of deferment for newlyweds being one year (Deut. 24:5).

Prototype of the Lie Dectector

Use of the lie detector, a device whose effectiveness depends upon physical reactions triggered by psychological factors, is not a twentieth-century innovation. A crude but probably effective ordeal based on the principle that guilt affects response was employed in Old Testament days.

A woman accused of adultery was led to a priest who created a charged atmosphere by escorting her into a holy place "before the Lord." Then he mixed dust from the floor of the tabernacle with consecrated water to form what he called "the bitter water that causeth the curse." With her head uncovered, the woman then took part in a ritual oath. "The Lord make thee a curse and an oath among thy people," said the priest, "when the Lord doth make thy thigh to rot, and thy belly to swell." Then the woman was required to say, "Amen, amen."

After the curse was written in a book and a special "jealousy offering" was made, the accused woman had to drink the water made potent by both incantations and dust from the holy place. "And when he hath made her to drink the water, then it shall come to pass, that, if she be defiled, and have done trespass against her husband, that the water that causeth the curse shall enter into her, and become bitter, and her belly shall swell, and her thigh shall rot. . . . And if the woman be not defiled, but be clean; then she shall be free, and shall conceive seed." (Num. 5:27-28.)

A Joker and a Jawbone

History and literature are filled with accounts of practical jokers and their exploits. If all such stories were compiled, they would form an immense book. But the most ancient of them all in such an anthology would come from Scripture.

The first habitual trickster whose pranks were recorded in literature that still survives (Judg. 14-16) was the hero of the tribe of Dan, Samson. Since his name is formed from the Hebrew word for "sun," it probably meant something like "child of the sun"—equivalent to "mighty prince."

A peasant with great physical strength but not too much brain power, Samson spent much of his life in the border region that separated the Israelite tribes from the Philistines, whose fortified cities dotted the plain to the southwest. In spite of the fact that the two peoples traded with one another and even intermarried, the fires of conflict never quite ceased to smolder.

Samson took advantage of his size and might to play numerous fiendish pranks upon the enemies of his people. Once he captured three hundred foxes. Then he tied them together in pairs, set fire to their tails, and turned them loose in the gardens and vineyards of the Philistines.

On another occasion he tricked his enemies by pretending to have lost his strength. Brought into the midst of his foes bound and apparently helpless, he suddenly broke his bonds and seized the jawbone of an ass. The choice of this weapon was not accidental; rather, it gave him special reason to laugh after he used it to kill a thousand Philistines.

Though some details in stories about his antics are suspect, the view that Samson was a mythological figure has generally been abandoned. Most experts think he was a rustic hero of an era somewhat like that of American frontier days—a prankster who derived equal pleasure from tricking his enemies, killing dangerous beasts, and conquering women.

First Account of Pretended Insanity

Contemporary law is just now catching up with practices that prevailed three thousand years ago in the treatment of the criminally insane. For under unwritten laws that were observed by Philistines as well as Hebrews, a man obviously demented was not subject to execution no matter how heinous his crime.

Seeking refuge from the wrath of King Saul, young David wandered into the territory of Achish, king of Gath. Servants of the enemy ruler recognized David as an aspirant for the throne of Israel; this placed his life in jeopardy, for the execution of captured enemy chieftains was taken for granted.

In this predicament the frightened David "changed his behavior before them, and feigned himself mad in their hands, and scrabbled on the doors of the gate, and let his spittle fall down upon his beard" (I Sam. 21:13). His demonstration was so convincing that Achish arrived at a verdict of insanity and in keeping with the code of the desert released his foe unharmed.

The vivid account in I Sam. 21:12-15 represents the earliest account of pretended insanity.

Music Used in Mental Illness

During the 1940's and 1950's groups of psychiatrists and students of mental health began experimenting with music to soothe their patients. Apparently this development began independently in several different centers at about the same time, and hence represents a case of the well-known phenomenon of simultaneous invention.

Dramatic results were reported by numerous researchers. Though it has not proved the cure-all that early practitioners hoped it would, music has won an established place in mental and emotional therapy. Some noted specialists feel that in some patients it can have a tranquilizing effect unmatched by any known drug.

Though he didn't use the vocabulary of modern psychiatry, one noted biblical figure endorsed the view that music can soothe a troubled mind. King Saul was a tormented man who exhibited many symptoms associated with schizophrenia. Ancient historians described his condition in theological terms; when he was less than rational "the spirit of the Lord departed from Saul, and an evil spirit from the Lord troubled him" (I Sam. 16:14).

Few of his courtiers could even approach the king when he was in a frenzy, but some of them believed in the curative power of music. So they found a skilled musician and asked him to spend a great deal of time with his half-mad ruler. David, son of Jesse, made his initial appearance at the court in the role of a harpist. In history's first account of the use of music in mental therapy, "it came to pass, when the evil spirit from God was upon Saul, that David took an harp, and played with his hand: so Saul was refreshed, and was well, and the evil spirit departed from him" (I Sam. 16:23).

Earliest Federal Capital: Jerusalem

American statesmen of the eighteenth century thought they had a brand new idea in planning Washington, D. C., as a capital city not included in the territory of any state, but the concept wasn't original. David used it when he chose Jerusalem as the seat of his government.

As ruler of both Judah and Israel, he felt his leadership would be jeopardized if he established a capital in either region. So he set out to capture Jerusalem from the Jebusites in order to make it a federal city—perhaps the first of the sort in the world. David's personal troops may have seized Jerusalem by slipping through a tunnel with little opposition, or they may have gone over the walls by means of grappling hooks. Hebrew terms used in the account are obscure.

Once taken by his men, Jerusalem was renamed the City of David (II Sam. 5:9). Largely populated by royal retainers—ancient forerunners of civil service workers and career military men—the capital that was outside tribal jurisdiction owed allegiance to no one but the ruler who headed the united nation.

Pioneer Experiments with Public Works

The idea of extensive public works designed and executed by the government with funds exacted from all citizens is often considered to be modern in origin. Actually, the beginnings of such enterprises are lost in antiquity. No one knows what ruler first conceived the idea of pooling national resources in order to undertake a building program designed to meet needs of the general public. (No harm was done if, by chance, this also served to satisfy ambitions of the head of state!) If the origin of the practice is too remote to be traced, the location of the first detailed record that is still universally accessible is not in doubt. Anyone interested can find it, scattered through the first half of the first book of Kings.

Though the temple that bore his name was by far the most spectacular and best known of his public works, Solomon gave personal attention to many other enterprises. At the fortress of Megiddo he pulled down an existing set of walls and erected massive new fortifications complete with defensive towers. In the name of national defense he spent a small fortune putting up a stable for the nation's war horses—horses that walked on cobblestone floors and ate from stone mangers.

Just as twentieth-century America has relied heavily upon scientists from Germany, Italy, and other lands, so Israel under Solomon turned to skilled Phoenician builders for help. They played a vital role in the erection of the temple and brought it to completion in seven years. By contrast, the royal palace required thirteen years. During this early building boom when national defense had a high priority, unemployment was virtually nil and the economy of Israel reached a level never before achieved.

Symptoms of Heart Attack Familiar

Contrary to widespread tradition, the people of the covenant did not think the location of a person's heart determined his wisdom or lack of it. This notion grew out of just one verse of Scripture: "A wise man's heart is at his right hand; but a fool's heart at his left" (Eccles. 10:2).

Here, the Preacher isn't giving a biology lesson. Instead he is making a poetic comparison based on the fact that the place of honor at a feast was on the right side of the host—a custom that still prevails. Various biblical writers use even more colorful language about the heart. It is said to melt (Ps. 22:14), to burn (Luke 24:32), and to break (Ps. 69:20).

Since metaphors like "heartsick" and "faint-hearted" are still very much a part of everyday speech, it is impossible to use them as an index to measure a culture's grasp of biology. Even if the Hebrews knew little about human anatomy prior to the period of their Egyptian captivity, they undoubtedly gained a working knowledge about the location of all major organs from the people who had practiced embalming for centuries.

The account of Nabal's death indicates that Abraham's descendants knew the symptoms of heart attack triggered by emotional disturbance. "It came to pass in the morning, when the wine was gone out of Nabal, and his wife had told him these things, that his heart died within him, and he became as a stone." (I Sam. 25:37.) He lingered in a comatose state for ten days—still a common period to live after a massive heart attack—and then died.

Oldest Record of Toll Road

The Romans had major overland transportation routes very early, but the name "highway" was first used to designate elevated roads that connected a few major English cities during the late Middle Ages. It was not until the beginning of modern times that westerners conceived the idea of charging fees for travel on major highways, long called turnpikes because their entrances were guarded by pikes that were moved to permit entry after prospective travelers had paid in advance.

Still, the basic concept underlying the modern toll road was devised long ago. Scripture preserves the first mention of such a system in a passing reference to "the king's high way" (Num. 20:17).

A caravan trade route so old that it had been traveled for centuries when Abraham was born, it connected Arabia with Syria and the coast of the region familiar to Bible readers as Palestine. Merchants who wished to take their goods to the Red Sea had no choice; they had to take this path because there was no alternative route. Important mineral deposits near the present Gulf of Aqaba added greatly to the strategic importance of the king's high way.

Chieftains and petty rulers whose names have not been preserved saw a golden opportunity. They erected a number of strongly fortified military posts along the frontiers of Edom and then charged all the traffic would bear in return for permitting merchants to pass unmolested. Returns from this toll road were important contributions to the economic prosperity of Edom during the period of the Hebrew monarchy.

Transformed by poetic metaphor into a route leading to eternal bliss, "the king's high way" is today commemorated in many hymns and songs that give no hint of the fact that in biblical times it was traveled by oxen, camels, and horses, as well as men.

Rachel's Recipe for Conception

Rachel, wife of Jacob, may be the first woman in history about whom we have a clinical account of effects from the use of a tranquilizing drug. In her case the potent stuff was self-prescribed.

Frantic because she was unable to present her husband with a son, Rachel took drastic steps (Gen. 30:14-15). She bargained with Leah for a supply of roots from a plant supposed to increase one's sexual potency. Leah's son Reuben had found a colony of mandrakes—plants that grow wild throughout the eastern Mediterranean region—in a wheat field. Once Rachel got her hands on them, she used them in a fashion prescribed by folk doctors of many cultures.

Since prehistoric times the mandrake has been valued for its alleged power to foster human fertility. In the Bible it is mentioned five times in connection with Rachel, once in the Song of Solomon. Recipes and charms linked with it remained current until comparatively recent times. Some medieval vendors even carved human features on mandrake roots. Then they claimed to have dug them from the ground, shaped by nature to resemble the babies they were supposed to bring. Such a mandrake image was known as a mannikin or *erdman* ("earthman").

Regardless of whether Rachel's mandrakes were carved or plain, she got results in the form of a son whom she named Joseph. Whatever its other effects may or may not be, the mandrake (distantly related to belladonna or "deadly nightshade") has a soothing effect upon the nerves of some who use it. Since some physicians now administer modern tranquilizers to foster conception, it may be that

Rachel's self-prescribed dose actually did enable her to become a mother.

Earliest Boy Kings

Beginning students of European history are sometimes startled to discover that adolescents and even children have been nominal rulers of France, England, Spain, and other nations. Actually, this practice isn't a recent innovation. Since ancient times there have been many instances in which the oldest son of a dead monarch has been named king—with a regent in control during his minority.

Scripture far antedates secular history in preserving a list of boy kings, some of whom ruled for half a century. Azariah, son of Amaziah, became titular ruler of Judah at sixteen (II Kings 15:2). Manasseh ascended the throne when he was just twelve (II Kings 21:1). But these potentates were mature by comparison with Josiah, whose reign began when he was eight (II Kings 22:1). Jehoiachin, who ascended the throne at eighteen, was deposed and taken prisoner by Babylonians after he had been in power just ninety days (II Kings 24:8-13). But Joash, who was made king at seven, controlled the destiny of Judah for forty years (II Chron. 24:1).

Except for Josiah, these earliest youthful potentates of whom we have records had completely undistinguished reigns. During the eighteenth year of his monarchy (about 622 B.C.) the young sovereign enacted a series of sweeping reforms. These grew out of accidental discovery of a long lost copy of the book of the Law in the temple (II Kings 22:8) and influenced the whole of subsequent Hebrew history.

Seventh Century B.C. Secretary

Baruch the scribe, brother of King Zedekiah's first chamberlain, was the world's first secretary to be mentioned by name in a written chronicle that is still read: the book of Jeremiah. His name is taken from a Hebrew word for "blessed."

Male secretaries, nearly always unnamed, played important roles at many ancient Near Eastern courts. Kings and rulers commonly entrusted the preparation of letters and proclamations to these men, skilled both in capturing the words of their masters and in writing legibly.

Jeremiah the prophet, who first began proclaiming the message of the Lord late in the seventh century B.C., was himself a man of high cultural background. Whether he was unable to write or simply preferred to concentrate upon speaking and entrust the preservation of his messages to Baruch is uncertain. In any case, he habitually used this member of a prominent Judean family to transcribe his prophetic warnings.

At Jeremiah's dictation Baruch wrote a series of oracles of destruction warning his countrymen of dire consequences that would stem from failure to put Jehovah first in their lives. King Jehoiakim ordered that the scroll be brought to him and read. It made him so angry that he took a knife, cut it in pieces, and burned it bit by bit (Jer. 36:23). Scholars surmise that Baruch must have used papyrus, for had his scroll been of leather, the odor would have stopped proceedings before destruction was complete.

Centuries after the time of Jeremiah, Paul also used secretaries to write his letters. But in his case their names were not preserved.

First Record of U.F.O. Sighting?

Unidentified flying objects didn't get into the headlines until the beginning of the Space Age, but a respected authority on these hotly debated phenomena has suggested that the first detailed record of a sighting appears in the Bible. Jacques Vallee made this proposal in his *Anatomy of a Phenomenon,* published in 1965 and widely regarded as the most thorough of all books on flying saucers.

In chapters 1-4 of his prophecy Ezekiel refers to the coming of a strange machine from the sky. He saw it land near the Chebar River in Chaldea (present-day Iraq) shortly before the end of the sixth century B.C. Since Ezekiel lived in a period when metal implements were scarce and complicated machines didn't exist, chariot and plow were the most sophisticated mechanical words in his vocabulary. It was natural for him to use them in a fumbling attempt to describe what he saw.

According to Vallee, the notion that Ezekiel saw a mirage must be ruled out. An attempt to reconstruct a model of the phenomenon he observed would produce an elaborate machine—not a vision such as that sometimes induced by sunstroke. So while he obviously cannot settle the question to the satisfaction of all parties, Vallee suggests that extraterrestrial craft made occasional contact with the earth in ancient times. One of them, sighted by Ezekiel, left its imprint upon Scripture.

Persons who reject such a point of view have difficulty with the poetic and flamboyant language of Ezekiel. If he didn't see a mirage or a space craft, could he have been under the influence of a plant-derived drug? If he actually heard a significant message from Jehovah, why was his report put in such form that for practical purposes it is unintelligible?

In the present state of knowledge about divine revelation, hallucinatory drugs, and unidentified flying objects, no final answers can be given.

Oldest Tale of a Traveling Salesman

Traveling salesmen, traditional subjects of American jokes, were common in New Testament times. Though this aspect of the story is usually overlooked, it was a commercial traveler who played the central role in one of the most famous of Jesus' parables.

The parable of the good Samaritan is only nine verses long (Luke 10:29-37). Still, the condensed account specifies that the hero of the story was a traveling man who had his own beast of burden. Unlike farmers and shepherds, who seldom had even one copper coin, this man was supplied with cash. And his promise to the innkeeper indicates that he expected to return home by the same route he was following when he rescued a stranger who had fallen among robbers.

Far from being rare, traveling merchants were numerous in first-century Palestine. Some made only one or two trips a year and covered wide territories while others worked in small regions and managed to be home most weekends. It was for the accommodation of these commercial agents that innkeepers maintained their establishments; when farm folk traveled, they took along their own gear and slept in the open air.

Death from Psychological Shock

Until recently there were few attempts to make scientific studies of human culture. Once the movement was launched, some long-cherished ideas were challenged. Among them was the notion that serious physical damage can be done by psychologically oriented rites such as voodoo and witchcraft. Today the trend has been reversed; most anthropologists agree that in primitive cultures it is indeed possible that a person can be frightened to death.

In the light of this view a familiar biblical story takes on fresh significance. Though there is no suggestion of occult rites or evil influences, the first-century story of Ananias represents the earliest objective account of death from mental-emotional-spiritual shock.

During a period when members of the Christian community "had all things in common," Ananias and his wife Sapphira concluded a real estate transaction. Instead of turning in the entire amount received, they kept part of the purchase price back and then made a great show of presenting the balance to leaders of the church. Peter accused Ananias of having lied to God, with the result that he "fell down, and gave up the ghost." Promptly buried, his body was hardly cold before his widow (unaware of what had happened) repeated the story told by her husband.

Peter told her of Ananias' death and warned that the same men were at the door to carry her out. "Then fell she down straightway at his feet, and yielded up the ghost: and the young men came in, and found her dead, and, carrying her forth, buried her by her husband." (Acts 5:10.)

Pioneer Account of Psychological Blindness

Late in the nineteenth and early in the twentieth century there were several reported cases of psychological blindness—total inability to see without a physical defect or illness to account for this condition. Until large numbers of Allied troops exhibited such blindness as a result of shell shock during World War I, most experts questioned the reality of the phenomenon.

Once it was recognized as genuine and a typical pattern of symptoms was cataloged, men discovered that detailed case histories of psychological blindness appeared long ago. There are brief references to "temporary blindness" in the Old Testament (Gen. 19:11; II Kings 6:18-20). But the earliest account that gives details consistent with what is now known about this affliction is found in the Acts of the Apostles.

On his famous journey to Damascus, undertaken with the purpose of taking captive any followers of Jesus whom he might ferret out, Saul of Tarsus was knocked to the ground by a light from heaven. He received a revelation from God that caused him to change his name to Paul and to espouse the new faith. A side effect of the encounter was psychological blindness: "And Saul arose from the earth; and when his eyes were opened, he saw no man. . . . And he was three days without sight" (Acts 9:8-9).

In the light of his own experience it is not strange that Paul later pronounced a curse upon a sorcerer and false prophet, condemning him to temporary blindness. So powerful was the force of his personality and so impressive was his formula that Bar-jesus succumbed. "Immediately there fell on him a mist and a darkness; and he went about seeking some to lead him by the hand." (Acts 13:11.)

First Organized Disaster Relief

Campaigns to aid victims of natural disasters are now so common in the western world that they are virtually taken for granted. Any time there is a hurricane, flood, earthquake, or other cataclysmic event leaving victims in its wake, religious and fraternal groups are likely to collect money to aid the work of formal relief organizations such as the Red Cross.

Even veteran readers of the New Testament do not always realize, however, that the earliest documented account of voluntary aid in time of disaster is reported in Acts 11:27-30.

Secular records of the period confirm and supplement biblical accounts of a great famine during the reign of the fourth Roman emperor, Claudius I (ruler from A.D. 41 to 54). Crop failures were so extensive that food supplies were exhausted in many regions. Before the critical condition of "great dearth throughout all the world" actually existed, a follower of Jesus named Agabus had a prophetic vision warning of it. He appealed to fellow believers in the big and wealthy city of Antioch. They heard his plea. "Then the disciples, every man according to his ability, determined to send relief unto the brethren which dwelt in Judaea: which also they did, and sent it to the elders by the hands of Barnabas and Saul."

Though there are records of famine as early as the time of the Hebrew patriarchs and crop failure was a constant threat throughout the Near East, neither secular nor religious chronicles report love gifts for famine relief before those made in the time of Claudius Caesar.

Queer Customs from Many Eras

Dietary Laws Without Parallels

Archaeological discoveries—most of them made since 1900—have shown that ancient codes of Babylon and other kingdoms included many provisions similar to those in the Law of Moses. But in some respects the body of rules Moses framed or collected is unique. None of the peoples with whom the Hebrews traded and fought had rules of diet and sanitation like those found in Deuteronomy.

Most anthropologists, professional students of culture, think regulations of this sort root in tribal prohibitions so old that their origin cannot be traced. As a rule, however, all the peoples of various cultures within a geographical region show the effects of similar influences. That is not the case with the Hebrews.

Scholars have never succeeded in finding among non-Hebrews of the Near East any trace of such regulations as those in Deut. 14:6-7: "Every beast that parteth the hoof, and cleaveth the cleft into two claws, and cheweth the cud among the beasts, that ye shall eat. Nevertheless these ye shall not eat of them that chew the cud, or of them that divide the cloven hoof; as the camel, and the hare, and the coney: for they chew the cud, but divide not the hoof; therefore they are unclean to you." Nor were there among other ancient peoples even the most remote parallels to the Hebrews' rules for keeping the camp clean (Deut. 23:9-14).

The unique features of biblical statutes support the view that though the Hebrews were involved in much cultural intermingling, they very early took steps to make themselves "a people set apart."

Aaron's Little Bull

Aaron's famous golden calf, made from earrings donated by men as well as by women (Exod. 32:2), wasn't really a calf. Instead it was a miniature bull whose size was determined by scarcity of the precious metal used in making it; thus "the little bull" entered many English translations as "calf."

Assyrians, Babylonians, Canaanites, Egyptians, and Hittites all worshiped bull gods. First in Memphis and later throughout Egypt the bull was among the most important sacred animals. Here he was usually depicted as black; in other lands spotted and tawny animals were venerated. Wherever bull symbolism was employed, the animal stood for strength and plenty because he was the only source of power with which to plow the land and practice agriculture. Frequently the divine bull was considered capable of bestowing sexual fertility upon his worshipers.

When Moses came down from Mt. Sinai and discovered his people engaged in a religious dance in honor of a miniature bull, he became so angry that he threw down and broke the stone slabs on which the Ten Commandments were engraved. Then he called for volunteers to help him and with their aid killed about three thousand bull worshipers.

But the cult of the animal revered by Israel's neighboring peoples did not die. At Bethel and Dan the Lord was worshiped in the form of a bull. In later generations Jehovah was symbolized by a bull which served as the pedestal upon which he stood invisible, and the famous temple of Solomon was decorated with great numbers of bulls made from olive wood and bronze.

Worship in the Holy Altogether

In many Near Eastern cultures all ordinary household articles, including clothing, were long considered contaminated. In order to achieve ritualistic purity, numerous holy men of various early sects regularly or occasionally approached the altar *in puris naturalibus* —stark naked.

The practice of ritualistic nudity in periods of prehistory was so widespread, many anthropologists speculate, that it may have given rise to the puzzling custom of taking off one's shoes before entering a holy place. Frequently mentioned in Scripture, the latter rite developed, according to some theorists, as a substitute for earlier abandonment of all clothing. Such token nudity could have served to symbolize and perpetuate earlier practices according to which all clothing was taboo in the tent or house of worship.

There is a passing reference to this custom in Exod. 20:26, where it is linked with worship of Jehovah himself. Later the band of refugees led out of Egypt by Moses danced naked before Aaron's little golden bull (Exod. 32:25). By this standard Moses himself was somewhat conservative; approaching the burning bush on Mt. Sinai, he removed his shoes in order to avoid profaning holy ground (Exod. 3:5).

Wearing a linen ephod (which may have been nothing more than a loincloth), David once performed an ecstatic dance before the ark of the Lord. From the fact that his wife Michal chided him for having uncovered himself before his servants' handmaidens (II Sam. 6:20), it seems likely that the king's exhibition was vulgar and revealing. Apparently as retaliation for her scolding, David fathered no children by Michal (II Sam. 6:23).

Moses' Magic Serpent

Epochal figure that he was in the search for the one true God, Moses in at least one instance practiced magic. He tried to solve the problem of snakebite by making a bronze serpent and setting it up on a pole where victims could see it; for all practical purposes this was indirect worship of the asp, long considered sacred by the Egyptians.

True, Moses thought he was acting in obedience to the instruction of Jehovah, for the idea of making the symbolic reptile came to him as a direct answer to prayer (Num. 21:7-8). According to the ancient account it actually worked, too. Farfetched as this seems from some viewpoints, the terrific psychological power of a faith-directed encounter with a magic talisman on the part of primitive people cannot be overestimated. It is within the realm of credibility that Moses' bronze serpent actually did save the lives of many snakebite victims. But the pagan character of its influence and of the rites connected with it is clearly indicated in Scripture. Members of the chosen people gave the metal figure a name—Nehushtan—and burned incense to it.

Regular or sporadic worship linked with the metal talisman continued for at least five centuries. Then in one of his most important reforms King Hezekiah "brake in pieces the brasen serpent that Moses had made" (II Kings 18:4).

Charms Worn to Win Divine Protection

During many centuries faithful Jews used Scripture as a sort of magic charm to ward off evil. In English, the devices employed are called phylacteries, adapted from the Greek for "amulet, or means of protection." This technical term came into the language through the Geneva Bible, where it had been taken from the Latin Vulgate.

A phylactery is a miniature prayer case, usually made of leather. One style is designed for use on the head and another on the arm. Both employ four passages of Scripture: Exod. 13:1-10 (the Mazzoth Law), Exod. 13:11-16 (the Passover Law), Deut. 6:4-9 (the Shema, or profession of belief in one God), and Deut. 11:13-21 (the command to love Jehovah alone).

A typical head phylactery has four compartments, each of which holds a miniature scroll. It is sewn with twelve stitches, symbolizing the twelve tribes of Israel. Handwritten letters plus symbolic knots spell out *Shaddai,* or "Almighty." The arm phylactery has only one compartment, containing a single parchment on which all four Scripture passages are written. It is fastened to the upper arm by means of straps in such fashion that it hangs at the level of the heart.

Orthodox Jews still wear phylacteries in obedience to scriptural injunctions. While the use of these devices is today symbolic, in late Old Testament times many persons wore them as talismans to bring good luck. In the only New Testament reference to them (Matt. 23:5), Jesus rebuked Pharisees for making their phylacteries conspicuously broad so that persons who saw them would be impressed by their great piety.

Clothing That Pointed to the Law

Modern distinctions between civil law and ecclesiastical law were unknown to the Hebrew, who for centuries treated church and state as a single entity. The all-absorbing importance of the Law of Moses was witnessed by the habitual use of clothing that pointed to it.

In somewhat the same sense that persons today sometimes tie strings around their fingers as reminders, early Jews followed Moses' injunction "that they make them fringes in the borders of their garments throughout their generations" (Num. 15:38). At first these ceremonial garments, rooted in reverence for the Law, were made with blue fringes whose purpose is clearly indicated in Scripture. Each time a person's eyes fell upon the symbolic strip of colored ribbon he was expected to "remember all the commandments of the Lord, and do them" (Num. 15:39).

Though it is nowhere fully described in the Bible, the garment prescribed by Holy Writ gradually became more and more complex. From their word for "covering," Hebrews called it the *tallith.* Tassels were hung at each corner; each tassel or fringe consisted of eight strands tied in five knots. Many rabbis read a special significance into these numbers. For the numerical value of Hebrew letters in the word for "fringes" is precisely 600. Add to this 8 for the number of strands and 5 for the number of knots in each strand and the total is 613—the total number of laws (religious and civil) that scribes counted in the Torah, or Five Books of the Law.

Persons particularly zealous for the Law didn't stop with wearing a fringed tallith as an outer garment. In New Testament times many also wore a small tallith or sacred undershirt. Customarily made of purplish-blue cotton and adorned with four tassels, this next-to-the-skin reminder of the Law was frequently regarded as symbolizing

Israel's badge of separation from the rest of the human race—all the uncircumcised who did not obey the Law.

Human Sacrifice by Builders

Because blood was considered the locus of life and because human blood was more potent than that of animals, ancients sometimes made special use of it when buildings were erected. A victim selected by virtue of special purity was killed, and his blood was poured over the foundation stone of the structure. As a modification of this practice the human sacrifice was sometimes walled up alive.

Though neither Scripture nor the findings of archaeology suggest that such rites were ever common among Hebrews, they were certainly practiced from time to time. Warning against any attempt to rebuild Jericho after the city was razed and burned, Joshua includes in his curse the provision that any man who disobeys "shall lay the foundation thereof in his firstborn, and in his youngest son shall he set up the gates of it" (Josh. 6:26).

Hiel of Bethel rebuilt the city in the days of Ahab, and, says the biblical historian, "he laid the foundation thereof in Abiram his firstborn, and set up the gates thereof in his youngest son Segub" (I Kings 16:34).

Bodies Laid Out, Bones Preserved

Only two persons mentioned in Scripture were embalmed: Jacob and Joseph. The bodies of others were buried. Had it not been for the strong Egyptian influence upon their careers, Jacob and Joseph would also have been buried with their fathers without any attempt to preserve their bodies intact.

Cremation was practiced by Canaanite inhabitants of the Promised Land, but was never sanctioned by Jews—though exceptions may have been made in time of pestilence (Amos 6:10). The bodies of Saul and Jonathan are reported to have been burned by the men of Jabesh-gilead, who retrieved these trophies hung on the wall of Beth-shan by Philistines. But the account clearly indicates that only flesh and entrails were burned. The bones of the slain leaders were solemnly interred (II Sam. 21:11-13).

Burial didn't necessarily involve placing the remains in the earth, however. Many bodies were laid out in niches of natural and artificial caves and left there until all flesh rotted away. When an occupied niche was needed for a new body, the bones from the preceding burial were gathered up and stored in a special limestone bone box or ossuary.

Bones were sometimes preserved for generations or even centuries, hence Scripture's many references to their importance. Apparently the special treatment given Jacob and Joseph created only temporary interest; there is no suggestion that their descendants treated the mummies with greater respect than that accorded ordinary bones.

An Obscure Form of Witchcraft

Magic was widely practiced among all the peoples of surrounding cultures, but the ancient Hebrews had so little to do with it that Biblical references aren't clearly understood.

In his prophecies "against the prophets of Israel," where "prophet" means any person who claims a special link with supernatural power, Ezekiel denounces a queer form of witchcraft. "Thus saith the Lord God; Woe to the women that sew pillows to all armholes, and make kerchiefs upon the head of every statue to hunt souls!" (Ezek. 13:18.)

"Pillows to all armholes," a clumsy translation only a bit clarified by growing knowledge of the original language, probably means something like "magic bands for all wrists." And no one knows whether "kerchiefs upon the head" covered the head only or the entire body; the latter alternative is considered more likely. Words naming these bands and kerchiefs occur nowhere else in Scripture and have not been found in secular documents of the period.

From what is known of witchcraft as practiced in other cultures, this obscure reference probably points to the very early use of dolls or puppets. Voodoo priests stick pins in such images in order to bring pain to the persons they represent. Witches of ancient Israel probably draped veils over clay statuettes and repeated incantations while wrapping magic bands about the wrists of victims whose souls they sought to capture.

Once-forbidden Blood Now Ceremonially Drunk

The Christian rite of Holy Communion developed as an offshoot of Jewish thought and worship, yet it violates one of the central laws of the Old Testament. Protestants and Catholics differ as to whether the meaning of the act is symbolic or literal, but both "drink the blood of Jesus Christ" despite centuries-old prohibitions against consuming any blood at all.

"Ye shall eat no manner of blood, whether it be of fowl or of beast, in any of your dwellings," runs the ancient statute. "Whatsoever soul it be that eateth any manner of blood, even that soul shall be cut off from his people." (Lev. 7:26-27.)

Most interpreters believe that this edict grew out of reverence for blood, for in the Old Testament, blood is literally the life of an organism. Recognition of this factor (Gen. 9:4) is linked with the prohibition of blood as a food, an edict which led to elaborate codes governing ways in which slain animals and fowls had to be drained of their blood before being cooked.

Blood was for centuries a major element in sacrificial rites. Priests had strict regulations that guided the way they dashed blood at the base of the altar of Jehovah, poured it out, smeared it upon the horns of the altar, and sprinkled it before the sanctuary (Lev. 1:5, 11; 4: 6-7).

Viewed through first-century eyes it is hard to conceive of a more incredibly radical transition than that involved in Jesus' demand that his disciples—ardent believers in the Law of Moses—should drink his blood to signify their acceptance of his new covenant (Matt. 26:28; Mark 14:24; Luke 22:20), and thereby gain eternal life (John 6: 53-56).

Praying in Reverse

Only the Gospels of Matthew and Luke preserve Scripture's most widely used prayer—and their versions are not identical. Even the universal title, the Lord's Prayer, does not appear in Holy Writ. But very early in Christian times the prayer came into virtually universal use for both private devotions and public worship.

It was regarded as having all but magical powers, with the result that persons who dabbled in the occult sciences put the prayer to their own uses. For the most part adopting it as found in prayer books rather than following the text of Scripture, medieval witches and sorcerers made it into a petition to the devil by repeating it backward.

This practice was still widely remembered by men and women of nineteenth-century England. In his famous novel *The Return of the Native* (1878), Thomas Hardy has Susan Nunsuch repeat the Lord's Prayer backward three times as she savagely burns a pin-stuck image of Eustacia Yeobright.

Cathedrals Pointing to Jerusalem

Jerusalem, mentioned by name many scores of times in Scripture, profoundly influenced what many persons consider the greatest flowering of architecture in history. Many medieval maps showed the holy city as the center of the world, with east rather than north appearing at the top.

Partly as a token of gratitude for the fact that the year 1000 passed without the end of the world, Europeans embarked on a fantastic campaign of cathedral building. From its superficial resemblance to a ship of the epoch (Latin *navis*) the central and principal architectural feature of a cathedral was called the nave. Because of the importance of Jerusalem in the biblical record, it was customary to design great houses of worship in such fashion that axes of their naves pointed directly toward the City of David. As a result worshipers always faced east.

Genealogical Table Taken Very Seriously

Though considered unimportant or even irrelevant by many Western Christians, Gospel references to Jesus' ancestry are highly significant to persons in the eastern world. All Moslems have special veneration for Abraham. Hence Matthew's mention of him in the first verse of his genealogical table fosters reverence for Jesus in Islam. (See Matt. 1:1-17; compare Luke 3:23-38.) There are many other New Testament references to Abraham; some of the most important are found in Matt. 3:9; 22:32; Mark 12:26; Luke 3:8; Acts 3:13; Rom. 4:1; II Cor. 11:22; Heb. 11:8-17.

Aside from Abraham's key role in the genealogical table reported by Matthew, the enumeration so monotonous to English readers is often regarded with great interest in sections of Asia and Africa. For in cultures where genealogies are stressed, the fact that Jesus has such a long and detailed list of ancestors is proof positive that he was a man of unique prestige!

Language Retarded by Bible

Reverence for the text of Scripture, transmitted over a period of centuries and hardened into opposition to other patterns of speech, retarded the development of the Hungarian (or Magyar) language.

Catholic ecclesiastics who settled in Hungary early in the eleventh century came to exert great political power. They established Latin as the predominant language of the court, higher schools, and public worship. Latin having become the tongue of the educated, there was little literature of significance in the Magyar tongue until the close of the eighteenth century.

In his volume *The Story of Language,* Mario Pei reports that the impact of scriptural Latin was so great that use of the vernacular in written form was an offense that was sometimes punished by death. As a result the group of oral dialects that constituted the Hungarian language did not merge to form a national tongue until the period from 1807 to 1830.

Nativity Scenes at Christmas

Tradition credits Francis of Assisi with having launched the worldwide custom of setting up nativity scenes during the Christmas season. Thousands of inexpensive ones are sold in variety stores every year, but others are lavish and costly. As a result of a gift establishing a trust fund for its support the city of Nashville, Tennessee, is annually treated to a glorified version that cost more than $40,000.

According to early stories, in the year 1223 Francis began decorating a stable at Christmas. He equipped it with simple representations of chief persons in the holy drama and probably used a few live animals. In this transformed stable he celebrated Mass and preached until the twelve days of Christmas were over.

From the Latin form of the Greek word for "manger" Italians called the Christmas scene *presepio.* In Old High German the name became *krippa;* among the French it took the form *crèche.* Regardless of how simple or how elaborate the presepio may be, Italians always bring the entire scene to focus upon the bambino.

Though inspired by the Bible, many nativity scenes in medieval as well as modern times were largely shaped by the imagination of their creators rather than the text of Holy Writ. Once a scene is exhibited for a period of years, however, community tradition frowns upon adding or removing animals or persons for the sake of adhering to meager details given in the Gospels.

Surgery and Dissection Forbidden

Many Old Testament passages support the view that the life of a person or animal is concentrated in its blood (see Gen. 9:4; Deut. 12:23). Hence the eating of meat with blood still in it was prohibited (Lev. 17:10-14) in edicts still observed by orthodox Jews. Frequently treated as equivalent to murder, the shedding of blood was strictly forbidden.

Once this point of view became firmly entrenched in Christian thought, it was logical to take one more step. It was not enough to abstain from acts of violence leading to bloodshed and death; faithful followers of Christ were taught that it was a sin to spill any blood whatever (unless the blood was that of an infidel such as a Moslem).

Without citing specific scriptural support but basing their whole argument upon the Old Testament view of bloodshed, popes and cardinals held it axiomatic that "the Church abhors the shedding of blood." Basing their decision on this principle, in A.D. 1248 members of the Council of Le Mans forbade monks under their jurisdiction to undergo any form of surgery.

Anatomists were subject to legal penalties if they attempted to practice dissection. As a result of this injunction, based upon a theory according to which mutilation of the body might interfere with resurrection of the soul, "body snatchers" built up a thriving business. For high prices they supplied surgeons with cadavers through bootleg channels. No substantial progress in human anatomy was made until religious scruples against dissection were withdrawn.

Even at the midpoint of the twentieth century, civil authorities occasionally interfere and issue a court order for surgery in the case of a minor whose parents believe it better for their child to die of acute appendicitis or strangulated hernia than to risk divine wrath by spilling blood.

Witches Weighed Against Bibles

Huge medieval Bibles, handwritten on vellum and stoutly clad in metal, were both cumbersome and heavy. Many volumes weighed sixty pounds or more; a few weighed as much as one hundred pounds. According to Pennethorne Hughes's scholarly study, *Witchcraft,* authorities sometimes employed one of these massive Bibles as a means of testing a person accused of witchcraft. After being freed from the pulpit to which it was chained in order to prevent theft, the Bible was hung from one arm of a big scale. Then the wretch accused of practicing black magic was fastened to the other arm of the scale in order to be weighed against the Bible.

Short of divine intervention to prove innocence, once the process of weighing began there was little doubt of the outcome. For even the skinniest old grandmother was usually heavy enough to tip the scales in her own direction—thereby demonstrating herself to be a witch and automatically drawing the death penalty.

Religious Names of Puritans

English Puritans of the late sixteenth and early seventeenth centuries were so obsessed with Scripture that many of them chose words and phrases from Holy Writ as names for their children. Lower's

English Sur-names reports that a jury list from Sussex County included these specimens:

Faint-not Hewitt	Seek-wisdom Wood
Redeemed Compton	Make-peace Heaton
God-reward Smart	Stand-fast-on-high Stringer
Meek Brewer	Search-the-Scripture Moreton
Peace-of-God Knight	Weep-not Billing
Kill-sin Pimple	Fight-the-good-fight-of-faith White
Be-faithful Juniper	

Throwing Dice for Gift Bibles

A village custom more than two centuries old was altered in 1880 because an Anglican bishop ruled that the Communion table was "No proper place" to throw dice for Bibles.

Robert Wilde, an eccentric member of the parish of St. Ives in Hampshire, England, was eager to foster the distribution of Scripture. At his death in August, 1678, he left fifty pounds as a special endowment. Interest earned by the money, he stipulated, should each year be spent for six Bibles "not exceeding the price of seven shillings and sixpence each." Then on the last Thursday in May six boys and six girls were invited to gather in St. Ives church and throw dice to determine which of them would receive copies purchased under the terms of the legacy.

Thrifty villagers invested Wilde's legacy in an orchard that inevitably came to be known as Bible Orchard. Since the yield from it came to be substantially more than was required to meet the conditions of the donor, parish officers began paying the vicar ten shillings for a special annual sermon "commending the excellency, the perfection, and divine authority of the Holy Scriptures."

After use of the Communion table was outlawed by the bishop of the diocese, a table erected at the chancel steps became the traditional spot for the annual dice-throwing on Bible Thursday.

Dipping for Good Fortune

In many parts of England, Scotland, and Holland the Bible was long put to special use on New Year's Day. With all members of the family gathered around a table before breakfast, the Book was laid upon it. Each who wished to consult it opened it at random, placed a finger on a verse, and read it in order to get a clue about what fortune had in store for him during the year ahead. Though often practiced by devout

Christians, such "dipping" was sometimes just a trifle removed from the occult arts of gypsy fortune-tellers.

According to Hone's *Every Day Book,* Hugh Latimer practiced a special form of dipping. One New Year's Day he departed from the usual courtier's practice of slipping a purse of gold into the hand of his ruler. Instead, Latimer offered King Henry VIII a New Testament with a leaf conspicuously doubled down at Heb. 13:4. If he used the Great Bible, as was likely, his New Year's bulletin to his much-married monarch read: "Wedlocke is to be had in honoure among all men, and the bed undefyled. As for whore kepers and advoutrers [adulterers] God shall judge them."

In 1555 Latimer was burned at the stake by Henry's daughter Mary.

Ecstasy by Way of Dung

From Old Testament times to the present day and in cultures that range from primitive to highly sophisticated ones, God seekers have sought ways to obtain divine messages. Some persons are able to enter a religious trance through concentration alone; others employ elaborate ceremonies and even drugs.

William Blake, the Bible-saturated, eccentric genius of English art and letters, spent so much time reliving Old Testament incidents that they were sometimes more real to him than events in the London of his day. Among several experiences each of which he entitled simply "A Memorable Fancy," Blake describes an evening on which "the Prophets Isaiah and Ezekiel dined with me, and I asked them how they dared so roundly to assert that God spoke to them; and whether they did not think at the time that they would be misunderstood."

Blake listened patiently while both men gave their interpretations of the nature of prophetic genius. Then when dinner was over he asked his guests to let him be the medium through which to give the world their lost books; both men told him "none of equal value was lost." After inquiring about Isaiah's motive for going naked and barefoot for three years, Blake reported, he inquired into what he evidently considered a primitive version of mind-stimulants whose function was not unlike that of modern psychedelic drugs: "I then asked Ezekiel why he ate dung, & lay so long on his right & left side? he answer'd, 'the desire of raising other men into a perception of the infinite: this the North American tribes practise, & is he honest who resists his genius or conscience only for the sake of present ease or gratification?' "

Blake probably misinterpreted the significance of Ezek. 4:12, for the prophets cooked with dung rather than ate it. But the context supports

Blake's conclusion that Ezekiel deliberately used techniques calculated to produce a paranormal state.

Mutilation of Scripture Avoided

During most of Christian history the act of mutilating or destroying Scripture has generally been regarded as an affront to deity. Lingering traces of this deeply entrenched point of view account for the fact that even today great numbers of persons refuse to destroy a Bible or Testament, no matter how badly worn it may be. Consciously or unconsciously accepting the idea that the willful destruction of Holy Writ brings bad luck, owners of battered Bibles frequently place them in drawers or upon shelves instead of dumping them in trash cans.

In earlier epochs dread of divine wrath as a result of physical damage to a copy of the Scriptures extended even to such acts as tearing out a page or cutting the binding. John Silver, arch villain of Stevenson's *Treasure Island,* simply echoes the verdict of his time when he warns his men of dire consequences sure to follow their rash act of cutting a flyleaf of a Bible in order to give him "the black spot," symbolizing revolt. To Silver, mutiny was not nearly as serious a matter as desecration of the Book.

Pilate Honored by Some Christians

Stories concerning Pontius Pilate's conversion to Christianity grew up very early and have been widely transmitted. Only one branch of the church, however, commemorates the Roman who sent Jesus to his death.

Approximately ten million persons are included in the Coptic Church of Ethiopia. Though classified as a Christian body, it includes elements from both Judaism and nature worship. For religious ceremonies priests employ a dead language called Geez, which is used only in worship. Historians consider it remarkable that any basic Christian emphases have survived in this isolated culture, subjected to ceaseless pressure from Moslem missionaries for nearly fifteen hundred years.

Ethiopian tradition asserts that Pontius Pilate ultimately regretted having yielded to popular demands in the trial of Jesus, repented, and himself became a follower of the slain Messiah. So the Coptic Church annually celebrates a feast in honor of the man all but universally condemned in western Christendom as a weakling and a coward.

A few scholars have gone so far as to question whether Pilate was a historical person. Lack of references to him in Roman documents have given some support to the view that his name was modified or even invented by early Christians.

This notion was dispelled in June, 1961. Italian archaeologists exploring ruins of the Roman theater at Caesarea found a stone slab whose Latin inscription mentions Pontius Pilate and identifies him as governor of Judaea. Carved during the reign of the Emperor Tiberius, this important find underscores the historical accuracy of the Gospels. In spite of it, though, there is no substantial evidence to lead other Christians to join Ethiopians in rejoicing that Pilate was converted before he died.

Bibles Bought with Tax Money

Customs by which religious and secular activities are strictly distinguished in the name of separation of church and state are of modern western origin. A totally different outlook prevailed in ancient times —and is still held in some regions, with the result that emerging nations of pagan background sometimes treat the Bible more generously than do those long labeled "Christian." At a period when the United States was engaged in controversy over court rulings that prohibited Bible reading in public schools, two of history's biggest orders for copies of Scripture were placed by governments.

One of them was for 200,000 copies of the Bible, bought with tax funds of Indonesian governmental agencies. Placed through the Indonesian Bible Society, the order was filled through the cooperation of the Japanese Bible Society. All the work of printing and book manufacture was done in Tokyo. Indonesian law requires that each student in the public schools shall enroll in a course designed to teach him the fundamentals of his chosen faith and that the textbook of the course shall be the sacred book of his religion—to be provided at government expense.

In 1965, a few months after the Indonesian purchase, the government of Ghana bought 500,000 copies of the Bible for use in the nation's schoolrooms. Placed through the Bible Society in Ghana, the order was so big that production had to be divided between plants in Europe and the United States.

At the very time these Bibles were being printed, lawmakers in the United States were attempting—unsuccessfully—to get Congressional approval of bills that would permit Bible reading and prayer in the public schools of this nation.

Law
Crime
and
Punishment

Cain Sentenced to Live in Guilt

Capital punishment, no longer practiced in some European nations and in some states in this country, is usually considered the most fearful sentence that can be imposed. But the first murderer was not given the death penalty; instead, God sentenced him to live in guilt and forbade anyone to take his life.

Confronted by God after his slain brother's blood "cried from the ground," Cain never did admit guilt. Nevertheless, God pronounced a curse upon him and banished him from the company of his fellows. Cain protested that as a fugitive he would soon be killed. So the Lord took steps to be sure he would live with his memories. "Whosoever slayeth Cain, vengeance shall be taken on him sevenfold. And the Lord set a mark upon Cain, lest any finding him should kill him." (Gen. 4:15.)

This enigmatic "mark of Cain" is frequently and erroneously considered to have involved the color of his skin and thus to have identified him as the first black man. Instead, it was almost certainly a physical sign corresponding to the pattern of tattooing that identified the clan of an ancient nomad and thereby gave him a kind of social protection. In the case of Cain the Genesis story clearly indicates that the mark set upon him was protective. Having sentenced him to be a fugitive for the rest of his life, the Lord took appropriate steps to guarantee that the sentence would not be commuted as a result of an attack upon Cain by human foes.

Builders Liable for Injuries

No European city had even the crudest approach to a building code until late in the Middle Ages. And the concept of public liability, according to which an owner is responsible for accidents that occur on his property, is usually considered to be a modern and rather sophisticated legal idea. Actually, both the basic notion of public liability and the rudiments of a building code are found in Scripture.

After the Hebrews ceased to live in tents and began to build houses concentrated within cities, rulers and persons of wealth insisted on having flat roofs sturdy enough to bear considerable weight. David "walked upon the roof of the king's house" on the occasion when he saw the wife of Uriah the Hittite bathing (II Sam. 11:2). In all probability she, too, was upon a rooftop, a favorite place for lounging and strolling. As late as New Testament times the roof was used for many purposes; messengers of the Roman centurion Cornelius reached Peter at a time when he was praying "upon the housetop" in Joppa (Acts 10:9).

Because the use of roofs involved the danger of falling, builders were very early required to shield them with parapets. "When thou buildest a new house," stipulated the earliest known building code, "then thou shalt make a battlement for thy roof, that thou bring not blood upon thine house, if any man fall from thence" (Deut. 22:8).

Two Views of the Sixth Commandment

Most persons who use the Bible reverently and habitually are deeply concerned to read its words as nearly as possible in their original sense. In spite of this emphasis centuries of cultural change have so distorted the sense of the sixth commandment that Moses would probably repudiate it as it is now frequently interpreted.

"Thou shalt not kill," he demanded as a result of his long vigil with Jehovah. But the Hebrew word used in Exod. 20:13 and Deut. 5:17 didn't have the present broad meaning of "to put to death; to deprive of life." Rather, it had connotations we today associate with the ideas of murder and manslaughter.

Far from forbidding acts of violence in self-defense, many Old Testament passages laud the heroes who surpassed their comrades in killing enemies. Not even the New Testament anywhere suggests that a person should refrain from killing animals for food. Still, the sixth commandment has been widely quoted as an argument against any act calculated to take the life of any creature, whether human or animal, under any circumstances whatever.

The force of tradition is so great that translators of "authorized" versions of Scripture (including the RSV) have hesitated to restore Moses' original meaning by modifying centuries-old language. But in his private translation of the Old Testament (1935) J. M. P. Smith boldly rendered the sixth commandment: "You must not commit murder." Similar usage is followed in the Jewish-sponsored, modern-language Torah, or Five Books of Moses (1962).

An Eye for an Eye

Measured by modern criteria, the Old Testament standard of justice symbolized by "eye for eye, tooth for tooth" (Exod. 21:24) seems cruel and vindictive. But when it was framed this code was a major step toward equal justice for all men.

Under most ancient legal systems a nobleman or chieftain did not receive the same punishment as that meted out to a servant or a slave who committed the same offense. This double standard was not simply a matter of tribal or community understanding; it was spelled out in detail in various written codes and was therefore a part of the established body of formal law.

Moses insisted that even in the case of an injury inflicted by a servant upon a member of the ruling class, punishment had to fit the crime. That is, instead of ordering a man's death because he put out an eye of his master, judges could hand down a maximum sentence of an eye for an eye.

This principle also served to reduce the severity of retaliation by persons who had suffered injury or assault. Under it even servants and slaves had legal rights. A master who knocked out an eye or a tooth of his manservant or his maidservant was required to confer liberty upon the injured one (Exod. 21:26-27).

Special Havens for Involuntary Killers

Jewish law in the time of the patriarchs included a provision that on the surface seems strangely contradictory. A person who committed involuntary manslaughter (clearly distinguished from willful murder) could flee to a city of refuge where relatives of his victim couldn't touch him. Primitive vengeance, the earliest principle of law, no longer applied. For practical purposes this established the world's earliest forerunner of today's practice of refusing to grant extradition papers for a wanted man.

Six special cities of refuge were established, three on each side of the Jordan (Num. 35:6, 13-14). In Josh. 20:7-8 these asylums are listed as Kedesh, Shechem, and Hebron on the Canaan side; Bezer, Ramoth, and Golan in the Transjordan. All were priestly or Levitical cities.

Precisely how they functioned and whether or not they became focal points of civil disorder resulting from the presence of numerous refugees isn't known. This much is clear: they were set up so that a person who had accidentally spilled another's blood would be safe from tribal retaliation that operated under the governing principle of an eye for an eye.

Upon the death of the local high priest all fugitives in a given city were free to return to their homes. Crude as it looks to modern eyes, this system incorporated many of the principles that govern our most advanced sets of legal procedures aimed at securing justice in cases of accidental homicide.

Centuries later, medieval cathedrals and churches provided sanctuary for hunted men. A person who succeeded in getting to an altar was immune from arrest in the holy place.

Four Degrees of Guilt

Contrary to widespread impressions that Hebrews in the time of the patriarchs were simple, naïve, and organized into a primitive society, they very early developed an intricate system in which homicides were divided into four distinct categories.

Murder was the most dreadful offense. But in order to establish a charge of premeditated murder it was necessary to show that a killer lay in wait (Exod. 21:13), that long-standing enmity existed between the principal parties (Num. 35:20-21), or that a deadly weapon was used (Num. 35:16-18).

Accidental homicide was second in gravity. Grave as this offense was, it did not carry the death penalty. A culprit could flee to one of several cities of refuge and take asylum there.

A third category grew out of the constant exposure of working men to the lethal horns of half-wild oxen. When a beast gored a man to death, prior circumstances governed the verdict of his fellow tribesmen. An animal not previously known to be vicious was stoned to death, and its meat could not be eaten, but no penalty was exacted from its owner. But in the event that an ox with a reputation for savage behavior succeeded in committing homicide, both the animal and its owner were judged guilty and sentenced to death.

Finally, Hebrew law had provisions for dealing with justifiable homicide. No blood-guilt was involved when a man killed in self-defense. Nor was there any penalty for slaying in battle or taking the life of a nighttime burglar.

Alone among peoples of the ancient Near East, Hebrews permitted no compromise in a case equivalent to first-degree murder. Egyptians, Babylonians, Assyrians, and others allowed many such cases to be settled; in keeping with the scriptural law Hebrews demanded the death penalty (Num. 35:31-33).

Sacred Dice for Reaching a Divine Verdict

At least until the time of David, Jehovah's people used an elaborate form of religious lottery to identify lawbreakers and gain answers to baffling questions. Though mentioned many times in Scripture under a variety of names, the equipment was guarded so closely that hardly anything is known about it even today.

Two objects roughly equivalent to modern dice and called Urim and Thummim were central in vivid ceremonies whose outcome often spelled life or death. Questions addressed to them were frequently shaped so that a clear "Yes" or "No" answer could be received. Occasionally termed "the ephod" (as in I Sam. 23:9-12) from the garment in whose pocket they were carried, the sacred dice probably bore inscriptions on some or all faces.

A detailed case history involved a "sin against the Lord" (equivalent to a crime against the state) in which Hebrews who defeated a band of Philistines killed and ate captured animals without having their blood ceremonially drained from them. This created a state of national emergency; the Lord was offended, and the culprit or culprits had to be found and punished.

As recounted in I Samuel 14, the matter came to King Saul's attention when the Lord failed to answer his plea for guidance. Saul called his army together and warned that the culprit would have to be found and put to death. His soldiers refused to give him any information. Seeking a "Yes" or "No" answer, Saul put his followers on one side, himself and his son on the other. When the sacred lot was cast, "Saul and Jonathan were taken [identified as guilty]: but the people escaped." With the suspects drastically reduced in this way, Saul then had another lot cast between himself and his son. "And Jonathan was taken." Sentenced to die, he was rescued by the people.

Sacred dice cast by Haman of Persia and called Pur (Esth. 3:7; 9:26) have been identified by archaeologists. Formed in quadrangular fashion, they were engraved with the numbers 1, 2, 5, and 6. Though their roles were similar to that of Urim and Thummim, precise techniques for their use are unknown.

Guilt Exposed Through Occult Powers

Law enforcement officers have only recently begun to acknowledge that many of them rely upon mediums and clairvoyants for leads in baffling cases. Though more widely developed in Europe than in the United States, the practice is spreading in this country because of the widespread publicity connected with such cases as that of the Boston Strangler.

History's first detailed account of crime-breaking by means of a psychic clue is recorded, not in a massive anthology of true police cases, but in Scripture (II Kings 5).

Gehazi, servant of Elisha, saw an opportunity for personal gain in the remarkable healing of Naaman the Syrian, whom his master cleansed of leprosy. From the fact that Naaman used horses and a chariot to seek out the mysterious Hebrew holy man, it may be inferred that the Syrian had considerable means.

Having himself arrived at that conclusion, Gehazi ran after Naaman and pretended that Elisha had sent him to request payment in the form of a talent of silver and two changes of garments. Naaman insisted that this was not enough; he handed Gehazi the clothing plus twice the weight of silver requested. Gehazi hid his loot and went in to Elisha as though nothing had happened. Questioned, he insisted that he had gone nowhere.

But through clairvoyance Elisha knew all about the clandestine incident. "Went not mine heart with thee, when the man turned again from his chariot to meet thee?" he demanded of his servant. His guilt exposed as a result of his master's occult powers, Gehazi made no further attempt to protest his innocence and as punishment was striken with the leprosy of the man whom he had defrauded.

Family Guilt from Individual Felony

Convicted as a result of Joshua's use of the lot as a form of oracle, an entire family suffered death because of one member's theft.

Repulsed in his assault on the fortress of Ai, Joshua was told by the Lord that the defeat was due to the fact that stolen things were carried into battle. Using a type of lottery not described in the vivid account, Joshua determined that guilt lay within the tribe of Judah. Clans within that tribe were brought forward one by one, and the lot fell on the Zarhites. Tested, the Zarhites were clear—with the exception of Zabdi. He brought his entire family forward and the lot was cast time after time until it fell upon his grandson Achan.

Convicted by this supernatural device, Achan confessed that at the sack of Jericho he couldn't resist "a goodly Babylonish garment, and two hundred shekels of silver, and a wedge of gold of fifty shekels weight" (Josh. 7:21). In taking these spoils Achan knew he was violating a specific edict of Jehovah. His loot was buried under his tent, he admitted.

Joshua sent messengers to check the story. They found the hidden booty—a potent source of evil to all Israel—and positively identified Achan as the thief. So the assembled Israelites seized Achan, his loot, "and his sons, and his daughters, and his oxen, and his asses, and his tent, and all that he had. . . . And all Israel stoned him with stones, and burned them with fire, after they had stoned them with stones." (Josh. 7:24-25.)

Community guilt having been removed by punishment of the individual offender and those most closely linked with him, "the Lord turned from the fierceness of his anger" (Josh. 7:26). At the next assault Joshua's forces captured and sacked the city of Ai.

Shoes Used in Making Contracts

Footgear played so important a part in the life of ancient desert folk that it came to have symbolic meaning. As a result, a detailed record is preserved showing how footgear was used to make a contract or pledge legally binding.

Seeking to buy a parcel of land belonging to Naomi because ownership of it carried the right to claim Ruth as wife, Boaz bargained with the relative who had first option on the deal. In the presence of ten elders of the city, who constituted official witnesses, Boaz insisted that the kinsman either exercise his rights or give them up. This man said it would jeopardize his other holdings to redeem the property and offered Boaz his claim.

"Now this was the manner in former time in Israel concerning redeeming and concerning changing, for to confirm all things; a man plucked off his shoe, and gave it to his neighbour: and this was a testimony in Israel. Therefore the kinsman said unto Boaz, Buy it for thee. So he drew off his shoe." (Ruth 4:7-8.)

Contrary to popular interpretations that stem from the awkward style of the King James Version at this point, Boaz did not take off his shoe to bind the contract. It was the relative who did so, as a sign that he was ready to forfeit his right to purchase. In Deut. 25:5-10 the law involved is reported in detail.

The gear with which the reluctant one indicated his willingness to give Boaz his option didn't resemble a modern shoe. It was a sandal consisting of a leather sole fastened to the foot by thongs tied between the first and second toes and then knotted around the ankle.

Death Penalty for Religious Trespassing

From the time of Moses, Jehovah was revered as tenderhearted beyond description. He was called a God whose "mercy endureth for ever" (I Chron. 16:34) and "a God full of compassion, and gracious" (Ps. 86:15). Yet as late as the time of Jesus, Abraham's descendants invoked the death penalty in cases when Gentiles were caught within forbidden areas of Jehovah's temple in Jerusalem.

Men who had not embraced the faith and ways of the Hebrews and thus were labeled the uncircumcised were permitted to promenade in an outer court of the temple. But a special barrier was erected to shield the sacred inner enclosure from the prying eyes of unbelievers. In Jesus' day notices written in Greek were posted at conspicuous points.

One of these, found in 1871, warned: "Let no foreigner enter inside the barrier and the fence around the sanctuary. Whosoever is caught will be the cause of death following as a penalty."

A high moment in the drama of Paul's dealings with the Jews occurred when men who had seen him in company with Trophimus of Ephesus accused him of bringing Greeks into the temple so that he "hath polluted this holy place" (Acts 21:28). A riot broke out, and it became necessary for Roman officers to intervene in order to prevent the crowd from killing Paul.

In its original intent the death penalty for intrusion into the sacred place by an unbeliever served as a device by which to guard the sanctity of the temple. An uncircumcised person who succeeded in catching a glimpse of holy rites would learn how to imitate them. At the same time, he would profane the holy place. Hence, the proper way to deal with an intruder was to execute him.

Scripture from the Pen of a Prisoner

In modern times several islands have played spectacular roles in the history of punishment. Napoleon was banished to the island of Elba. French penal authorities created and maintained Devil's Island as an escape-proof prison for incorrigibles. Until recently the strongest of all United States prisons was Alcatraz—deliberately erected upon an island.

Far from being a new idea, the concept of safeguarding enemies of the state by placing them upon islands was familiar to the Greeks and Romans. According to the New Testament its strangest and, in some respects, most sublime book was produced by a prisoner serving time in a penal colony located on the island of Patmos.

About ten miles long by six miles wide, this rocky and inhospitable bit of land lies off the western coast of Asia Minor. It was virtually escape proof, for armed guards could easily repulse any boat used in an attempted rescue. Hence the caesars reserved it for especially dangerous prisoners—that is, persons who threatened the peace of the empire by political agitation.

According to Rev. 1:9, John was banished to Patmos because he refused to cease stirring up trouble by his testimony concerning Jesus Christ and "the Word of God." His zeal for the faith made him an enemy of the empire, for worship of the emperor was consistently challenged by Christians. John may have been exiled under Domitian, shortly before or after A.D. 95. Since only the emperor had authority to sentence a man to spend the rest of his days on Patmos, John must have been considered a source of real threat. Forced to cease preaching, he took up his pen and produced the Revelation.

Biblical Impact upon English Law

Many kings and rulers have shown great interest in the Bible, but only one potentate of any significance acquired considerable skill as a translator. Alfred the Great, known to his subjects as Aelfred, not only holds this distinction, but went so far as to incorporate snatches of his translation into the laws of England.

Since he was the fifth son of King Aethelwulf, Aelfred was not regarded as a likely successor to his father so he received an education more suitable for a churchman than a sovereign. An accomplished Latin scholar, he rendered a number of secular books into Anglo-Saxon. Then he turned his talents to Scripture and translated at least fifty psalms and other favorite passages.

Two of his brothers died during his adolescence and the third when he was about twenty-two. As a result Aelfred ascended the throne in April, 871, and took over the full responsibility of defending his country from Danish invaders.

Though he spent much of his life on the battlefield, the royal scholar did not abandon his interest in the Bible. He spent far more time with the Old Testament than with the New Testament, and considered Exodus 20–23 to constitute "the Golden Rule." Using his own translation, he incorporated Exod. 21:12-15 into the laws of the kingdom (much as Scottish law concerning incest was later taken bodily from Leviticus 18).

Scriptural injunctions that governed the conduct of his subjects became known as Alfred's dooms. Expanded and modified in succeeding centuries, these brief verses played a key role in shaping the development of English and hence of American law.

"Christ's Murderers" Banned from England

Because Jesus' antagonists in the Gospels are so frequently labeled simply "the Jews," the people who gave the world the Bible and the Saviour were legally barred from England during a period of nearly four centuries.

Jews reached the island kingdom at least as early as 1066, for some came at the express invitation of William the Conqueror. But after the Conqueror's death William II—called Rufus because of his fiery complexion—ascended the throne. Using the scriptural record as an excuse for repudiating his father's policies, Rufus made it a crime for "Christ's murderers" to become converts to Christianity.

Legends multiplied. It was whispered that some Jews used the blood of murdered Christians for their Passover feast. Persons who refused to believe that tale often endorsed the story that Jews habitually broke into churches and cathedrals in order to steal consecrated wafers used in Communion services.

Public opinion reached such a fever point that in 1290 all Jews were expelled from England simply for the crime of having been born Jews—the people who had sent Jesus to the cross. France, numerous independent German states, and eventually Spain and Portugal followed England's lead. Though a few returned a bit earlier, until the middle of the seventeenth century it was a violation of the law for a Jew to set foot on English soil. In 1801 when Isaac D'Israeli became an English citizen, he chose to have his children baptized into the Anglican Church—with the result that his son Benjamin became England's first prime minister of Jewish descent.

Bible-based Execution of Witches

No one knows how many thousands of persons were put to death during the late Middle Ages and early Renaissance for the crime of witchcraft. But the number was so great that Exod. 22:18 has no rival for the title of the deadliest verse in the Bible. It makes no exception or qualification to the rule: "Thou shalt not suffer a witch to live."

Men divided on practically every other issue agreed in accepting this verse as a base of both ecclesiastical and civil laws. In 1490 Roman Catholic authorities issued the *Malleus maleficarum,* an elaborate textbook for the examination and extermination of witches. "I would have no compassion on the witches," Martin Luther said. "I would burn them all." Some of John Wesley's theological opponents challenged the reality of witchcraft. "I cannot give up to all the Deists in Great Britain the existence of witchcraft," said the founder of Methodism, "till I give up the credit of all history, sacred and profane."

When authorities lagged in their zeal for enforcing the law of Exod. 22:18, common folk took matters into their own hands and burned any witch they could find—and then boasted that they had been faithful to Holy Writ.

Contrary to popular tales no person convicted of witchcraft in seventeenth-century Salem, Massachusetts, were burned to death. But about twenty were hanged on Gallows Hill, and two other accused persons died in prison.

Animals Tried by Old Testament Laws

Scripture repeatedly stresses the fact that animals lack the capabilities of humans. Still, Old Testament law held dumb creatures responsible for crimes. Violations entailed severe penalties that included capital punishment.

An ox that gored a man or woman so severely that death ensued was considered guilty without a trial. Law prescribed that the animal be stoned, but even in death its flesh was held to be taboo and could not be eaten (Exod. 21:28). For the crime of trespassing upon the holy ground of Mt. Sinai, the offender "whether it be beast or man" was "stoned or shot through." But the text in Exod. 19:12-13 doesn't indicate whether a carcass could be eaten or had to be abandoned.

Since the Bible was the chief legal code of the Middle Ages, animal trials were held at frequent intervals for centuries. At Lavegny, France, in 1457 a sow and her brood of pigs were brought into court on charges of having killed a child. Brilliant work by the defense attorney led to the release of the six young animals on probation, but the sow was sentenced to be hanged by the neck until dead.

Cats, goats, chickens, and dogs were among lawbreakers brought to justice. A horse was executed for homicide at Dijon in 1639, and a mare guilty of the same offense was burned at the stake at Aix in 1693. Near Moissy, France, a bull gored his master so severely that death resulted. As was customary with larger animals accused of crime, the bovine prisoner was locked up in the local jail until court convened. On conviction of premeditated murder, he was hanged on the village gallows.

By the eighteenth century most courts took the position that the ancient law of Deuteronomy was no longer binding. The last known formal trial and execution of a dumb creature, that of a cow, took place near Munster, Germany, in 1740.

Literacy as the Key to Life

About 1087 King William II of England set in motion a program aimed at fostering literacy. By royal decree a person subject to the death penalty could appeal for "benefit of clergy." Nominally in force as late as 1700, this judicial procedure involved the use of a Bible.

A prisoner who showed his ability to read it saved his neck—literally, and not figuratively. A magistrate might open the Book at random for a test. But it was more common for the bishop's representative, appointed for the purpose at each prison, to stipulate that the accused man read a particular verse. At Newgate it was nearly always Ps. 51:1: *"Miserere mei, Deus, secundum magnam misericordiam tuam; et secundum multitudinem miserationum tuarum, dele iniquitatem meam."* Very early this became known as the neck-verse.

If the ecclesiastical official said, *"Legit ut clericus"* ("He reads like a clerk"), the offender was only burned on the hand. But if he bungled his neck-verse, he was executed on schedule. Some unknown hack poet summed up the whole matter in verse:

If a clerk had been taken
For stealing bacon,
  For burglary, murder or rape,
If he could but rehearse
(Well prompt) his neck-verse
  He never could fail to escape.

Executed for Religious Obstinacy

A sixteenth-century English rebel against the church used Scripture as an argument against capital punishment. Nevertheless, she was tortured and executed in the presence of the Bishop of London.

Anne Askew, born about 1521, was the second daughter of a petty nobleman. Her elder sister, Martha, died after being betrothed to a Lincolnshire justice of the peace. In obedience to scriptural marriage codes, her parents forced Anne to take Martha's place and marry Thomas Kyme.

They quarreled frequently and violently. Anne became fanatical in her zeal for Bible reading, and in pursuing her studies became convinced that some doctrines of the church were wrong. Her chief objection was to the view that the wafer of the Mass literally becomes the flesh of Jesus. At least twice in 1545 she was examined for heresy, then released.

But on June 18, 1546, she was brought before a commission that included the Bishop of London, the Lord Mayor, and three other notables. No jury was impaneled and no witnesses were called. On the basis of interrogation she was condemned to be burned; her judges concluded her to be "very obstinate and heady in reasoning of matters of religion."

Taken to London Tower and tortured on the rack, she refused to change her views. She insisted that she had searched the Bible through "and never found that Christ or his disciples had put anyone to death." So she challenged the Lord Chancellor to prove her wrong or to release her. With her query still unanswered, on July 16 she was burned at Smithfield in the presence of the dignitaries who had condemned her.

Strangled for Translating Scripture

Henry VIII, king of England and Ireland, was not the uncouth man often depicted by novelists. On the contrary, he was a highly educated scholar, linguist, and musician. Tradition has it that in early manhood, being deeply interested in theology, he seriously considered taking holy orders in order to become a priest. Still it was he who signed the death warrant of pioneer Bible translator William Tyndale.

Tyndale violated both civil and ecclesiastical law by publishing a New Testament on the continent of Europe and then smuggling copies into England. To make matters worse, he criticized Henry's numerous divorces and remarriages so he had to take refuge outside Great Britain.

After a period in the Netherlands he was forced to flee because Henry demanded his surrender from Emperor Charles V "as one who was spreading sedition in England." In May, 1535, the Bible translator was betrayed by a young protégé. Imperial officers imprisoned him at Vilvorde Castle, six miles from Brussels. He remained there for a year and 135 days; a letter begging for a lamp and his Hebrew books so that he could continue his work on the Bible has been preserved.

Not only was his request refused; he was formally tried on the charge of heresy—a religious rather than a civil crime. Convicted, he was strangled at the stake on October 6, 1536. Then his body was burned.

Tyndale's chief regret was his failure to complete the task of rendering Scripture into English so that common men could read with understanding. As was the custom in the period, the condemned man was permitted a final statement. He chose to bow his head and pray, "Lord, open the King of England's eyes!"

Burned Because of Irregular Views

John Calvin was only twenty-seven when he wrote a famous theological treatise translated into English as *Institutes of the Christian Religion.* His Bible-based set of doctrines proved so inflammatory that he was banished from Paris and took refuge in Switzerland. Under his leadership Geneva was organized as a theocracy, or political unit "governed directly by God." Yet in this Bible-based state a Spanish physician lost his life because he held irregular views of the Trinity.

Michael Servetus exchanged letters with Calvin as early as 1545 and expressed a desire to visit Geneva. Though deeply interested in Scripture, Servetus was unable to accept traditional formulas defining God as "Father, Son, and Holy Ghost"—one God expressed through three personalities. He put his doubts into print and stirred up a furor of indignation.

The New Testament nowhere conveys the doctrinal formula as such; it was shaped by church councils of the fourth and fifth centuries. Still, Servetus was interrogated by the inquisitor-general at Lyons, France, on March 16, 1553. Two weeks later he was arrested and "examined." He escaped, spent four months as a fugitive, and on Saturday, August 6, rode into a village on the French side of Geneva. The next morning he walked into "the city governed by God," was recognized at church, and arrested.

John Calvin suggested that so vile a foe of the Bible and its faith should be promptly beheaded. But followers of the great theologian insisted upon a lengthy trial so that all Servetus' heretical views could be properly recorded. Hearings ended on October 26 when sentence was passed. As a result, agents of Protestant leaders took Servetus to Champel the next day and burned him at the stake until his body was totally reduced to ashes.

Condemned for Saying the Earth Moves

The grandeur of God the Creator is stressed throughout Scripture. He is infinite and his power has no limit. His majesty is beyond human imagination. Yet defenders of Holy Writ used the Bible as a weapon with which to attack an astronomer who tried to help men develop a more exalted concept of the Creator's work in shaping the universe.

As a result of having discovered ways to improve the quality of telescopes, Galileo turned his attention to the heavens. With self-made instruments, he found that the moon shines with reflected light, that Jupiter has four large satellites, and that there are countless stars in the Milky Way. Soon after 1610 he began observing sunspots and their movements and in 1613 published *Letters on the Solar Spots*. This treatise used scriptural as well as scientific arguments to support the view that the earth and other planets revolve about the sun.

But in 1615 Galileo appeared before the Inquisition at Rome. After a month of examination his proposition that the sun is the center of our system and does not revolve about the earth was condemned "as foolish, absurd, false in theology, and heretical, because expressly contrary to Holy Scripture." The scientist was called back to Rome late in life and forced to recant, or publicly announce that his earlier conclusions were false. Legend has it that after he finished taking a solemn oath avowing that the earth is fixed in position as the center of the universe, he whispered, "It still moves!"

Except for members of obscure sects, few Christians today regard Holy Writ as a handbook of astronomy that supports the system named after the second-century astronomer-mathematician Ptolemy, who taught that sun, planets, and stars revolve about the earth.

Intolerance in Massachusetts

Though it never used the name officially, the Massachusetts Bay Colony was for all practical purposes a Bible commonwealth—one of the few Scripture-based modern political experiments that succeeded for more than a half-century.

Puritans aboard the *Mayflower* reached Cape Cod on November 9, 1620. But before proceeding toward the new land of freedom before them, they drew up a solemn compact stipulating the terms of their government. Membership in the church was required as a condition for voting, and the clergy were given great power both in selecting new church members and striking recalcitrant old ones off the rolls. As a result, Plymouth was never a democracy. Instead it was an oligarchy sometimes ruled by as few as one fifth of the population. Founded in 1630 as an offshoot of Plymouth, the Massachusetts Bay Colony was based on the same governing principles.

Puritan leaders used biblical standards in establishing their written and unwritten laws—and employed harsh measures in enforcing them. One servant who was convicted of having uttered "foul, scandalous invective against the churches and the government" was severely whipped. Then his ears were cut off, and he was banished from the colony.

Such multiple punishments probably weren't common. But Roger Williams was banished because of his religious views, and all Quakers were automatically persecuted. Expressing the general attitude of the Bible-based group whose members at least theoretically held their wealth in common, the Rev. Nathaniel Ward wrote that persons of other religious beliefs "shall have free liberty to keepe away from us."

"Blue Laws" Reflected Unwritten Codes

Settled in 1638 by a company from London, the Colony of New Haven was greatly influenced by the Rev. John Davenport. In the nearly thirty years of its independence before it united with Connecticut, New Haven's unwritten legal code was largely drawn from or shaped by Scripture.

Very early, hecklers and wits of less than pious turn of mind made fun of the community. In the tradition of the American tall tale, actual practices were magnified and distorted and then reported as authentic. Though there is no documentary support for the claim that this or any other Connecticut settlement had a formal set of blue laws, the force of tradition is so great that the term has entered common speech to name any group of puritanical regulations. Richard Peters' *General History of Connecticut* (1829) made public a long list of statutes. Though their authenticity has long since been disproved, they actually may represent a reasonably good interpretation of the unwritten moral code that prevailed in the colony noted for its strict application of "the general rules of righteousness."

As late as the period just after the Civil War it was generally believed that Bible fanatics really had ruled New Haven with an iron hand. Some of the laws reputed to have been in effect there but actually fabricated by Peters are:

No priest shall abide in the dominion: he shall be banished, and suffer death on his return. Priests may be seized by any one without a warrant.

No one shall run on the sabbath-day, or walk in his garden, or elsewhere except reverently to and from meeting.

No one shall read common-prayer, keep Christmas or saint-days, make minced pies, dance, play cards, or play on any instrument of music except the drum, trumpet and Jews-harp.

If any person turn Quaker he shall be banished, and not suffered to return, but upon pain of death.

A Woman Guilty of Talking Too Much

Scripture has furnished support for many movements aimed at securing liberty and freedom, but male Puritans of the Massachusetts Bay Colony employed it to defend their tyranny over women. Though it was never included in the official articles that governed the commonwealth, Paul's standard as set forth in I Cor. 14:34-35 was unofficially treated as binding. In the Geneva Bible, used by members of the colony, the key verses read: "Let your women kepe silence in the Churche: for it is not permitted unto theme to speake: but [they ought] to be subject, as also the Law saith. And if thei will learne anie thing, let them aske their housbands at home: for it is a shame for women to speake in the Churche."

Mrs. Anne Hutchinson, who ignored this principle and created considerable turmoil, was brought to formal trial in 1637. When she demanded to know what law she was charged with breaking, elders of the colony cited the fifth commandment—which requires that children honor their fathers and mothers. By talking too much, judges ruled, Mrs. Hutchinson had brought reproach upon the fathers of the commonwealth!

Found guilty, she was sentenced to be banished from Massachusetts, never to return. She took refuge in Rhode Island, and then migrated to what is now Westchester County, New York. There she died with her children and grandchildren in an Indian massacre of 1643. When Governor John Winthrop learned of it, he meditated for a time before turning to his diary and writing: "God's hand is the more apparently seen therein, to pick out this woeful woman to make her and those belonging to her an unheard of heavy example of the Indians' cruelty."

"Franklin's Rods" Condemned

Though he didn't do it deliberately, Benjamin Franklin stirred up such a commotion among churchmen that some publicly denounced him as a rebel against God. The ire of defenders of the faith was not evoked by Franklin's less-than-orthodox religious views but by his invention of the lightning rod.

Immediately after he drew electricity from the clouds in his famous kite experiment of 1752, the Philadelphia inventor suggested equipping buildings with iron rods so that lightning could run into the ground without doing harm. But the prevailing interpretation of Scripture made thunder and lightning tokens of divine wrath—the artillery of heaven, to be accepted without protest or interference. Especially in Massachusetts, some churchmen argued that erection of "Franklin's rods" on a few buildings had so angered the Lord that he sent the earthquake of 1755 as punishment.

Though spires and steeples of churches make them especially vulnerable to lightning, they were the last public buildings to be equipped with conductors. Americans adopted them relatively quickly, but no

English house of worship was equipped with lightning rods before 1762. Bible scholars of France, Germany, Italy, and Spain united in denouncing the American invention as heretical.

A single bolt of lightning finally converted church leaders of all faiths to the use of conductors. For years the Republic of Venice had used the huge vaults of the church of San Nazaro, at Brescia, as a storage place for gunpowder. Approximately one hundred tons of it were on hand when lightning struck in 1767. More than three thousand persons were killed in the subsequent explosion, and a great section of the city was leveled.

In the aftermath of this catastrophe, scriptural references to lightning (mentioned about thirty times in the Old Testament but not once in the New Testament) were reexamined. Interpreters revised their judgments, concluded that nothing in Holy Writ expressly forbade the use of conductors, and sanctioned their use on cathedrals, churches, and meeting houses.

Jailed for Vending the Scriptures

Persecution of Bible distributors has been frequent and violent in non-Christian lands, but it was the constitution of a Christian nation that was revised following publicity aroused by the case of a lone missionary.

Born in northern Italy, Francisco Penzotti emigrated to Uruguay as a boy. On the way out of a dance one evening he bought a copy of the Gospel of John. Penzotti read it through before he went to sleep, experienced a conversion to Protestantism, and became a preacher and Bible society agent.

He took his wife and children to Callao, Peru, in 1888, where he served as that country's only evangelical missionary. Harassed for street-corner vending of Scripture portions, he was eventually arrested and thrown into the "Casa Mata" (House of death). This foul dungeon, seventy by twenty-two feet in size, already held thirty-six other prisoners of both sexes. All of them slept on the filthy dirt floor.

An American mining engineer managed to snap a single picture that revealed conditions in the Casa Mata. Published in the New York *Herald,* it created such a stir that both the United States and Queen Victoria's government asked for an investigation. As a result of it Penzotti was released from prison on the day before Easter, 1891. He immediately resumed his work of distributing the Bible and preaching, and the constitution of Peru was amended by a clause granting religious liberty.

Fined for Teaching Darwin's Theory

America's most famous legal case involving Scripture led to the conviction of the defendant. But in spite of the fact that the sentence imposed upon the convicted amounted to a fine of just one hundred dollars, the Scopes trial (or the monkey trial) is known around the world.

Tennessee legislators became alarmed because they felt biology teachers were undermining the authority of the Bible by teaching their pupils Charles Darwin's theory of organic evolution, so they passed a law forbidding the teaching of the theory in public schools.

John Thomas Scopes, a teacher in Dayton High School, deliberately violated the law. No atheist, agnostic, or attacker of the sanctity of Holy Writ, Scopes felt that intellectual honesty demanded some treatment of one of the most controversial topics then being discussed.

Arrested and brought to trial, the obscure Tennessee teacher became the focus of national controversy. William Jennings Bryan volunteered his services as aide to the prosecuting attorney; Clarence Darrow came to the defense of Scopes. Much testimony was false to the teachings of Darwin, himself educated for the ministry, who nowhere suggested that humans are the descendants of monkeys. But in an emotion-charged atmosphere, sparked by zeal for defending a literal interpretation of the Genesis story, the jury returned a verdict of guilty.

There was worldwide reaction in scientific and academic circles, yet the law under which Scopes was convicted remained on the statute books of Tennessee until 1967. That year vigorous debate resulted in a compromise that permits the teaching of evolution as a theory, but not as an established fact.

How It Started

Olive Branch as Emblem of Peace

Olives grow only in comparatively narrow geographical bands. Small variations in temperature and annual rainfall are sufficient to make a region barren of olive trees. As a result, only a small fraction of the countries of the world produce this fruit in commercial quantities. Yet through the impact of Scripture persons who have never seen an olive tree use "olive branch" to mean an overture toward peace and harmony.

This nearly universal figure of speech grows out of the fact that in ancient Mesopotamia the olive was sometimes depicted as the tree of life. But the modern proverbial phrase stems directly from a single incident. As described in Genesis 8, the universal flood was halted through the mercy of God. After Noah's ark came to rest on the top of the mountains of Ararat, water continued to recede steadily for week after week. Seeking to determine whether to abandon ship and seek dry land, Noah sent out a raven. This bird failed to return, so he released a dove that circled fruitlessly and then came back to her perch on the ark. Seven days later Noah tried again. This time the dove "came in to him in the evening; and, lo, in her mouth was an olive leaf plucked off: so Noah knew that the waters were abated from off the earth" (Gen. 8:11).

This incident was stressed as symbolizing the end of wrath on the part of God and the beginning of peace. Depicted by countless painters and described in poems composed in every major language of the western world, the olive leaf of Genesis was transformed into *olive branch* and treated as an emblem of peace or gesture of conciliation. Most paintings of the eagle as the symbol of United States power and peacemaking show the bird clutching arrows with one foot and holding an olive branch with the other.

Formation of the Name "Hebrew"

After centuries of investigation scholars remain divided concerning the etymology of the name "Hebrew." But though they differ concerning the factors that produced it, most concur in saying that the Hebrews gained their name through secular rather than religious influences.

Twentieth-century archaeological finds in Syria and Mesopotamia have yielded many secular inscriptions. Among them are notations made by Israel's earliest rivals—who described the chosen people as itinerant tradesmen using donkeys to transport their wares. William F. Albright says that as a result of continuous travel between the big trading centers of the Middle East these merchant people became known as the *'Apiru,* or "dusty ones." According to Albright the ancient tradesmen's title became *Ibri* in the speech of the Israelites and then entered English as Hebrew. Early scholars (who didn't have access to the inscriptions studied by Albright) considered *Ibri* to mean simply "one from the other side of the river."

Roland de Vaux stresses the fact that in Scripture the name Hebrew is seldom applied to an Israelite except when he had forfeited his freedom by semivoluntary slavery. Israelites who entered the service of Philistines are also labeled "Hebrews" (I Sam. 14:21). This usage prevailed in a period considerably later than that in which the "dusty ones" gained their name, however.

Complete agreement concerning the origin of this now universal title may never be reached. But regardless of differences on other scores, all present interpretations suggest that the Hebrews didn't get their name as a result of religious zeal.

Consecrated Oil Adopted from Egyptians

During most of Hebrew history Egypt has symbolized everything hateful and abominable. This view developed during the long period of captivity and oppression that was ended by divine deliverance and the Exodus into the desert. Though anything and everything Egyptian was despised by the Israelites, much evidence indicates that practices associated with the use of holy oil in anointment were borrowed from these people.

Generations or even centuries before their Egyptian sojourn, the Hebrews were acquainted with aromatic gums and fragrant leaves. One such substance obtained from trees on the plateau of Gilead is still famous as "balm of Gilead." It was an important item of commerce at a very early period. (See Gen. 37:25.)

But the official practice of going through rites of consecration and purification by means of sacred oil is never mentioned until the Hebrews were liberated from their long period of captivity in Egypt. Moses' first ark, or portable altar, was designed so that incense could be burned upon it. Like the perfume that was reserved for Jehovah alone (Exod. 30:34-38), the holy anointing oil was so important and sacred that its formula has been preserved (Exod. 30:23-25).

Made in great quantity, it was eventually used for a multitude of purposes. Vessels and furniture of the place of worship, the altar itself, and even the priests were made holy by means of the consecrated ointment. Use was so general that it became proverbial that "the odor of sanctity" marked a person or thing set aside for service of the Lord. Later generations of Israelites showed implacable hatred of everything Egyptian, so it is particularly ironic that their use of consecrated oil didn't start until they had been in the land of the Nile long enough to see it used in worship and learn how to compound it.

How Palestine Got Its Name

Though the ultimate origin of their own title is lost in antiquity, abundant evidence shows that it was the people today called Philistines who named the most fought-over region in the world—Palestine.

Philistia (Hebrew *pelesheth*) figures prominently in ancient records as the land of the Philistines. Documents produced at the court of Egypt's Ramses III (1195-64 B.C.) refer frequently to both the people and the land. They once nearly succeeded in invading the kingdom of the Nile but were repulsed in a great battle whose details are recorded in a series of inscriptions still clearly legible. After this defeat the Philistines settled down in Philistia, and though they resisted many efforts to subdue them never again set out to achieve world conquest.

A unique geographical feature of Philistia is the Shephelah—a long range of low, limestone foothills which include a series of longitudinal valleys. These serve to divide the low hills from the central range of Samaria. Geographers have found few counterparts elsewhere. Dotted with fortified towns from very early times, the Shephelah served as "an outer bulwark and a moat of the fortress of the uplands of Judah."

Even before the Philistines were firmly entrenched in this region, Greek sailors and explorers used the name Syria to label the land mass that included it. Syria, in turn, was later divided into three parts: Upper Syria, Coele Syria ("hollow" or low Syria), and Syria *pelesheth*. In time the Hebrew name for the region of the Philistines was modified by Greeks into *Palestina*. Passing from Greek into English, this became the now familiar Palestine. Since few persons of medieval or modern times have had a clear understanding of the geography of the Holy Land, it was easy to use the sonorous label (actually pointing to the Philistines rather than the Hebrews) as an all-inclusive term for Canaan or the Promised Land of Moses.

"Amen" Borrowed from Hebrew Worship

Persistent legend has it that the ejaculation "Amen" was born in the great open-air meetings that marked England's eighteenth-century Wesleyan Revival. Not so. It originated in ancient Hebrew worship, and has remained in continuous use at least as long as any other common expression in the religious vocabulary.

In the time of King David, and probably generations or centuries before his reign, persons who assembled to pay tribute to Jehovah were accustomed to shout "Amen" ("It is true" or "So be it") at intervals. At first, priests probably gestured to indicate that this response was appropriate (see Deut. 27:15-26). Later the vocal outburst was included in a few ritualistic hymns (Pss. 41:13; 72:19; 89:52; 106:48). Firmly established in oral usage by the time of Jesus, it appears in the New Testament far more frequently than in the Old Testament. The English form "amen" represents as close an approximation to the original Hebrew as can be achieved by using Roman letters without accents.

Part of the unmatched tenacity of this Hebrew term, so deeply embedded in English that it is often regarded as native to it, stems from the fact that it is sonorous. It lends itself well to unison response and rolls so majestically from the lips of worshipers that it remains hale and hearty in spite of its great age.

Body-based Units of Measurement

All the small units of length employed by the early Hebrews were based upon the human hand or arm. The fingerbreadth or digit (*etzba*) was often considered equal to the breadth of six grains of barley at their thickest points. Though the "finger" figured in ancient commercial transactions, there is no reference to this unit in Scripture.

Four fingers formed one *topah,* or palm. Three palms made one span, or *zereth,* and two spans were equal to one cubit (*'ammah*). This was a logical stopping point, for most persons who actually try this handy system of measurement find that one cubit is also the length of the arm from the fingertips to the elbow. Yardsticks and tape measures don't have to be remembered when these units are employed; every adult of average size takes his built-in system of measurements with him wherever he goes.

But other weights and measures of the Bible world would create some difficulties today. Area was measured by the amount of ground a team of oxen could plow in one day. And wholesale merchants calculated cargo in terms of the *homer* (Hebrew for "ass"), which consisted of the amount that could be loaded on the back of a pack animal.

Background of the Name "Jew"

Israel's tribes were united in a single kingdom for only a brief period that began with the rise of Saul. By the tenth century B.C. internal friction had reached an explosive point. Under Rehoboam, Solomon's son and successor, the nation divided into two separate units: Israel and Judah. It was the latter kingdom that provided a base for creation of the now universal title "Jew."

Hebrews probably weren't responsible for the formation of the name. It was seldom used until Babylonians seized control of Judah in 586 B.C. Until then most citizens of Judah referred to themselves simply as Israelites, commemorating the Kingdom of Israel which had been wiped out in 721 B.C. Captors among whom the people of Judah settled probably first called them Judahites; in time the name was adopted by the Hebrews themselves in the form *Yehudhi.* Passing into Greek it became *Ioudaios.* Then it entered Latin, from which tongue the venerable title became *gyu* in Old French and eventually Jew in the modern English form.

Though every reference to a Jew testifies that Judah long outlived Israel, it also constitutes a linguistic monument to the ancient rivalry that led to the division of the kingdom of David.

Formation of the Bible's Title

A pagan city, famous for its worship of a fertility goddess and renowned as an ancient "melting pot of the world," is the ultimate source of the Bible's name.

Located on the coast of the Mediterranean about twenty-five miles north of modern Beirut, the port of Gebal was the most important of Phoenician cities until about 1000 B.C. Mesopotamian, Egyptian, and Mycenaean cultures met and fused here, for merchants came from the entire known world to purchase cedar and copper. A pagan goddess dominated the religious life of the Gebalites, as they are called in Scripture. Yet Solomon employed gangs of their carpenters and masons to help erect his temple.

Papyrus was far the most important commodity brought to the international trading center by Egyptians. Enormous quantities of it were kept in warehouses of the city, from which Phoenician ships took it to ports as distant as one thousand miles. Greek merchants who imported papyrus found it hard to pronounce the name of the city and gradually came to call it Bublos or Byblos. It was natural that the commodity distributed from Byblos should be named for its source; as *biblos* it was the most important writing material of the Greek world. Passing through Greek into Latin and so transformed that the Gebal of Holy Writ was no longer recognizable, *biblos* came to mean "little books of papyrus" which in turn became the Bible.

Why Jews Won't Eat Pork

Though Scripture lists the pig (or swine) as an unclean animal (Lev. 11:7; Deut. 14:8), no special stress is given to it as a greater source of evil than other forbidden foods. Jewish abhorrence of pork seems to be rooted not so much in the Law of Moses or tradition of the patriarchs as in political, economic, and religious struggles.

Before Abraham's descendants settled in Palestine, people of the region made free use of the pig as a meat animal. Remains from ancient sites suggest, however, that it may have been connected with pagan feasts. This point of view is strengthened by the fact that Babylonians treated pork as sacred to various deities and ate it only during religious ceremonies. Syrians considered swine holy because the animal was dedicated to their god Tammuz.

At least as early as the time of Isaiah some Israelites who dabbled in magic made a special point of using swine (Isa. 65:4) or blood from the animals (Isa. 66:3) in their pagan rites. Some went so far as to eat the forbidden flesh (Isa. 66:17).

Greek expansion that began in the fourth century B.C. under Alexander the Great continued for generations at an accelerating rate. Greek commerce, culture, and religion threatened to engulf the Hebrews. Some of their own leaders were so deeply involved in compromise with the enemy that it seemed all Palestine would become Greek in outlook. Alexander Jannaeus, one of the worst of Jewish kings, assumed the throne about 103 B.C. Pro-Greek influence is indicated even by the form of his name. During his rule the sacrifice of young pigs, linked with the worship of Adonis, was practiced by some Hebrews.

But instead of winking at this practice, devout Jews elevated swine to the head of their list of animals forbidden in any form. So strong was the religious-political-economic taboo that among the orthodox it has persisted unchanged for more than twenty centuries.

"Hell" Born in a City Dump

Garbage disposal—a ceaseless source of headache for administrators of modern cities—created problems long before the time of Christ.

A perpetually burning dump on the outskirts of ancient Jerusalem contributed to the development of the view according to which hell is a place of eternal fire.

Hebrew *Ge-Hinnom,* rendered into Greek and Latin and thence into English as Gehenna, was probably an abbreviation for "valley of the son of Hinnom." This deep ravine flanked the western boundary of Old Jerusalem and skirted the whole of the city's southern edge. Before the Hebrew conquest of Canaan it may have belonged to a Jebusite named Hinnom.

Pagan rites were long practiced in Gehenna's shadows; child sacrifice was probably associated with the shrine of Topheth that was located there. (See II Kings 23:10; II Chron. 28:3; 33:6; Jer. 7:31; 19:2; 32:35; etc.) Jeremiah, who frequently denounced evil practices that took place in the great ravine, referred to it simply as "the valley" (Jer. 2:23).

As the population of Jerusalem expanded, it was natural to turn to this place for garbage disposal. During centuries of accumulation so much refuse was dumped into it that the rubbish-heap burned continuously. Hence, this city landmark became synonymous with the place of fire (Matt. 18:9; Jas. 3:6)—a fire that was literally unquenchable.

Partly through influence of curses pronounced upon it by Jeremiah (Jer. 7:32; 19:6) and other prophets (I Enoch 27:2; 90:26), the valley of the son of Hinnom came to be regarded as the worst place to which a soul could be sent. Consigned to it, a rebel against God was considered to burn like straw (I Enoch 48:9) in the process of being destroyed body and soul. To Jesus and his disciples it was a fit place for Pharisees (Matt. 23:15, 33). As a result of its impact upon man's thought, the foul-smelling place where fires never went out helped to shape the modern concept of hell.

Jesus' Name Rooted in Antiquity

Rather than being unique or even distinctive, the name Jesus was quite common in the first century. Josephus, noted Jewish general and historian of the era, mentions nineteen different men who bore the name. A man's place of birth or residence was often used as part of his title. That is the case with Jesus of Nazareth, but in Christian history the title "Jesus Christ" has been even more widely employed.

In its English form, "Jesus" goes back to church Latin *Iesus* which is a transliteration of the Greek *Iesous.* But in its original Hebrew form it was *Y'hoshua'* ("Yahweh saves"), frequently abbreviated to *Joshua.* Since the original Joshua, son of Nun (Josh. 1:1), was an ardent patriot and brilliant military leader, rising nationalism on the part of Jews under Roman tyranny may have given the name Jesus special popularity in the last decades before the beginning of the Christian era.

Among English-speaking people biblical names have been enormously influential, but Jesus has rarely been used. That is not the case in Spanish cultures, for even today Jesus is one of the names most frequently encountered in Latin America.

The Fish as a Christian Symbol

A title compounded of biblical ingredients gave rise to the use of the fish as an early Christian symbol.

New Testament writers employed a great variety of terms and metaphors in speaking of the One whose mission and message they reported. Many were borrowed from the Old Testament—usually somewhat modified. Others such as "Light of the World" seem to have been coined at or soon after the beginning of Christianity as a movement separate from Judaism.

Among the many titles applied to the man whom contemporaries knew as Jesus of Nazareth, three emerged into special prominence: Christ (Greek for "anointed"), Son of God, and Saviour. Though the precise combination occurs nowhere in the New Testament, it was inevitable that in worship his followers should refer to their risen Lord under the elaborate designation: Jesus Christ, Son of God, Saviour.

In Greek this title was *Iesous Christos, Theou 'Yios, Soter.* When the initial letters of all these words are combined, they do not form a hopelessly scrambled pattern. Instead, they spell *ichthys*—or fish! (Through Greek influence the scientific study of fishes is still called ichthyology.)

Whether this special acrostic arose as a result of chance arrangement of terms or whether biblical titles were selected and arranged so their initial letters would spell "fish," no one knows. Whatever its origin, the effect was highly significant during centuries of persecution. A Christian who wished to identify himself to another member of the faith without saying things that might be understood by Roman persecutors would stealthily draw the outline of a fish. His sketch instantly identified him as a follower of Jesus Christ, Son of God, Saviour.

Birth of the Book in Modern Form

Various methods of writing were employed centuries before the time of Christ. But the modern book, consisting of sheets covered with words on both sides and sewn together at one edge, is a by-product of early enthusiasm for the Scriptures.

Clay tablets, rolls of papyrus or parchment, and occasionally thin sheets of copper were used as writing material. Jews employed leather rolls—sometimes as long as thirty feet—for copies of their law. Pagan religious works were typically written on papyrus scrolls of the same general design.

At least as early as the second century, Christians made a radical change. Partly in order to make their holy books physically distinctive, partly because they wanted to locate quickly and easily certain scattered passages, they either invented or adopted the codex. To make it, a papyrus roll about nine inches wide and thirty-five feet long was cut into pages. The sheets were either folded once and stacked or stacked singly before they were stitched together at the left side. Both surfaces of a page were used for writing, rather than the single surface customarily employed for a scroll. Placed in a special carrying case, such a codex could be transported easily and safely. If Jesus used a typical scroll when he read from the book of the prophet Isaiah in his home community, he had to unroll about twenty-four feet in order to find Isa. 58:6 and perhaps an additional two feet to reach Isa. 61:1-2. (See Luke 4:16-20.)

Practically all early codices consisted of Scripture portions or other Christian writings. This supports the conclusion that if Christians didn't actually launch the most radical of all changes in the production of written records, they used it so effectively that the codex displaced every competitor, and the book was born.

Use of the Bible in Ceremonies and Oaths

In many nations statutes and long-standing customs make the Bible central in civil ceremonies. Before being allowed to testify, a witness may be required to place his hand on the Book and "solemnly swear to tell the truth, the whole truth, and nothing but the truth." Kings and emperors, governors and presidents use the Bible in taking the oath of office or the royal pledge to their subjects.

This practice grew out of ceremonies used by ancient pagans. Both Greeks and Romans customarily used the names of their gods in taking oaths. In particularly solemn rites the oath taker was accustomed to put his hand upon an object associated with some temple or shrine.

Early Lombard converts to Christianity placed their hands on consecrated weapons in order to attest lesser oaths; for important vows, a copy of the Gospels was used. A passage in one of John Chrysostom's sermons reveals that by the fourth century the custom of swearing with one's hand on an open Bible was well established.

Many local variations developed in later centuries. Among the English it became mandatory that a ruler or high public official should reverently touch his lips to a Bible before completing his oath of office. This practice of "kissing the Book" still rates an entry in dictionaries of law.

Some potentates added color to their vows by verbal phrases of their own choosing. William the Conqueror kissed the Book and swore "by the splendour of God"; Richard I swore "by God's legs"; and John Lackland, twelfth-century English king, swore "by God's teeth."

While no such eccentricities ever flourished in America, ritual rooted in ancient pagan practices requires the use of a Bible in oath-taking ceremonies by persons ranging from witnesses to Presidents. Volumes used in major events are often treasured as heirlooms. Some persons present at the ceremony say that John F. Kennedy's personal Bible was used when Lyndon B. Johnson took his oath of office; others insist that a Roman Catholic missal was used. Whatever its nature, the book employed disappeared and has never been recovered.

The Sea Properly Called "Dead"

What criteria determine whether a body of water should be called a lake or a sea? Modern geographers have reasonably precise standards, but ancient ones did not. Hence a remarkable salt lake located at the mouth of the Jordan River and acknowledged as one of the world's strangest physical features was to biblical writers a "sea."

Most of them referred to it as the Salt Sea (see for example Gen. 14:3; Num. 34:3; Deut. 3:17; Josh. 3:16). Translators of the Revised Standard Version use Sea of the Arabah to render an obscure title that in the King James Version appears as "sea of the plain" (see Deut. 3:17, Josh. 12:3). And because the body of water lay on the eastern boundary of the territory of ancient Israel, it is sometimes called the East Sea (Ezek. 47:18; Joel 2:20).

None of these names suited other writers, who preferred instead

Sea of Sodom or even Sea of Asphalt. Greek and Latin writers of the second century A.D. adopted still another label—Dead Sea.

Of all the names applied to the body of water that figures so prominently in Scripture, Dead Sea is clearly the most appropriate. Water escapes from it only by evaporation—at an estimated rate of seven million tons per day. As a result the land-locked body holds water that is five times saltier than average sea water. Suspended and dissolved chemicals account for about 27 percent of its weight. A quart of it weighs thirty-nine ounces—six ounces more than a quart of fresh water.

The concentration of chemicals is so high that no fish have lived there for centuries. Great numbers of them are annually swept in by the Jordan River—but die within minutes after being immersed in the toxic waters. No one knows exactly when the tiny "sea" was first called dead or by whom—but once the title was introduced into literature it stuck and eventually displaced all others.

Origin of Hot Cross Buns

Hot cross buns, once baked throughout England on the morning of Good Friday, were long used for medicine as well as food.

William S. Walsh thinks the prevalence of the custom is due to the fact that British Christians took over and modified a pagan rite. In Roman times, he says, the altar of Diana of the Crossways stood at the spot where two great roads crossed—Icknield Street and Armynge Street. On holy days sacred cakes were offered to the goddess by Britain's conquerors.

When the Roman Empire fell, Christians in the region about the ancient shrine of Diana began baking their own buns with religious symbolism. The brown surface of this small and rather heavily spiced product of the oven was marked with a sugar cross. Until comparatively recent times every Englishman wanted a supply—piping hot —on Good Friday. Street vendors had numerous standard sets of appeals to purchasers. One of them ran:

One a penny, two a penny,
  Hot cross buns.
If you have no daughters,
  Give them to your sons;
But if you have none of these merry little elves,
Then you may keep them all for yourselves.

At the Old Bun-house in Jews' Row, Chelsea, as many as fifty thousand persons formerly congregated to buy hot cross buns on Good Friday. Though most buns were eaten hot, good mothers always saved one or two for use as medicine. A small portion of the Good Friday cake marked with the chief symbol of Christendom was grated into water and used as a general remedy. Particularly potent in cases of diarrhea, it was considered a sure cure for that malady.

Stations of the Cross Established

Protestant readers of the New Testament familiar with the four Gospel accounts of Jesus' last hours often find Roman Catholic veneration for the stations of the cross a bit puzzling. There is no evidence that the number was originally fixed at fourteen.

During the long period of Moslem rule in Jerusalem, monks of the Franciscan order were given responsibility for guarding the holy places. Since they didn't actually control spots made sacred by association with Jesus' death, monks began making statues which provided visual interpretations of them. A member of the order who found it impossible to make a pilgrimage to the Holy Land could travel the stations of the cross in order to make the visit in imagination. In 1694 Pope Innocent XII declared a special indulgence for any Franciscan who prayerfully visited each station of the cross—regardless of the cathedral in which this "pilgrimage" was made. In 1726 Benedict XIII extended the indulgence to include "all the faithful."

The decision to represent neither more nor less than fourteen (twice the mystical number, seven) New Testament incidents was not reached quickly. Some churches included the finding of the cross by Helena and as a result exhibited fifteen: in Vienna at the end of the eighteenth century only eleven were customarily shown.

In modern usage the stations of the cross nearly always fall into a pattern suggested by combining elements from the various Gospel accounts: (1) the condemnation by Pilate; (2) Jesus' reception of the cross; (3) Jesus' first fall; (4) the meeting with his mother; (5) Simon of Cyrene carrying the cross; (6) Veronica wiping the face of her Lord; (7) the second fall; (8) Jesus' exhortation to the women of Jerusalem; (9) the third fall; (10) Jesus being stripped of his clothing; (11) the crucifixion itself; (12) death of the Saviour; (13) descent from the cross; and (14) Jesus being laid in the tomb.

Biblical Roots of Modern Drama

Mystery and miracle plays of the late medieval period were usually drawn directly from the Bible. Elaborate cycles of them were developed in more than one hundred English towns; each such group included twenty to fifty separate plays.

Very early plays, of which a few twelfth-century fragments survive, were written in Latin and performed by members of the clergy. About 1276 the town of Chester shattered all precedents by staging miracle plays under the sponsorship of mercantile guilds. Other towns followed suit; some of the more notable biblical dramas of England emerged from Norwich, Lincoln, Leeds, Worcester, Coventry, Winchester, Canterbury, and London.

Unlike today's outdoor dramas, staged chiefly for the benefit of tourists, biblical tragedies and melodramas employed only amateur actors and relied upon the simplest of stage props. They received only token pay for performances, but the records of guilds which sponsored some dramas suggest that the scale of pay depended upon popularity with the crowds rather than special ability.

In Coventry, the Guild of Smiths paid both "Herod" and "Caiaphas" three shillings fourpence—but the stipend for "God" was only two shillings.

"Jehovah" Coined About 1520

Regardless of whether it is considered a title of God or a proper name, and in spite of the fact that it appears hundreds of times in many English Bibles, Jehovah is not in the Hebrew original of the Old Testament.

When God revealed his name to Moses at the time of the Exodus, it was held as a closely guarded secret. To be able to call upon the Lord by name, thought men of that day, was a sure way to gain a hearing impossible to a person unfamiliar with the divine name.

In the earliest Hebrew the sacred name was written as a tetragrammaton—or grammatical form made by the combination of four letters, all consonants. Though the language barrier between ancient Hebrew and modern English can never be fully bridged, the divine name was roughly equivalent to JHWH or YHWH. Many modern translators insert vowels and render the name as Yahweh.

Even when it was written in cryptic and abbreviated form, the Hebrews regarded the divine name as possessing sacredness in itself—apart from the Sovereign to whom it pointed. So they customarily wrote beside the consonants of the potent name a set of vowels corresponding to modern *adonai*—"my Lord." When reading orally from the Law or the Prophets it was *adonai* that was pronounced, rather than JHWH.

This state of affairs persisted for generations. Then about A.D. 1520 a scholar thought to have been Petrus Galatinus conceived the idea of combining the two titles of God. He took the consonants of JHWH plus the vowels of the Hebrew word we render as *adonai* and formed a new name: JeHoVaH. Completely artificial and never having any counterpart in ancient Hebrew speech or worship, the name Jehovah has been so firmly established by the impact of the King James Version that many moderns use it as a favorite name for God.

Chapter and Verse Divisions

Most authorities think the work of dividing Scripture into segments for convenience in reference was done by three men widely separated in time and viewpoint. Cardinal Hugo de Sancto-Caro is credited with having done most of the work on the chapter divisions, said to have been completed about 1236. Rabbi Mordecai Nathan is usually mentioned as the man responsible for chopping the Old Testament into bite-size verses. And a persistent story has it that verse division of the New Testament (first used in Greek editions) was accomplished by the French printer-editor Robert Estienne (or Stephanus) while fleeing on horseback from Paris to Lyons in 1549. Though one or two New Testaments of local influence included verse divisions earlier, it was the influential 1557 edition of Stephanus that set the pattern of verses as universally known today.

Anyone who observes the way in which many sentences are arbitrarily divided in order to make verses is likely to conclude that this piece of scholarship could have been accomplished *only* on horseback. Awkward from a literary standpoint but essential for the purpose of citing passages and making quick reference to them, the existing pattern of chapters and verses is so firmly fixed that there is little likelihood of any significant change in future generations.

From Helper to Helpmate

Eve was created especially to be Adam's companion and proved to be of great help to him, but was never his helpmate. This title for the first woman evolved slowly over a period of centuries as a result of difficulty in dealing with subtleties of language.

Scholars who prepared some early English translations had a difficult time with Gen. 2:18. John Wycliffe, intent upon framing a vivid expression to indicate God's intention of making a suitable helper for Adam, rendered the phrase: "Make we to hym help like hym." Working 150 years later and conscious of changes in English speech patterns, Miles Coverdale tried to convey the idea of the original text by describing Eve as "an helpe, to beare him company."

By the time an official committee of experts pooled their resources to frame the King James Version, it was obvious that the language used by both Wycliffe and Coverdale was already obsolete at many points. So in the famous version of 1611 God's monologue about the lonely man he had created was rendered: "I will make him an helpe [helper] meet [suitable] for him." In popular speech the two terms describing Adam's mate were quickly pulled together. Though the word nowhere appears in any version of Scripture, Eve came to be universally known as Adam's helpmate.

No Corn in Egypt

"Joseph's ten brethren went down to buy corn in Egypt" (Gen. 42:3), and this cereal is mentioned one hundred additional times in Scripture. But there was no corn in Egypt. Nor was there at any time a single grain of it anywhere in the ancient Near East.

From the Teutonic term for "a worn-down particle," the word "corn" became the general label for such grains as sand, salt, and gunpowder. Then it was attached to tiny grains of wild cereals, and from this usage became the standard label for cultivated grain of all kinds. At the time the King James Version was translated, Englishmen customarily used corn as their name for wheat, while Scots applied it to oats. In the New World it quickly supplanted maize as the standard name for a grain native to the western hemisphere and everywhere cultivated by American Indians.

The global importance of Indian corn—now the world's largest single source of calories for human consumption—gradually separated the ancient name from smaller grains. Today it is universally understood that corn grows on cobs arranged above the middle of tall, heavy stalks, but in 1611 the name hadn't yet attached to the New World grain. Biblical incidents that mention corn actually refer to millet, wheat, barley, or spelt—the only cultivated cereals known to the Hebrews either in Egyptian exile or in the Promised Land.

Influence of the Jordan River

By all odds the most sung about and probably the most talked about river in the world, the Jordan gets its name from an ancient Hebrew word for "the downrusher," or "the descender."

In terms of its capacity to transport goods and to furnish water, it is insignificant, and it is not listed among the great rivers of the world.

But because it is so frequently and so highly praised in Scripture, water from the river Jordan has been prized during many centuries and throughout much of Christendom. Warriors in the Crusades tried to bring home special trophies—miniature bottles filled with water from the Jordan. So many of these found their way back to England that from the characteristic shape of the bottle the name Jordan became attached to a pot or vessel used by an alchemist or physician. Then it transferred to a much bigger container of roughly the same type. As a result, generations of persons referred to any chamber pot as a jordan, without knowing they were alluding to "the downrusher" the Bible mentions by name almost two hundred times.

Salem, Massachusetts

Long one of America's most important ports that often bristled with armed ships, Salem, Massachusetts, is so called because in Scripture the name Salem means "peace." Ironically, during the Revolutionary War at least 158 privateers, mounting more than two thousand guns and carrying not fewer than six thousand men, fitted out from the town of peace. These vessels captured 445 prizes and brought nine tenths of them into port in safety.

But in 1629 new settlers from Britain were not thinking of armed struggle against their mother country or any other nation. They were greatly disturbed that natives knew the port as Naumkeag, for legend had it that this was a corrupt form of an American Indian name for a tribal god. Others insisted it wasn't so; they held that Naumkeag was a modification of Hebrew for "comfort haven" and had survived as a memento of wanderings on the part of Israel's lost tribes.

A semiofficial public meeting was called to debate the question of a suitable name. Someone reported that he had been struck by the way Ps. 76:1-2 seemed to pertain to their trek to this strange land, so he read it aloud with a flourish: "In Judah is God known: his name is great in Israel. In Salem also is his tabernacle, and his dwelling place in Zion." Hoping that the sonorous biblical term would serve as an omen promising that their settlement would never know strife, settlers chose Salem, and the name has stuck through war and peace.

Philadelphia, Pennsylvania

Though the prominent Roman city of Philadelphia figures in the book of Revelation (3:7-13), America's city of brotherly love got its name from Paul's letter to the Romans. In that epistle *philadelpheia* appears as a compound form of a Greek verb.

Three times imprisoned for nonconformity (1666, 1669, 1670), a visionary member of the Society of Friends dreamed of founding a new city that would be a genuine utopia. In order to fulfill that purpose, it needed an appropriate name. So William Penn turned to his Greek New Testament and found it in Rom. 12:10. In the Geneva Bible, which Penn knew well, this passage exhorts: "Be affectioned to love one another with brotherlie love."

Laid off foursquare like the New Jerusalem described in Scripture, Penn's city was for him the center of the universe. Writing in his later years of the choice of its name, the Quaker recalled: "Thou, Philadelphia, the virgin settlement of this province, named before thou wert born, what care, what service, what travail has there been to bring thee forth!"

Birth of Modern Bible Societies

On March 7, 1804, the world's largest organization for the distribution of Scripture was founded—in a London pub. Churchmen who launched it met in Bishopsgate Tavern in response to a challenge by Thomas Charles.

Visiting Wales in connection with the evangelical revival, Charles found the movement lagging because Welsh-language Scriptures were practically unobtainable. In the winter of 1802 he laid the problem before a committee of the Religious Tract Society.

Members of the society pondered the need and concluded it to be bigger than they could handle. A new organization was required, they concluded, whose sole purpose would be to provide Bibles for Wales. But once this judgment was reached, Joseph Hughes insisted on a broader goal. If Bibles could be provided for Wales, he argued, why not for the entire United Kingdom? Then, carried away by his own oratory, he enlarged his own suggestion: "If for the United Kingdom, why not for the whole world?"

Wealthy laymen, among whom William Wilberforce and Zachary Macauley were prominent, were consulted. They gave enthusiastic endorsement to the proposal that a society be organized with the purpose of making global distribution of Scripture "without note or comment." It was a meeting called with their support and convened in a tavern not far from the Thames River that gave birth to the British and Foreign Bible Society.

Sex Love and Marriage

Wives on the Tax List

According to the Law of Moses a woman is her husband's property —not figuratively, but literally and legally. This point of view is spelled out in one version of the Ten Commandments, in which the God-fearing are warned against the sin of covetousness. Here is the list of property items that must be respected: "Thou shalt not covet thy neighbour's house, thou shalt not covet thy neighbour's wife, nor his manservant, nor his maidservant, nor his ox, nor his ass, nor any thing that is thy neighbour's" (Exod. 20:17).

Viewed against the backdrop of biblical life, the admonition concerning a neighbor's wife centers upon property values rather than the evils of lust. Had ancient tax assessors called upon the patriarchs, they would have listed a man's wives along with his other belongings. Only in the light of this attitude does it become understandable that Lot should have offered to give his daughters to the men of Sodom in exchange for the honor of his male guests (Gen. 19:8) and that Abraham lent his wife to Pharaoh in a gesture calculated to save his own life (Gen. 12:10-20). Echoing the attitude of Lot, an elderly householder of the city of Gibeah offered to give his daughter to a gang of prowlers in exchange for the safety of a guest (Judg. 19:24).

Despite the low legal status of Hebrew women in Old Testament times, their social prestige was higher than that enjoyed by women of surrounding cultural groups.

Early Marriage Engagements

Until the rise of the modern newspaper there was no equivalent of the present practice of putting a girl's picture in the paper at the time her engagement is announced, but formal agreements that constituted preliminary steps toward marriage were known long ago. The earliest account of customs equivalent to announcing an engagement appears in Deuteronomy.

Though not yet married to his fiancée, a man whose hand was pledged could use this as a reason for asking to be temporarily excused from military service (Deut. 20:7). No records indicating the way engagements were made public have been preserved from this period. Still, the military provision indicates that an engagement had legal standing.

Once a girl was betrothed, her future husband had an important property right. Hence, if she was seduced or sexually attacked, in addition to her own purity the property rights of her fiancé were violated. Recognizing the significance of engagement, the Hebrews developed specific laws to fit cases of this sort (Deut. 22:23-27). If an engaged woman was violated within a city, both she and her attacker were stoned—on the theory that she could have cried for help, had she wished to do so. But if she was attacked in open country, the woman had no way to call for rescue. She was therefore not punished, while the man who violated the rights of her fiancé was stoned.

When David became engaged to the daughter of Saul, his future father-in-law used a formula that indicated the bargain was sealed: "Thou shalt this day be my son in law" (I Sam. 18:21). Such a public announcement was deferred until after agreement had been reached concerning the *mohar,* or purchase price to be paid by the future bridegroom.

Special Privileges for Husbands

Though the New Testament gives much greater stress to the solemnity of marriage vows than does the Old Testament, this emphasis is prominent in many of the prophetic writings. Nevertheless, one of the earliest sets of regulations governing the issuance of a writ of divorce is found in Scripture.

During the period of the patriarchs a man could put away his wife for no reason except that he was displeased with her. But he was required to "write her a bill of divorcement, and give it in her hand" so she would be free to find another husband (Deut. 24:1-3). Reference to this custom by Isaiah (Isa. 50:1) supports the view that it prevailed for generations or even centuries. In an exalted figure of speech preserved in Jer. 3:8, the prophet declares that Jehovah has given Israel a bill of divorce for her "adultery" (idolatry).

The vague language of the stipulation in the key passage of Deuteronomy created a situation in which ancient ecclesiastical lawyers could hardly avoid reaching varied interpretations. Members of the strict rabbinical school of Shammai sanctioned divorce only in cases of adultery and gross misconduct, but the more liberal school of Hillel reached conclusions that sound strangely like those of some modern divorce courts. According to Hillel and his followers, the scriptural regulation was intended to make it possible for a man to sever his relationship with his wife if she proved to be a poor cook.

In the apocryphal book of Ecclesiasticus, or the Wisdom of Jesus the Son of Sirach, husbands are given blunt advice (25:16, 25-26). "I had rather dwell with a lion and a dragon, than to keep house with a wicked woman," admits the writer of the book. "Give the water no passage; neither a wicked woman liberty to gad abroad," he advises. "If she go not as thou wouldest have her, cut her off from thy flesh, and give her a bill of divorce, and let her go."

Romantic Love in Ancient Israel

The concept of falling in love as a prelude to marriage is relatively modern. As late as New Testament times parents typically took the initiative and arranged marriages for their children. Still, the concept of romantic love is not as modern as might be assumed. Scattered biblical allusions indicate that it was familiar in ancient Israel.

Shechem, son of the Hivite prince Hamor, clearly took the initiative in the courtship of Dinah the daughter of Jacob. Eventually he demanded of his father: "Get me this damsel to wife" (Gen. 34:4). Jacob's own courtship of Laban's beautiful daughter Rachel grew out of a case of love at first sight (Gen. 29:10-18).

And though they must have been rare, there were occasional instances in which girls "set their caps" for the men of their choice. Saul promised David the hand of his elder daughter Merab and then broke his word. In this dilemma another of Saul's daughters, Michal, sent word to her father that *she* loved David (I Sam. 18:17-20). Eventually she won him for her husband, but their union was not a happy one (I Sam. 25:44; II Sam. 3:14; 6:16-23). The story of Ruth and Boaz, a romance by any standard, has all the features of a modern short story in which hero and heroine live happily ever after.

Levitical Law and the Fertility Cycle

Ceremonial laws of Israel, attributed to Moses, afford internal evidence that the man who received the Ten Commandments, or those who succeeded him in leadership, knew far more biology than was once thought. Lev. 15:16-33 (along with many other passages) centers directly upon matters related to human reproduction. "If a woman have an issue, and her issue in her flesh be blood [that is, if she is in the process of menstruation] she shall be put apart seven days," the holy law prescribed.

After this time of isolation she went through another seven-day period of ceremonial uncleanness. At the end of the fourteen days during which she was unclean and no man could touch her, a woman was required to make an offering; two turtledoves or two young pigeons were acceptable. Cleanliness restored, she was permitted to return to the marital bed.

Modern studies indicate that approximately fourteen days after the beginning of menstruation, a woman's chance of conception is close to its maximum. All this could be written off as purely coincidental —were it not for the fact that Scripture over and over stresses the central importance of parenthood. Was it pure chance or strangely accurate understanding of the human fertility cycle that shaped laws restraining men from approaching their wives until the season when reunion was most likely to cause them to "replenish the earth"?

Male Prerogatives in Divorce

Christian scholars, pondering the Law of Moses in the light of historical and literary evidence, have gone through a complete cycle. For centuries it was taken for granted that the biblical code was unique, completely free of influence from non-Hebrew cultures—or even dictated word by word by God himself.

During the latter half of the nineteenth century and the first half of the twentieth, the pendulum swung to the opposite extreme. Many experts pondered an increasing mass of evidence from the ancient Near East and were struck by the fact that similar emphases appear in various legal systems. The famous Code of Hammurabi was frequently compared with the Ten Commandments. During the 1930's and 1940's some historians and linguists went so far as to say that everything in the Law of Moses was borrowed directly from earlier legal codes.

Today the pendulum has once more swung toward the view that Moses and his immediate followers were, after all, strikingly original. One small but significant bit of evidence comes from regulations governing the all-pervasive and all-important institution of marriage. Among the Hebrews a man who took a wife and failed to be satisfied with her could prepare a writ of divorce "and send her out of his house" (Deut. 24:1). This was a one-sided arrangement; the dissatisfied bride had no right to divorce her husband.

Twentieth-century archaeological finds, some of them only recently deciphered, indicate that this double standard on the part of the Hebrews was unique. Neither the Egyptians, the Babylonians, nor the Assyrians had anything like it.

Marriage a Civil Contract

Most Christian groups today regard marriage as both a religious and a civil contract. Among those branches of the church which have a formal list of holy ceremonies requiring a priest or minister, marriage is frequently listed as a sacrament along with baptism, the Lord's Supper, and other rites.

In the light of this widespread contemporary view it is strange that in the seedbed from which Christianity sprang no such concept ever gained root. From the days of the patriarchs to the time of the early Christian church, marriage was considered to be a purely civil contract. It was conducted without a priest, and no religious rites were linked with it.

There is a possibility, but no certainty, that written contracts of marriage were drawn up quite early. Scripture preserves only one specific reference to such a document in Old Testament times. Raguel, father of Sara, arrived at an understanding with his prospective son-in-law, Tobias. Then he formally gave the girl to her suitor after which "he blessed them; and called Edna his wife, and took paper, and did write an instrument of covenants, and sealed it." This account appears in the seventh chapter of the apocryphal book of Tobit, written about 200 B.C.; no Old Testament book generally accepted by Protestants has a similar account.

It is reasonably clear, however, that formal marriage contracts were frequently drawn up. As for the ceremony itself, the whole burden of responsibility was upon the bridegroom. In the presence of witnesses he declared, "She is my wife and I am her husband, from this day for ever." No vow was taken by the bride.

Bigamy on High

If a report of the prophet Ezekiel were to be taken literally, we would have to admit that God is a bigamist.

There were two sisters, the Lord told Ezekiel, whose names were Aholah the elder and Aholibah her sister. In the King James Version the text continues "and they were mine, and they bare sons and daughters" (Ezek. 23:4). J. M. P. Smith translates this passage "they became my wives" and Ronald Knox renders it "both I espoused."

Since the speaker here is Jehovah, the only way around the difficulty is to recognize that the entire passage is poetic and figurative. Even so, the fact that such a statement would be attributed to the Lord makes it clear that polygamy was so deep-rooted in the ancient Hebrew culture that it was taken for granted as a way of life. Solomon is credited with an all-time record of having a thousand women in his harem: "seven hundred wives, princesses, and three hundred concubines" (I Kings 11:3).

In spite of the fact that "the wisest man who ever lived" set such an example, common folk never failed to recognize polygamy as a seedbed for trouble. This is indicated by the common Semitic name for a second wife, which in the Hebrew original occurs in I Sam. 1:6 and the apocryphal book of Ecclus. 26:6; 37:11. The root meaning of the title bestowed on any second wife was "to vex, to show hostility toward." In the King James Version it is rendered "adversary."

Adolescent Marriages Encouraged

At least as early as the time of David, Hebrew parents were concerned about the problem of teen-age marriages. But their focus was 180 degrees away from that of present-day American society. Mothers and fathers—especially those who had daughters—considered it a family crisis if their children weren't married before the end of adolescence.

Scripture gives no direct information at this point but preserves numerous indirect clues. Historians who compiled the books of Kings frequently gave the age of a ruler at the time he ascended the throne. They then indicated the length of his reign and the age of the son who succeeded him. From these records it appears that Josiah married at fifteen (II Kings 22:1; 23:31). His father Amon became a bridegroom at fourteen (II Kings 21:19; 22:1). By these standards Jehoiakim was a confirmed bachelor, for he didn't marry until he was seventeen (II Kings 23:36; 24:8).

Girls frequently married a bit younger than boys, but the contemporary western custom according to which the typical bridegroom is older than his bride had not yet been established. It was not unusual for parents to work out a mutually profitable marriage agreement under whose terms the bride was considerably more mature than the groom.

There are no biblical standards to govern the suitable age for marriage. But many centuries after the times with which the earliest historical sections of Scripture deal, rabbis worked out practical rules. According to them, the minimum age for marriage was twelve for girls and thirteen for boys.

Double Standard on Adultery

Under Old Testament law it was possible for a married man to engage in sexual relations with a woman other than his wife without commiting adultery.

This state of affairs, strangely tangled from the perspective of New Testament standards of morality, resulted from the fact that in the time of the patriarchs a woman was legally the property of her husband. Adultery was both a violation of sexual standards and the abuse of another man's property rights. This meant that illicit relations did not constitute adultery if the woman was unmarried, for there could be no violation of a husband's property rights in such a situation.

A married woman who engaged in a clandestine affair was automatically guilty since she belonged to her husband, but a married man who found a paramour in a woman not married was comparatively free from reprisal. Under the long-accepted definition he did not commit adultery and so faced none of the severe penalties associated with it.

An act of fornication with a Hebrew woman of previously good character did involve property damage with respect to her father. This could usually be settled by payment of an appropriate settlement, however. Where the woman involved was a slave, even if she was engaged to be married, the man who violated her purity could settle the score by presenting a ram as a trespass offering (Lev. 19:20-21).

As a result of this (to us) curious instance of a double standard, practically all recorded cases of stoning to death for the crime of adultery involved women as the culprits.

Vital Role of the Bridal Veil

Though the ancient Hebrew bride did not wear a garment equivalent to the modern wedding gown designed especially for use on a single occasion, her clothing was highly important. One item of it, the veil, played a particularly vital role. It was this accessory that enabled a crafty father to palm off Leah upon Jacob after he had worked seven years for Rachel (Gen. 29:23-25).

A marriage was an occasion for tribal rejoicing, with the amount of food and drink consumed being dependent upon the economic level of the bridegroom. In lieu of anything approaching a modern wedding ceremony, certain customs were rigidly observed. His head adorned with a makeshift diadem, the bridegroom and his friends made their way to the bride's house (or tent) to the accompaniment of music (Song of Sol. 3:11; I Macc. 9:39). She wore the finest clothing her father could provide. Occasionally in literal fashion and more often in symbolic ways, she was adorned with precious stones (Isa. 61:10). Entranced by her beauty, her bridegroom addressed her in poetic fashion: "Behold, thou art fair, my love; behold, thou art fair; thou hast doves' eyes within thy locks" (Song of Sol. 4:1-2; see also 4:3; 6:7).

Custom dictated that the veil should be taken off only in the bridal chamber. This lovely custom—a symbolic way of emphasizing the fact that the beauty of the bride was reserved for her bridegroom alone—proved the undoing of Jacob. Though the ancient account doesn't say so, he may have been drinking somewhat heavily from jars of wedding wine. For though Jacob undoubtedly lifted the veil from his bride after taking her into his tent, it wasn't until the next morning that he learned he had married Leah rather than his beloved Rachel.

Pagan Rites During Pregnancy

Archaeological finds made within this century suggest that some early Hebrew women who were devout worshipers of Jehovah may have dabbled in pagan rites during a special period: pregnancy.

Amulets, which are half-religious and half-magical symbols worn on the person, have been known since antiquity and are still used in many cultures. Before the period of Hebrew occupation they were plentiful in Canaan. Most which date from this epoch are believed to be Egyptian in origin and have been recovered chiefly from graves.

Regardless of the shape in which it was carved, an amulet constituted a graven image whose use was forbidden under the Law of Moses. Nevertheless, a number of them have been found in the ruins of early Hebrew cities at levels indicating they were used by the Israelites rather than the Canaanites who held these sites at earlier periods. Most such magic charms associated with the Hebrews are of a single type. Somewhat surprisingly, in view of its long and almost universal distribution, the beetle-like scarab is rarely found. Instead, mounds from the time of the patriarchs and several centuries afterward have yielded numerous talismans, plaques, and figurines that depict the goddess Ashtoreth—or Astarte.

Ashtoreth played a prominent role in pagan fertility rites. Practices associated with worship of her were so gross that devout Hebrew scribes wrote her name with the vowels of their word for "shameful thing." The extent of her cult may be estimated by the fact that Scripture refers to it several times (see Josh. 9:10; 13:31; Judg. 2:13; 10:6; I Sam. 7:3; 12:10; 31:10).

Renowned scholars, including William F. Albright, have pondered the evidence and concluded that to some Hebrew women the appeal of Ashtoreth was overpowering during the months when they carried children in their bodies. If this view is correct, women who walked the straight and narrow path of devotion to Jehovah during most of their lives just couldn't resist paying homage to the goddess of fertility in periods before their children were born.

Earliest Birth Control

A crude method of birth control practiced by Onan the son of Judah is reported to have cost him his life. Upon the death of his older brother Er, Onan was required by the Hebrew law to take the bereaved widow as his wife. This law was reinforced by a specific order from his father.

Onan resisted, however. He wasn't enthusiastic about raising up seed for his dead brother. So "it came to pass, when he went in unto his brother's wife, that he spilled it on the ground, lest that he should give seed to his brother" (Gen. 38:9).

Termed *coitus interruptus* by modern analysts of human sexual behavior, this way of attempting to prevent conception is now regarded as psychologically dangerous. Numerous reports suggest that it may be a precipitating factor in mental breakdown. But in the case of Onan consequences were even more dramatic. His refusal to play the role of procreator to sons who would bear his brother's name angered Jehovah—"wherefore he slew him" (Gen. 38:10).

Strangest Marriage Present

Warriors in many cultures have followed the practice of cutting off some portion of a slain enemy's body as a trophy—and perhaps also as a good luck talisman. European explorers who first penetrated the New World were aghast to find that American Indians took the scalps of those they killed in battle, but this practice was comparatively civilized when viewed against the backdrop of ancient Hebrew customs.

Over a long period fighting men made a practice of cutting off the foreskins of foes whom they had overcome in combat. Besides proving the descendants of Abraham, Isaac, and Jacob to be more powerful than their uncircumcised opponents, this practice provided a handy way of getting an exact tally of enemy casualties.

To test young David, King Saul offered him the hand of his daughter Michal. No marriage present of gold and precious stones was expected, the ruler said. Instead David was required to bring back the foreskins of one hundred slain Philistines in order to claim the princess as his bride (I Sam. 18:25; II Sam. 3:14).

A Dainty Dish for David

In his declining years the great King David entered a common pattern of gradual physical deterioration. Perhaps due to loss of appetite and low intake of calories, perhaps as a result of heart or circulatory trouble, his body energy dropped to a low level. "Now king David was old and stricken in years; and they covered him with clothes, but he gat no heat" (I Kings 1:1).

In this critical situation court doctors met for consultation and decided to secure an appropriate remedy. They sent envoys through the whole land searching for the loveliest young woman who could be found. But the girl who was chosen was not a Hebrew. Perhaps as a deliberate ruse to increase the potency of their prescription by employing a woman whose foreign blood made her more exotic, David's servants selected Abishag the Shunammite. Then they acted on their proposal to "let her stand before the king, and let her cherish him, and let her lie in thy bosom, that my lord the king may get heat" (I Kings 1:2).

Far more was involved than appears on the surface, for it was an article of faith that the fertility of animals and the soil plus the general prosperity of the land were bound up with the virility of a ruler. This was, therefore, a deliberate attempt to induce David to "get heat" in order that he might foster the reproduction of sheep and goats and bountiful harvests of wheat and barley, olives and grapes.

Nothing came of the scheme; "the damsel was very fair, and cherished the king, and ministered to him: but the king knew her not" (vs. 4). Still, Solomon regarded Abishag as his father's widow and had Adonijah executed for treason when he requested her for his wife (I Kings 2:13-25).

Absalom Seizes a Harem

Absalom's attempt to seize the throne of his father was symbolized not by military defiance but by his act of taking possession of David's harem. He acted on the advice of Ahithophel, himself an aspirant for power. "So they spread Absalom a tent upon the top of the house; and Absalom went in unto his father's concubines in the sight of all Israel." (II Sam. 16:22.) Unlike wives, most concubines were of foreign birth; many were slaves.

Once this public breach was accomplished by what amounted to an act of treason, Absalom vacillated. Acting on the advice of Hushai (secretly loyal to David), he refused to let Ahithophel take a small force in order to pursue and kill the king. This gave David time to gather his forces and prepare to quell the revolt. Overruled in this instance, the man who had persuaded Absalom to signal his defiance by taking over his father's bed saw that the rebellion couldn't succeed, and so went home and hanged himself (II Sam. 17:23).

Psychology of Sexual Assault

Long before Sigmund Freud and his followers developed formal theories about the psychology of sexual assault, a detailed clinical account was inserted in Holy Writ. Salient features stressed by modern analysts are conspicuous: lust for the forbidden culminates in physical attack, but instead of gaining satisfaction, the assailant is overcome by guilt that produces violent revulsion for the woman taken by force.

"And it came to pass after this, that Absalom the son of David had a fair sister, whose name was Tamar; and Amnon the son of David loved her. And Amnon was so vexed, that he fell sick for his sister Tamar; for she was a virgin; and Amnon thought it hard for him to do any thing to her." (II Sam. 13:1-2.)

With the connivance of a friend, Amnon feigned illness and then asked that Tamar be sent to nurse him. Pretending that he was too sick to have visitors, Amnon asked everyone but Tamar to leave. Then he tried to seduce her. She rejected his overtures and suggested that the matter be referred to King David.

"Howbeit he would not hearken unto her voice: but, being stronger than she, forced her, and lay with her. Then Amnon hated her exceedingly; so that the hatred wherewith he hated her was greater than the love wherewith he had loved her. . . . Then he called his servant that ministered unto him, and said, Put now this woman out from me, and bolt the door after her." (II Sam. 13:14-15, 17.)

Castration for Religious Purposes

Like rulers of most other peoples with whom they came in contact, ancient Hebrew kings followed the practice of appointing castrated males, or eunuchs, to important positions. Such officers, whose nature does not always appear in English translations, were known as early as the time of David (I Sam. 8:15; I Chron. 28:1) and at least as late as the last period of the Judean monarchy (II Kings 24:15; 25:15; Jer. 38:7). Kings frequently took the precaution of placing their wives and concubines under the care of eunuchs. Because of their close association with monarchs, men of ability were often transferred to places of strategic importance outside the royal household.

Jesus referred to various types of emasculated men in Matt. 19:12: "There are some eunuchs, which were so born from their mother's womb: and there are some eunuchs, which were made eunuchs of men: and there be eunuchs, which have made themselves eunuchs for the kingdom of heaven's sake. He that is able to receive it, let him receive it." Whether Jesus' language was strictly literal or laced with a figurative element is unknown, but on the basis of this scriptural injunction castration was widely practiced.

Many early Christians voluntarily emasculated themselves; tradition has it that the great preacher-scholar Origen did so. By the third century a special sect was formed whose membership was open only to men who had undergone the operation. These Valesii, as they were called, never gained the official approval of the church. But until the accession of Pope Leo XIII in 1878 some of the choir boys of the Sistine Chapel in Rome were castrated to prolong the period in which their voices remained in the soprano range. Spokesmen who defended this practice cited the Gospel passage as proof that it was really an act of kindness to perform emasculation, since this increased one's chances of entering the kingdom of heaven.

Sex Cult Sanctioned by Solomon

Canaanite and Phoenician fertility cults, involving gross absorption with sex, won many adherents among the Israelites. Prophets, judges, and kings of the chosen people were continually plagued by waves of enthusiasm for gods worshiped in surrounding cultures. During the reign of Rehoboam one such movement became so popular that Israelites "built them high places, and images, and groves, on every high hill, and under every green tree" (I Kings 14:23).

This enthusiastic support of temple prostitution by masses of persons in the nation "set apart for God" was simply a continuation and extension of practices that prevailed during Israel's days of greatest material glory. During the same period when Solomon was building his temple to Jehovah as a world showplace he was also erecting shrines to pagan deities as a concession to popular demand.

Many generations later a long-lost copy of the Law of Moses was found, and as a result King Josiah attempted to stamp out idolatry. "And the high places that were before Jerusalem, which were on the right hand of the mount of corruption, which Solomon the king of Israel had builded for Ashtoreth the abomination of the Zidonians, and for Chemosh the abomination of the Moabites, and for Milcom the abomination of the children of Ammon, did the king defile. And he brake in pieces the images, and cut down the groves, and filled their places with the bones of men." (II Kings 23:13-14.)

At the time Josiah tried to check the movement that had flourished because it had the support of "the wisest man who ever lived," he was just eighteen years old.

Nonbiological Concept of Inbreeding

Though frequently practiced for political reasons (as among ancient Egyptian royal families) or because of geographical isolation (as among contemporary colonies of mountain people), inbreeding has long been recognized as potentially dangerous. We know today that the chances of having defective children are greatly magnified if husband and wife are descended from immediate common ancestors.

Inbreeding was strictly forbidden in Old Testament times. "None of you shall approach to any that is near of kin to him," the law warned (Lev. 18:6). On the surface this seems to indicate that the patriarchs had some dim understanding of biological dangers involved. But a closer look at the concept of consanguinity as detailed in Leviticus 18 shows that socially established bonds, rather than biological impediments, often forbade procreation.

It was illegal for a man to unite with the daughter or granddaughter of a woman he had married, whether or not she was also descended from him. Marriage between brother-in-law and sister-in-law was forbidden, and a man could not take his uncle's wife (or widow?) as his mate. Though no blood bonds were involved, an impediment existed between a son and his stepmother as well as between a father and his daughter-in-law.

Many of the unions forbidden by Old Testament law are now recognized to be free of biological hazards. But the force of Scripture-shaped western customs is so great that violation of these ancient standards is still regarded as a form of inbreeding and carries great social stigma in all cultures except those untouched by biblical patterns.

Xerxes' Harem

Though the United States in the twentieth century is often condemned as a sex-saturated culture, no present practice even challenges a record set by a ruler described in Scripture. Ahasuerus of Persia, better known under the Greek form of his name, Xerxes, required members of his harem to spend an entire year in preparation for a single night with him. This period of "purification" was centered upon making the body soft and sweet-smelling under the ministrations of eunuchs who gave daily massages with oils and then applied perfumes. "Every maid's turn was come to go in to king Ahasuerus, after that she had been twelve months, according to the manner of the women, (for so were the days of their purifications accomplished, to wit, six months with oil of myrrh, and six months with sweet odours, and with other things for the purifying of the women;)." (Esth. 2:12.)

Does the report in Esther constitute authentic history, or is it an example of Oriental hyperbole? Final answers are suspect; perhaps it was compounded from both ingredients. Whatever the case, there's no arguing over the fact that the inclusion of the account helped make the Bible a book that would have given many censors trouble had it not been treated as divinely inspired.

Male Prostitution

Many persons have puzzled over the fact that Scripture prohibits making a gift to the Lord of money realized from the sale of a dog. "Thou shalt not bring the hire of a whore, or the price of a dog, into the house of the Lord thy God for any vow: for even both these are abomination unto the Lord thy God," the ancient law stipulates (Deut. 23:18).

This enigmatic prohibition stems from the fact that in Elizabethan English "dog" was used as a euphemism for a male sex deviate. So in translating it was natural to employ the term for what in the original Hebrew meant "male prostitute."

Paul's warning to stay away from dogs and evil workers (Phil. 3:2) almost certainly refers to sexual deviates, common in Greek cities of his day. But the old usage is so firmly established—or translators are so fearful of public reaction—that most modern versions of Scripture preserve language by which faithful ones seem to be cautioned to avoid selling one of man's best friends. The difficulty of interpretation is compounded by the fact that numerous appearances of the word "dog" (such as those in the Gospels) are literal and matter-of-fact, referring strictly to the four-legged animal.

Censored Bibles Unsuccessful

It takes only a casual glance through the Bible to see that it includes some very plain language. Some linguists insist that there never has been an unexpurgated translation in English, and that it would create a great uproar to issue such a version. But even the restrained style of the King James Version has offended so many readers that a number of persons have prepared special editions leaving out all the naughty words and stories. One of the earliest was issued in the eighteenth century by the Rev. Edward Harwood, D.D. Since then he has had many imitators. No censored version has ever won a wide following, however. Divided as they are on some issues, most churchmen seem to agree that the basic nature of Scripture is altered when it is stripped of references to fornication, incest, homosexual acts, and other behavior condemned in blunt words by prophets and lawgivers.

Unsolved Riddles

No Apples in Eden

There's a reasonable possibility that the forbidden fruit which led to Adam's fall was an apricot or a pomegranate—or it could have been a lemon, orange, citron, olive, fig, or grape. One of the least likely contenders for the questionable honor of playing a central role in the fall of man is the apple. It's highly doubtful that this temperate zone fruit was known in the ancient Near East.

Since the Genesis story doesn't specify the variety of fruit involved, western Europeans jumped to the conclusion that it must have been their own common favorite. Once the story got started, there was no stopping it. Folk lore put such stress on the part supposed to have been played by a red or yellow apple that the lump said to have stuck in the first man's throat gave the Adam's apple its name.

Special Symbolism of the Serpent

Generations of persons have puzzled over the role of the serpent in the Genesis story. Why should this particular creature and no other, out of the thousands that teem the earth, be portrayed as the villain responsible for the fall of man?

Archaeology has yielded a partial answer, supplemented by comparative mythology, for in both Mesopotamia and Syria the serpent was very early linked with rites dedicated to the nude goddess of fertility. As a symbol of sex the crawling one was also regarded as a source of life. This usage accounts for the emergence of the serpent as a symbol of healing—portrayed by Greeks as a companion of the divine healer Asclepius. Hence the still-perpetuated tradition according to which the physician's insignia of office, or caduceus, shows a staff around which two serpents are curled.

Though this throws a great deal of light upon ancient and modern symbolism, it does not account for original development. Here psychology offers the only plausible conjecture. In ancient mythology, some say the serpent was treated as a projection of the male organ of procreation. If this theory sounds crudely absurd, remember that in the saga of original sin great care is taken to specify that it is Eve—not Adam—who submits to the lure of the serpent (Gen. 3:4-5). Described in words, the suggested symbolism isn't particularly vivid. But in paintings and sculpture the evil and sensuous serpent that beguiles the first woman is easily viewed in the fashion suggested by Freudian psychology.

Ark's Contents Not Known

There are numerous Old Testament references to a central piece of equipment used in early Jewish worship: the famous ark of the covenant. As described in Exodus 25 it was built of wood overlaid with gold inside and out measured about 3′9″ by 2′3″ by 2′3″.

This portable chest, or box, was carried before the Hebrews when they marched into battle. It was the first piece of gear to cross the Jordan after the wilderness Exodus. And it was to the ark that troubled persons came seeking divine answers to personal questions. Eventually it was placed in the temple of Solomon.

Many allusions suggest that the chest actually contained something —perhaps one or more fetish stones from a sacred place like Sinai. But precisely what was in the ark—if anything—no writer says in any of the approximately two hundred times it is mentioned.

Any Chance That Jonah Could Have Lived?

No biblical story—not even that of Noah and the ark or Jesus' feeding of the five thousand—has excited more fervent debate than that of Jonah the son of Amittai. According to the brief account that probably took form about the fourth century B.C., Jonah spent three days and three nights in the stomach of a great fish.

The identification of that "great fish" as a whale rests upon the translation of Matt. 12:40; in the book of Jonah, the precise creature that swallowed him is not specified.

Matthew (and only Matthew) has Jesus comparing his own entombment with Jonah's sojourn in the belly of the whale (Matt. 12: 39-41). In spite of this support from the Saviour himself, the whole story of the ancient adventurer has frequently been dismissed as a deliberate allegory or an outright myth. Scholars who have supported one of these conclusions have usually underscored the fact that whales have never been seen in waters anywhere close to Palestine, and the digestive juices of most whales are so potent that any man who succeeded in being swallowed would almost certainly meet instant death.

Contemporary recognition that the Bible is more accurate than nineteenth-century scholars thought has revived the riddle of Jonah and his hair-raising escapade. The American naturalist Peter Farb, writing in *The Land, Wildlife and Peoples of the Bible,* suggests that there may be a kernel of historical fact behind the story of Jonah.

According to him, the man-eating white shark (which attains a length of sixty feet) has the queer capacity to "store food in its belly for many days without digesting it." How Jonah could have survived without air for even a brief period (to say nothing of the seventy-two hours indicated in the book that bears his name) Farb does not say. But the fact that a contemporary naturalist insists on taking a new look at the story shows that regardless of what professional Bible scholars may say or think, the question of whether Jonah was really swallowed and somehow survived is still very much alive.

Selah: Still an Enigma

Our oldest Hebrew versions of Scripture include the word *Selah* seventy-four times—seventy-one times in Psalms and three times in Habakkuk. Yet after having been pondered by generations of scholars, the word remains an enigma.

Luther considered it to mean "Silence!" But the learned Rabbi Kimhi studied it for years and concluded that it was a signal to elevate the voice. Gesenius explained it as ancient shorthand for "Let the instruments play and the singers stop."

Many contemporary experts insist that it is a cue showing the conductor of the ancient symphony when to signal in order that a clash of cymbals should interrupt the even flow of chanted music. Others think it a cry used by worshipers—somewhat like "Hallelujah!" and "Amen!" There's continuing debate concerning whether it originated in pure Hebrew worship or was borrowed from the Persians.

Eric Werner, professor of liturgical music in New York's Hebrew Union College, believes the word was originally a marginal explanation, or gloss, that crept into the sacred text over a period of centuries. In *The Interpreter's Dictionary of the Bible* he suggests that the "most expressive" occurrence of the term is *Higgāyôn Selāh* in Ps. 9:16—"indicating the end of the main thought by a soft whispering of strings, followed by a clash of cymbals."

Despite its uncertain origin and meaning, *Selah* still appears dozens of times in many versions of the Old Testament.

Why No Mention of the Cat?

According to a centuries-old tradition that circulates among peoples of the eastern Mediterranean, there was no cat aboard Noah's ark. As a result of this sad state of affairs, mice and rats thrived on Noah's supply of grain, brought aboard to feed his animals. Eventually matters grew so bad that at Noah's command the lioness gave a mighty sneeze and produced a cat.

This yarn seems to have been produced because of a biblical vacuum, for the common cat is nowhere mentioned in the Old Testament or the New. Silence concerning the animal supports the supposition that it was not known in Palestine. But such negative evidence is far from conclusive. Cats were abundant in Egypt from the beginning of recorded history. In time they came to be closely associated with the sun god Ra and in some places and periods were themselves regarded as sacred. Many thousands of these feline representatives of deity were mummified; enterprising English merchants of later centuries shipped great numbers of them to Britain where they were used as fertilizer.

Reticence of biblical writers may stem, then, from abhorrence of the animal revered by Egyptians rather than from lack of acquaintance with it. Whatever the case, folk lore of the Levant supplies the omission by continuing to transmit the story of a lioness who sneezed and produced the first cat when rodents threatened to overrun the ark.

Jonah and the Monster

Until the Bible was translated into English, no one had ever heard the story of Jonah and the whale. For the great fish that's mentioned in Jonah 1:17 was considered by ancient and medieval scholars to be a sea monster and was designated accordingly in Greek and Latin Bibles.

One of the great art finds of modern times is a group of eastern Mediterranean sculptures dating from the late third or early fourth century A.D. Produced in a period when it was long thought that Christians carved no statues at all (in obedience to the commandment forbidding graven images), three of these works of art give a complete summary of the Jonah story. They were placed on the market in secrecy, and thus their point of origin is not known, but Antioch is the best guess.

Whoever he was, the Greek-trained sculptor who made these pieces followed the earliest known text of Scripture and portrayed Jonah in the process of entering the belly of a sea monster. In his version the beast of the deep has feet like a lion and huge elongated ears. He doesn't remotely resemble any type of whale or dolphin, by then well known to seamen. Hence the interpretation is faithful to Greek *ketos,* which designates a sea dragon or monster.

Just what creature was in the mind of the original writer of Jonah's saga remains a matter of conjecture. Probability points to some semi-mythical sea serpent rather than to the shark or humpback whale included in early illustrated editions of English Bibles. Many twentieth-century versions and translations reject "whale" and use "sea monster" or "dragon" in rendering the ancient account.

What Forces Shaped the Nature of Satan?

Though the Old Testament and the New have organic bonds, there are important differences between them—quite aside from the fact that the New Testament centers upon the story of an actual rather than an anticipated Saviour. One of the sharpest, and in some respects most puzzling, differences lies in the fact that the Satan of the Old Testament is far from identical with the Satan of the New Testament.

The root meaning of the Hebrew original is approximately "obstacle" or "adversary." But in some instances the superhuman adversary is regarded as actively on the side of the Lord—an agent in his employ. For an example of this point of view, see the story of Balaam, especially as in Num. 22:22.

Though Satan plays various roles in the Old Testament, nowhere in it does he appear as the personification of evil. Linguistic evidence supports the view that for the patriarchs and their descendants, Satan was a title rather than a personal name. Any angel who happened to be cast in the role of "the adversary" was, for the moment at least, Satan.

In the New Testament, the whole tone changes. Here he is a distinctive personality, regardless of whether he is serving as "the tempter" (Matt. 4:3), "the prince of the power of the air" (Eph. 2:2) or simply "the enemy" (Luke 10:19).

Precisely how this transition from officer to person was accomplished in Jewish thought and why the transition took place remain mysteries. The most likely explanation links ancient changes in theological thought with military and political events. Israel's prophets had traditionally associated national disaster with divine wrath; this view became increasingly hard to support during centuries when Greece and Rome put Israel into eclipse. Confronted with the problem of why God's people suffered, Jewish theologians found comfort in the theory that the world was presently in the clutches of a superdemon, an avowed enemy of God. As a result the office of heavenly "adversary" attached permanently to a single Evil One—and the modern concept of Satan was born. Until a better theory is devised, this one will have to serve.

Was Moses a Leper?

Leprosy, whose basic cause is now known to be a strain of bacteria discovered less than a century ago by the Norwegian scientist Armauer Hansen, is still considered the world's most stubborn chronic disease. Though it has been studied and treated for at least four thousand years, there are relatively few complete cures on record—and most of them have involved gradual improvement over long periods. Yet some contemporary scientists interpret the biblical record to indicate that Moses' role in history stems from a sudden and dramatic cure from leprosy.

There are sufficient references in Scripture to indicate that Hebrews were well acquainted with the malady from the earliest times. Writing in *Man, Nature and Diseases,* Richard Fiennes voices a conclusion reached by various investigators when he suggests that Moses was a victim of leprosy.

As reported in Genesis the fugitive from Egypt was ordered by Jehovah to thrust his hand under his cloak. He did so "and when he took it out, behold, his hand was leprous as snow." God then commanded him to repeat his action. "And he put his hand into his bosom again; and plucked it out of his bosom, and, behold, it was turned again as his other flesh." (Exod. 4:6-7.) This stupendous sign was one of the badges of authority conferred upon Moses, so that the Hebrews would accept him as their leader.

According to Fiennes, this passage implies that Moses was a victim of leprosy who experienced a remarkable cure while living the healthy outdoor life of a shepherd, "perhaps aided by some profound emotional experience." This conjecture concerning one of the factors that helped launch Moses on his road to world-shaping influence is strengthened by the fact that a few present-day lepers have experienced "spontaneous remission" with climactic religious experiences serving as contributing factors.

Date of the Exodus Uncertain

The Exodus of the Israelites from Egypt under the leadership of Moses marked the beginning of their nation and is *the* crucial point in Jewish history. Nevertheless, centuries of research have failed to reveal the date when it took place.

According to I Kings 6:1 the Exodus occurred 480 years before Solomon built the temple in Jerusalem, but this figure probably represents an estimate based on twelve generations of forty years each. Another possibility is that the total of 480 years was obtained by adding fifty years (the approximate period of the Babylonian Exile) to the total length of the Judean monarchy as reported in Deuteronomy.

Many scholars of the last century, recognizing that the best they could produce was an educated guess, borrowed from western history. To help fix the approximate date of Moses' leadership, they compared him with Columbus and gave the rule: "Fourteen hundred and ninety-two (B.C.) is an easy date to remember, and, as the date of the Exodus, is near enough for all ordinary exactness."

This date, however, would place Moses' people in Egypt during the reign of the great conqueror Thutmose III. Mention of the store cities Pithom and Raamses in the book of Exodus (1:11) indicates that the Jews were in Egypt when the city of Raamses was built by Ramses II (1290-1224 B.C.). Hence the present tendency is to reject the notion that Moses was an ancient mariner of the desert who functioned as many years before Christ as did Columbus after Christ and to date the Exodus of the Jews somewhere in the period of 1290-1260 B.C.

Lost Books of the Jews

Numerous ancient chronicles mentioned in the Bible have been lost. Presumably familiar to those who shaped the Old Testament record, these accounts (which may have been transmitted orally from generation to generation by memory rather than by means of clay tablets or leather scrolls) would fill in a great many gaps if they could be recovered.

There are brief quotations from some of them in Holy Writ, but for the most part only their names are known. For example, the Prophecy of Enoch (see the Epistle to Jude, vs. 14); the Book of the Wars of the Lord (Num. 21:14); the Book of Jasher (Josh. 10:13; II Sam. 1:18); the Book of Iddo the Seer (II Chron. 9:29; 12:15); the Book of Nathan the Prophet and the Prophecy of Ahijah the Shilonite (II Chron. 9:29); the Acts of Rehoboam in the Book of Shemaiah (II Chron. 12:15); and the Book of Jehu the Son of Hanani (II Chron. 20:34).

God's Feathers

According to the writer of psalm 91, God's body is covered with feathers. The distressed seeker after the Lord is comforted by the promise: "He shall cover thee with his feathers, and under his wings shalt thou trust" (vs. 4).

While this reference can be regarded as poetic and figurative, its original meaning may have been literal—due to the influence of Egyptian belief in Horus, the hawk god, who was revered as the ancestor of the pharaohs and was thought to protect these rulers in battle. Ancient Jews repudiated Egyptian idolatry, but cultural intermingling led to the assimilation of many Egyptian words and ideas.

Though the hands of God are mentioned in Scripture far more often than his wings, allusions to the latter are too numerous to be ignored. Boaz promises Ruth that she will be fully rewarded by "the Lord God of Israel, under whose wings thou art come to trust" (Ruth 2:12). Other references to God's wings are found in Pss. 17:8; 36:7; 57:1; 61:4; 63:7; and Mal. 4:2.

Jericho's Walls Tumbled Down

Joshua's conquest of the heavily fortified city of Jericho is one of the most intriguing—and puzzling—stories in the entire Bible. Largely because men were eager to find out whether its walls really fell and, if so, why, the site of the ancient city lying 820 feet below sea level was one of the earliest to be studied seriously by biblical archaeologists.

Ernst Sellin and Carl Watzinger worked there from 1907 to 1911. This was long before pottery had been found to be an accurate source of a crude "calendar" for ancient times so these pioneers had no way to date the remains they uncovered. John Garstang started digging into the ruins of Jericho in 1929 and worked there for seven years. According to his findings, the city conquered by Joshua covered at least four acres and was surrounded by massive fortifications. Garstang's work suggests that a few years before or after 1394 B.C., a great fire practically leveled the city. Some analysts think the conflagration occurred as a result of an earthquake that actually leveled the city walls. According to this theory, Hebrew soldiers had Jericho under siege at the time of the disaster and interpreted the crumbling of enemy defenses to direct intervention by Jehovah, in whose name they fought.

Others challenge the notion that an earthquake could have razed Jericho's double brick walls. For while the outer wall was about thirty feet high and six feet thick, excavations indicate that the inner one was about the same height and more than twelve feet thick.

In the present state of knowledge no universally acceptable interpretation is likely to be developed. Neither is an accurate chronology available; Garstang's dates, if accurate, would place the Exodus from Egypt considerably earlier than the period usually assigned to it. But in probing the source of one of history's strangest military campaigns, diggers working since 1950 have found positive proof that the site was inhabited several thousand years earlier than previously imagined. Regardless of what made them topple, when Jericho's walls fell, they helped destroy one of the oldest, if not indeed the very oldest, city known to man.

What Was the Star of Bethlehem?

No other event or phenomenon described in the New Testament—not even Jesus' miracle of raising Lazarus from the dead—has excited such intensive research as Matthew's almost incidental mention of the star that led the Wise Men from the East to Bethlehem (Matt. 2:1-2).

In the seventeenth century Johannes Kepler sifted evidence and concluded that the "star" was actually due to a meeting of Jupiter and Venus. This "conjunction" of the planets, which occurred in 7 B.C. under the sign of the fishes, takes place only once every 794 years. Other astronomers and mathematicians have made their own suggestions, but like Kepler's insurmountable objections can be raised to them. Because no known pattern involving the movement of heavenly bodies is adequate to account for the brief appearance of a "star of wonder," many scientists of past decades dismissed the story as a folk-tale.

But evidence accumulated by physicists, chemists, and astronomers since the end of World War II has reopened the whole question. It is now generally believed that our universe includes antimatter which is exactly opposite in properties to the matter previously known to science. Theoretical conclusions point to the probability that chunks of antimatter occasionally collide with matter and form brief-lived but brilliant sources of light. Since such encounters are haphazard rather than orderly, there is no way to chart the times or regions where they occurred in the past or will take place in the future.

So the best guess science can offer suggests that light from a collision between a distant star or planet and a mass of antimatter may have caused veteran eastern astronomers to seek out the Babe of Bethlehem. If this highly tentative hypothesis is rejected, the riddle of the star of Bethlehem is narrowed to two choices: myth or miracle.

How Did Wise Men Travel?

Manger scenes used at Christmas in American homes and churches frequently include the Wise Men and almost always show them leading camels or mounted on them, but the New Testament account gives no support for this custom. As far as the Gospel record is concerned, it is well within the realm of possibility that they walked.

Camels entered the story because the general region of Persia is so closely linked with these animals that early readers assumed they played a part in the journey to Bethlehem. According to a widespread Mexican tradition, each Wise Man rode a different animal, with the result that their party included a camel, a donkey, and an elephant.

Because camels are unknown among peoples of some island cultures, the publishers of an illustrated edition of the Christmas story for use in the Philippines ran into trouble. Eventually they settled on an animal familiar to potential readers and issued the booklet with a cover drawing of Wise Men astride water buffalo.

Was Salome Really Beautiful?

Long-entrenched opinion to the contrary, the New Testament does not identify Salome as the woman responsible for the death of John the Baptist. Herod, the ruler who honored a dancing girl's request for John's head as a gift, did have a stepdaughter named Salome, so it was natural for the ancient historian Josephus to conclude that she performed the famous dance reported in Matthew 14.

In the first edition of the *American Encyclopedia,* Salome is identified as "a young girl, who is instigated by her mother Herodias to ask of Herod Antipas the execution of Saint John the Baptist." Numerous reference works give similar accounts, but others qualify their versions.

Regardless of whether it actually was this girl, a sister, or a half sister of hers, nineteenth-century writers labeled her as the chief villain in the ancient story. Oscar Wilde's play *Salome* was refused a license by English authorities—but Sarah Bernhardt played in a French version of it in 1894. Richard Strauss used the same name and the same emphases for his celebrated opera first performed in Dresden in 1905. England barred it for a period, but in 1910 it was performed several times at Covent Garden under the direction of Thomas Beecham.

So little is known of the historical Salome (nowhere mentioned by name in Scripture) that practically everything said about her is a product of the imagination. There is no evidence whatever—in the Bible or outside it—that she ever executed a "dance of the seven veils" like that made famous in theaters and opera houses. So far as authentic information about her is concerned, it is altogether possible that instead of being an agile temptress, Salome may have been a clumsy hag.

Did Jesus Speak Hebrew?

In spite of the fact that Jesus came from the stream of Jewish life and thought, there is no certainty that he could read or write Hebrew. Instead, he may have used a vernacular tongue now generally called Aramaic.

The roots of Aramaic are thought to go very deep; it was probably the language of ancient Aramaeans before they settled in Palestine. But it was not widely known among the Jews at first. In the period of the patriarchs both Hebrew and Assyrian officers used it fluently, but common folk didn't understand it (II Kings 18:26).

By the sixth century B.C. Aramaic was the most widely used of all Semitic languages. It became the common language of the Persian empire and the official language used by many diplomats. Great numbers of Jews—especially those living outside Palestine—lost all touch with Hebrew. This made it necessary to translate the Scriptures into Aramaic versions, known as Targums.

Within a century after the Babylonian exile began in 587 B.C., Hebrew ceased to be a vital, thriving language. It continued to be used in some formal religious services, much as Latin was later used for centuries in the Roman Catholic Church. But men without special training couldn't read or write the language of their ancestors. While there is no documentary proof to support the view, it is possible that Jesus' reading from the book of the Prophet Isaiah (Luke 4:17-20) was done from an Aramaic version. This conjecture is strengthened by the fact that when Jesus quoted Ps. 22:1 from the cross as reported in Matt. 27:46, he spoke in Aramaic rather than in Hebrew: *"Eli, Eli, lama, sabachthani?"* ("My God, my God, why hast thou forsaken me?")

Mark's Gospel also quotes Jesus as speaking Aramaic (5:41; 7:34). William Barclay ventures to guess that these examples represent firsthand information secured by Mark from Peter, who was present and heard the phrases.

How Did the First Christians Baptize?

Few debates centering about New Testament rites and ceremonies have produced as much heat and as little light as that over the mode of baptism practiced by the earliest Christians.

Because John the Baptist took his converts to the Jordan River, it was long assumed that he administered baptism by immersion. But if that was the case, Paul probably broke the precedent, for his midnight baptism of a jailor and his family in the city of Thyatira strongly suggests sprinkling or pouring (Acts 16:33).

Nor is there any clear conclusion as to whether Jesus practiced baptism. In John 3:22 he is said to have administered the rite himself, but in John 4:2 this is contradicted. Matthew Henry, seventeenth-century commentator who is still widely read, got around the difficulty by concluding that "he himself baptized not, with his own hand, but his disciples by his orders and directions. But his disciples' baptizing was his baptizing."

The famous Manual of Discipline, now counted among the Dead Sea Scrolls of the Qumran community, describes baptism as a ceremony in which waters of ablution are sprinkled for the cleansing of the soul. Whether or not the very earliest Christians followed this practice remains an unsolved riddle.

Neither literary nor archaeological research is likely to bring all followers of Jesus to accept the same conclusions about this central ceremony in Christianity. References in the New Testament itself are too few and too brief to afford any final answers. Despite this situation, a nineteenth-century American edition of the King James Version was published in which "immerse" was used in many passages where "baptize" ordinarily occurs.

Spiritual or Psychological Sources of Stigmata?

Persons of great piety whose bodies develop the stigmata, or wounds of Jesus, are often venerated as saints. But most of them are more greatly influenced by tradition than Scripture—for their bleeding sores seldom fall into a pattern compatible with the most plausible concept of Jesus' crucifixion.

Original readers of the documents that fused to form the New Testament knew all about crucifixion; the ordeal was so common and familiar that Gospel writers give few details. St. Francis of Assisi, first known stigmatic, developed bleeding sores in the palms of his hands. Others have had "wounds" in their feet.

Not having access to details, medieval Christians drew on their imagination when picturing the crucifixion. Many paintings and statues showed Jesus with one nail driven through his crossed feet and one piercing each palm. Largely under the influence of a famous ivory "Crucifixion" by Michelangelo, the majority of modern sculptors and painters show the feet of the crucified Jesus separated, with a nail through each.

Practically all historians now agree that Romans typically drove nails through the forearms of their victims and seldom fastened feet to a cross except by means of leather straps. Detailed knowledge of executions carried out in this manner has been accumulated in recent decades as a result of archaeological and literary finds. Modern medical study indicates that it wasn't bleeding from nails or other instruments that caused the death of Jesus. Though the precise reason remains an unsolved mystery, the best conjecture is that he choked to death. Unmoved by the historical reconstruction of actual events, most stigmatics continue to bleed at four points: the palms of both hands and the tops of both feet.

What Made Matthew Misquote?

Whether the author of the Gospel of Matthew is responsible or error crept into the text as a result of a mistake by some early scribe is unknown. But Matt. 27:9-10, part of the account of the downfall of Judas Iscariot, contains a monumental boner. In all known manuscripts it reads: "Then was fulfilled that which was spoken by Jeremy the prophet, saying, And they took the thirty pieces of silver, the price of him that was valued, whom they of the children of Israel did value; And gave them for the potter's field, as the Lord appointed me."

Jeremiah never said anything about thirty pieces of silver; the passage is a free paraphrase of Zech. 11:13. Some scholars have found in it faint echoes of Jer. 18:2-3 and 32:6-15, but even the most ardent defenders of Matthew admit that here he should have spoken of Zechariah rather than Jeremiah.

Quotation from memory was a common practice by New Testament writers, and there are many instances in which Old Testament passages are used in slightly modified form. New Testament writers were careful with proper names, however, and the error in Matt. 27:9 has no counterpart. (Mark 2:26 has Jesus referring to Abiathar the high priest rather than to Ahimelech his son, who actually held the office at the time. This reference to II Sam. 8:17 may also represent an error on the part of a Gospel writer; this conclusion is not certain, however, since some manuscripts omit the reference entirely. This suggests the possibility that the error was made as a scribal gloss added to the original text of Mark. In the case of Matthew's misquotation, all manuscripts are in agreement.)

Was Jesus Luminous to the Eye?

New Testament writers gave emphasis to Jesus' radiance and paid homage to him as the Light of the World. Yet the Gospel record nowhere makes specific reference to an idea made familiar by generations of biblical artists—the concept that Jesus was marked by a visible halo.

A radiant envelope, at first called a nimbus and later a halo, is sometimes depicted as covering Jesus' entire body. This usage is especially prominent in medieval paintings of the infant Saviour. But a majority of Christian artists have suggested that a luminous circle was seen about the head of Jesus.

Indian coins of the first century B.C. showed halos about the heads of some gods and kings. After having spent forty days with the Lord, the face of Moses shone so brightly that his appearance frightened tribesmen, and he was forced to put on a veil (Exod. 34:29-35).

Some students of culture think the basic concept of the shining face represents a survival from ancient astrological beliefs, in which a glorified person was identified with the sun. But numerous present-day seers and prophets of various backgrounds insist that though science can't detect it, the eye of faith can sometimes see a luminous disk surrounding the head or body of a person who has achieved great sanctity.

Whether or not Jesus was physically luminous to sensitive observers on special occasions, as hinted by numerous Gospel references and affirmed by artists and sculptors, remains an unsolved mystery of the faith.

Why Did John's Name Become So Popular?

At least nine different biblical characters are named John. Some of them, like John the Baptist, John the apostle, and John Mark, are central characters. Others are mentioned only in books of the Apocrypha or incidentally in familiar books.

In spite of the fact that Peter clearly dominated the thought of the early Christian Church, his name has had far less impact upon the English-speaking world than has that of John. As early as A.D. 1300 it was estimated that one Englishman out of every five was named John. Today the name is still bestowed upon about 15 percent of American boys—and more than one hundred variations and adaptations of the biblical name are also in current use.

No one knows why John, rather than Peter or Paul, happened to catch the imagination of generations of parents who wanted their sons to have biblical names.

How Freely Did Shakespeare Use Scripture?

Every student of literature knows that there is an organic connection between the Bible and the plays of Shakespeare, but no expert can give an exact summary of scriptural influence upon the bard of Avon. Though tallies differ, it's generally agreed that Shakespeare refers to or quotes from the Bible about 1,200 times. In the famous First Folio edition more than fifty biblical proper names are attached to characters in his plays. One list enumerates 151 Shakespearean references to the Gospel of Matthew, 137 to Psalms, 64 to Genesis, and 42 to Job.

But in numerous instances the scholar is confronted by an insoluble set of questions: Is Shakespeare actually quoting from Scripture? Has he used a proverb based upon a biblical source? Or is the similarity of ideas and language the result of coincidence? Some of the more vexatious passages of this sort are:

Bible (II Cor. 11:6)—But though I be rude in speech, . . .

Shakespeare (*Othello,* Act I, sc. 3)—Rude am I in my speech, . . .

Bible (Ps. 39:6)—Man walketh in a vain shew: . . .

Shakespeare (*Macbeth,* Act V, sc. 5)—Life's but a walking shadow, . . .

Apocrypha (II Macc. 15:28)—Nicanor lay dead in his harness.

Shakespeare (*Macbeth,* Act V, sc. 5)—We'll die with harness on our back.

Bible (Ps. 8:4*a*-6)—What is man, that thou art mindful of him? For thou hast made him a little lower than the angels, and hast crowned him with glory and honour. Thou madest him to have dominion over the works of thy hands.

Shakespeare (*Hamlet,* Act II, sc. 2)—What a piece of work is a man! how noble in reason! how infinite in faculty! in form and moving how express and admirable! in action how like an angel! in apprehension how like a god! the beauty of the world! the paragon of animals!

Did Adam and Eve Have Navels?

Most readers have been untroubled by the Bible's failure to specify whether the stomachs of Adam and Eve were flat or dimpled by navels. Probably it didn't occur to early Christian artists that questions might be raised. The first man and his mate are described as having been created by processes that didn't include an embryonic period with the vital umbilical cord attached for feeding. But painters typically showed the first man and woman with familiar buttons formed as a result of natural birth.

Thomas Browne, a noted seventeenth-century physician, gave considerable attention to this issue in his book on *Religio Medici.* His arguments were chiefly theological rather than biological, however, and failed to convince painters that they should omit navels from portraits of Eden's central characters.

William Blake, the poet-artist who executed a series of water colors to illustrate an edition of *Paradise Lost,* followed artistic tradition and showed Adam and Eve as though they had been born rather than created. A notable exhibition of his works in 1939 led to the reproduction of his "Creation of Eve" and "Temptation of Eve" in numerous American newspapers and magazines. So publicized, his nude Eve with long hair and a prominent navel prompted numerous readers to write letters to the editors in which they questioned the painter's interpretation. So far, no one has offered a universally acceptable theory concerning the shape of Eve's stomach.

Who Carved Dighton Rock?

Dighton Rock, which lies at Assonet Neck, Massachusetts, has been the subject of inquiry and controversy for nearly three hundred years. Present opinion is weighted in the direction of the conclusion that inscriptions on it represent a deliberate hoax, perpetrated to support a strangely twisted interpretation of the Old Testament.

Just when the strange symbols cut into the face of the rock at the mouth of Taunton River were first seen is not known, but they were the object of very early speculation. By 1690 so much interest had been aroused that the famous Cotton Mather visited the spot and wrote a description of the message that seemed to be engraved in some ancient language. Many symbols, he noted, were reminiscent of those associated with the Near East.

Early in the nineteenth century a Maryland teacher, Ira Hill, announced that he had solved the riddle. He called attention to the fact that in the time of Solomon several expeditions were sent to the land of Ophir for gold. A successful voyage is noted in II Chron. 8:18, while the record of a naval disaster is preserved in I Kings 22:48. Dighton Rock, said Hill, either represented a story of a biblical expedition that started for Ophir and somehow wandered to North America, or was an elaborate practical joke played upon persons who identified American Indians with the "lost tribes of Israel."

Hill himself thought the carvings were genuine; no scholar of repute has supported this theory. Several have concluded that the inscription was actually made to bolster the lost tribes tradition. But the hoax theory has its shortcomings. Why would anyone go to the trouble of cutting a dozen lines of mysterious characters into a solid rock on the perpendicular side of a steep bluff where there was no certainty anyone would ever find the message? Unless new facts are uncovered, it is unlikely that any completely satisfactory explanation will ever be framed.

Just Which Verse Is in the Middle?

E. W. and Catherine Smith who lived in Rochester, New York, about the turn of the century, are credited with having made a discovery about the Bible. Though rabbis of ancient times may have noticed it, none are known to have called attention to the fact that of all the women mentioned in the Bible, only one has her exact age at death specified. This woman, pointed out the Smiths, is Sarah, who laughed when she received a divine message that she would bear a son in her old age. According to Gen. 23:1 she lived to be 127 years old.

There is no indication that Scripture's departure from the general rule of silence concerning the age of women (as contrasted with men, whose ages are frequently specified) represents an attempt to punish Sarah for her amusement.

Again according to the Smiths, the middle verse of the Bible is Ps. 18:8. But in spite of their zeal for accuracy and their triumph concerning the age of Sarah, they may have been dizzy from reading when they recorded the latter observation, or perhaps their pronouncement could have suffered from a printer's typographical error. For other reseachers, whose names are not preserved, have insisted that the middle verse of the Bible is Ps. 118:8.

Will Noah's Ark Ever Be Found?

Was Noah's ark a huge sailing vessel that actually rode out the great flood—or was it a small craft whose size has grown in telling and retelling the story? Few unsolved questions of biblical scholarship have attracted more attention since this one was first debated in the twelfth century.

As described in Gen. 6:14–8:19 the ancient vessel was huge and cumbersome—more like a floating house than a ship. It had three decks and measured 300 cubits long (about 450 feet), 50 cubits wide (about 75 feet), and 30 cubits high (about 45 feet). Much evidence indicates that ancient techniques were inadequate for the construction of so large a vessel.

In the light of this problem, plus the obvious fact that however large it may have been no ship could possibly have contained pairs of all the earth's multitudinous living creatures, many persons have scoffed at the whole story. They regard it as an ancient folktale with a religious moral that somehow got incorporated into the holy writings of the Hebrews.

Others not only insist that the ark was actually built and used; from time to time various explorers have claimed to find portions of its remains. Most searchers have concentrated in the region of 16,873-foot Mt. Ararat, in present-day Turkey.

About 1840 a party of mountain climbers reported having discovered the bow of an ancient wooden ship sticking out of permanent ice at the 13,000-foot level. Late in the century James Bryce brought back from that spot a piece of wood about four feet long and five inches thick, "evidently hewn by a tool." Dr. Nouri, Archdeacon of Jerusalem and Babylon, in 1893 reported sighting the wrecked vessel and asserted that he saw "beams of dark red wood joined by twelve-inch nails." At intervals ever since, explorers have claimed that they have sighted Noah's ark, but no pictures or fragments have been pronounced authentic by skeptical experts.

This leaves the matter exactly where it was centuries ago. Some think Noah never built a ship of the size and type described in Scripture; others cling to the hope that its ruins will yet be discovered. Some scholars dismiss the whole story of Noah as a myth and scoff at the notion that he built a boat of any sort.

What Triggered Ezekiel's Visions?

Linguists are far from united concerning the meaning of a Hebrew noun used only three times in Scripture—in Ezek. 1:4; 1:27; and 8:2. Ronald Knox, one of the few scholars to translate the entire Bible single-handed, follows the usage of the King James Version and reports that the prophet saw the "colour of amber." Translators of the Revised Standard Version use "gleaming bronze" to render the same word. Whatever it was, it played some part in Ezekiel's mystical visions.

Curt W. Beck, chemistry teacher at Vassar College, has recently made scientific headlines with his study of amber—which is fossil rosin deposited by evergreen trees about sixty million years ago. Beck's studies show that a prehistoric stand of conifers in Scandinavia produced a unique kind of amber. Such "Baltic amber" was a very early and important item in international trade. It was used not only for ornamentation, but also for warding off evil spirits and for healing.

Since it was credited with magical powers, there's a reasonable possibility that instead of merely drifting into a trance as a result of gazing at gleaming bronze, the visionary prophet who lived by the river Chebar in Babylon actually experimented with the effects produced by intense visual concentration upon exotic amber imported from northern Europe. In the entire scriptural record no other historian or seer mentions the substance—whatever it may have been—that figured in some of Ezekiel's ecstatic experiences.

Life in Bible Lands

Moses Wrote with Hammer and Chisel

Jehovah originally wrote the Decalogue upon tablets of stone with his own finger. Later Moses served as scribe to rewrite "upon the tables the words of the covenant, the ten commandments" (Exod. 34:28).

This central moment in the history of the chosen people represents a case in which the hammer was mightier than the pen, for details of the account clearly indicate that Moses' "writing"—a job that required forty days—was done with hammer and chisel.

When he was through with his world-shaping work, Moses probably had nothing more than a brief set of words or phrases that represented condensed laws. It is highly unlikely that he or any other artisan could have chiseled out so lengthy a code as that quoted in Exodus 20 and Deuteronomy 5.

Regardless of how brief they may have been and how lacking in orderly structure by modern standards, these maxims had one important quality. In a land where many materials decayed rapidly and in an epoch when enemies were prone to destroy anything they could capture, the Decalogue cut into solid rock was designed to last. Moses' stone writing transmitted its message so long and forcefully that it became the foundation of all western law.

A Flint Knife for Circumcision

As a central religious ceremony with side effects in the field of hygiene, circumcision almost certainly originated in the Stone Age. Just before the Battle of Jericho, long after metal had come into common use, the leader of the Israelites was ordered by the Lord to make flint knives for use in the rite.

"So Joshua made flint knives, and circumcised the people of Israel at Gibeath-haaraloth." (Josh. 5:3 RSV.) Translators of the King James Version, not nearly as well versed in Hebrew and archaeology as some of their successors, mistakenly translated the key words in this and the preceding verse as "sharp knives."

Practically every major archaeological expedition to Palestine has yielded at least one stone knife. Before 3500 B.C. the size and shape of the blade used in circumcision became standardized in a form about six inches long, with a double edge and a raised central ridge. Though flint implements must have been recognized as inferior to fine copper blades in cutting capabilities, generation after generation of Abraham's descendants continued to insist that the only proper way to cut off a foreskin was with a stone blade.

Land Purchased for a Cemetery

Land ownership, often a vague and tenuous matter among nomads and herdsmen, became of crucial importance when men wished to bury their dead. As a result of this factor, the first piece of property owned in the region Jehovah promised to the descendants of Abraham was a burial place.

When Sarah died at Hebron, about nineteen miles southwest of Jerusalem, Abraham persuaded Ephron the Hittite to sell him the cave of Machpelah (Gen. 23:7-16). This sole plot of ground owned by the chosen people served as the family sepulcher of Israel's patriarchs and matriarchs. Eventually it became the last resting place not only of Sarah, but also of Abraham, Isaac, Jacob, Rebekah, and Leah (Gen. 49:31; 50:13).

Much evidence from archaeology supports biblical stress upon the antiquity of Hebron as a city. Jar handles of the eighth century B.C. stamped with the name of the city and the inscription "to the king" are believed to have been broken from ancient equivalents of the modern standard quart and standard gallon, now so carefully guarded by the United States Bureau of Standards.

Greeting Cards from Broken Pots

It was once thought that written communications were rare during Old Testament times; this view has been demolished by the discovery of trememdous hoards of ancient documents.

One of the earliest such finds took place by accident in 1877 on the site of Egypt's famous "City of Crocodiles." Grave robbers hunting valuables in ancient tombs were disappointed to find one big crypt filled with mummified crocodiles. A workman who struck a blow in disgust found the crocodile he hit to be stuffed full of bills, receipts, personal letters, contracts, and other documents. Tens of thousands of such remnants from highly developed cultures have since been uncovered and deciphered.

Hebrews were short of papyrus and used much of their leather for rolls of Scripture, so ordinary folk scribbled memos and invoices on bits of broken pottery. Most such *ostraca* eventually ended in dump heaps, but many are so well preserved that they clearly indicate that early Israelites were accustomed to sending bills for merchandise bought on credit as well as clay "greeting cards" to the sick.

Earliest Impersonal Signatures

The production of signatures by printing or other mechanical methods is usually considered a modern innovation but actually antedates the custom of writing one's name in order to seal a bargain or complete a legal document. If he did not own and use one himself, Abraham was undoubtedly familiar with ancient prototypes of devices designed to give a distinctive and unduplicated "mark" indicating approval of an agreement.

Excavating the site of Erech, mentioned in Genesis 10:10, archaeologists found button-like stamps used by ancient merchants to "sign their names" and assume responsibility for carrying out transactions. The use of these devices preceded by many centuries the custom of affixing personal signatures.

Long before that stage was reached, stone cylinder seals were in use throughout the Near East. Considerably more sophisticated than the "buttons" employed at Erech (or Uruk), cylinder seals bore designs or pictures engraved in relief. Rolled on a tablet of soft clay, such devices left distinctive impressions and served to make contracts binding. Clay marked by a button or cylinder seal was baked so hard that many documents remain legible after three thousand years of exposure to weather.

Tools that made marks which served the role of signatures obviously created an atmosphere conducive to forgery. To fake a contract or other document, all one had to do was to get temporary possession of another person's seal. In order to execute her plot against Naboth, Jezebel forged letters in King Ahab's name and then "sealed them with his seal" (I Kings 21:8).

Bare Feet for Holy Ground

Removal of one's sandals as a mark of respect for deity became customary so early that no one knows how it started. Early footgear was clumsily made and often became dirty in use; hence some scholars assume that unwashed bare feet were considered more respectful than those shod in leather or cloth.

Scripture has little to say about sandals—presumably because they were worn only by the wealthy and powerful of Old Testament times—and gives no description of them. Secular monuments and inscriptions indicate that though most sandals were simply made, rulers sometimes wore boots with upturned, pointed toes.

On Mt. Sinai the Lord specifically ordered Moses to take off his shoes (Exod. 3:5). This indicates not only that the mountaintop was considered holy ground but also that Moses was a man of considerable means; otherwise he would not have been wearing "shoes" while tending flocks of his father-in-law.

Priests of Israel are presumed to have performed their ministrations barefooted, since footwear is nowhere mentioned in connection with detailed descriptions of other ecclesiastical apparel. Even today Muslims customarily remove their shoes before they go into their mosques.

Though all theories about the origin of this custom are tentative, ideas which focus upon clumsy and muddy footwear have one important rival. Some interpreters think the practice of taking off one's sandals in a holy place was a result of insistence upon preserving the ways of the past when no one, not even a chieftain, wore shoes of any kind.

Jacob's Treatment of Esau Legal

Among various neighboring peoples as well as the Hebrews, a man's first son occupied a special position. He inherited the bulk of his father's estate and at the death of his father became the head of the clan even though he might have brothers close to his own age. This right of the firstborn, familiar to Old Testament readers as birthright, was far more than a custom that members of a family could choose to accept or reject. Rather, it was an important feature of organized society and had the status of law.

To dramatize the importance of the birthright, sons who ate with their father were customarily seated in the order of their ages (Gen. 43:33). Some patriarchs had several wives, all of whom bore sons. In the case of a man whose favorite wife was not the first to present him with a boy, normally the father was not permitted to give the birthright to a son of his choice; it had to go to the first male child whom he sired (Deut. 21:15-17). Abraham's treatment of Ishmael (Gen. 21:9-14) was based on the fact that the boy's mother was a bondwoman; here the law of birthright apparently did not apply or was deliberately violated.

Along with social status and property rights the firstborn was entitled to a special blessing from his father. In early periods this was a semimagical formula thought to confer special potency and a protection against death. The blessing was treated as a closely guarded secret and transmitted orally from father to firstborn for generation after generation.

Small wonder, therefore, that Jacob coveted the birthright that belonged to Esau. Scholars once questioned the validity of the account of Esau's hasty sale on the basis of the conjecture that birthright was purely biological and could not be transferred. But archaeological finds at the site of ancient Nuzu indicate that a birthright was negotiable property. Documentary evidence concerning this attitude among their contemporaries strengthens the likelihood that it prevailed among the Hebrews, too. Though Jacob was greedy and crafty, he probably stayed well within the law when he used his brother's hunger as an opportunity for profit.

Trees Listed as Property

Westerners familiar with long-established systems of ownership according to which a purchaser of land usually gets everything on it and under it have puzzled over a queer set of details in the records about an ancient sale. Primarily because he wanted a cave for use as a family tomb, Abraham bought the field of Ephron. He got the field and the cave, but that didn't end the matter; "all the trees that were in the field, that were in all the borders round about, were made sure" (Gen. 23:17).

This oddly precise stipulation has been clarified by study of the Hittite code recovered from the ancient capital city of Bogazköy (in modern Turkey). According to the code, trees were so valuable in the ancient Near East that it was a standard Hittite practice to enumerate each one included in a real estate transaction. With the great significance of green property recognized, it becomes clear why both Ephron the Hittite and Abraham took care that all the trees involved in their transaction were "made sure," or individually counted and listed.

Praying with Open Eyes

There are occasional instances in which the Bible associates kneeling with prayer (Ezra 9:5; Ps. 95:6; Dan. 6:10; Luke 22:41). But the overwhelming weight of scriptural evidence supports the theory that a person ordinarily prayed in an upright position with his eyes wide open (I Sam. 1:26; I Kings 8:22; Matt. 6:5; Mark 11:25; Luke 18:11).

This attitude for prayer is prescribed rather than optional in the Bible-based code of laws familiar to the modern world as the Talmud. A man engaged in earnest prayer, standing upright in the approved manner, typically looked toward heaven and raised both his hands

(I Kings 8:22; Isa. 1:15; II Macc. 3:20; Pss. 28:2; 63:4; 134:2; 141:2; Lam. 2:19; I Tim. 2:8).

References to bowed heads and closed eyes aren't totally missing from Scripture (Gen. 24:26; Neh. 8:6; Exod. 34:8; I Kings 18:42). Archaeological discoveries from the Greco-Roman world indicate, however, that this mode of prayer didn't become dominant until well after the second century A.D.

Palestine's Predator: The Goat

Seeking to unravel the riddle of how broad sections of once fertile land in Palestine have become denuded, agricultural experts now indict a four-legged villain: the goat. At the time Moses' followers first entered Canaan the land was described as "flowing with milk and honey." Great bodies of evidence, some of it in the Bible but much more from archaeology and secular history, support the view that the description was once accurate. But now the region includes vast areas of desert and semidesert.

Gradual changes in climate were long considered to have brought about this change. Modern studies quashed this theory by showing conclusively that the climate of Bible lands hasn't changed greatly in four thousand years. At the same time, careful observation has revealed that the goat differs from all other domesticated animals. Cattle, sheep, and horses browse on vegetation and often crop it close to the ground. Goats do the same thing—but in addition, use their sharp hooves to dig up roots in order to eat them. As a result they can subsist in regions where other animals perish.

Large numbers of goats, most of them black, were kept in the period of the Hebrew patriarchs. Prosperous tribal leaders often owned great herds of them; a gift of 7,700 he goats to Jehoshaphat is recorded (II Chron. 17:11). Goats were used as peace offerings (Lev. 3:12), burnt offerings (Lev. 1:10), guilt offerings (Lev. 5:18), and sin offerings (Lev. 4:23). The animal so important to Hebrew life and worship is now believed to have engaged in systematic stripping of the land over a period of centuries. So gradually that its impact was never apparent to those who considered it valuable, the goat reduced great districts from pastures and vineyards to dustbowls.

"Improper" Psalms

Methodism's founder, John Wesley, urged congregations to omit some sections of the book of Psalms because he considered them "highly improper for the mouths of a Christian congregation." Many other scholars before and after Wesley have echoed nearly the same point of view, but few agree concerning precisely which of the "psalms of violence" should be deleted.

Measured by any standard, the most flagrant endorsement of brutality in the Psalter grew out of the period of the Babylonian captivity of the Jews. After stressing the way in which exiles sat down by the rivers of Babylon and wept, the psalmist concludes: "O daughter of Babylon, who art to be destroyed; happy shall he be, that rewardeth thee as thou hast served us. Happy shall he be, that taketh and dasheth thy little ones against the stones." (Ps. 137:8-9.)

Repugnant as is the notion of seeking divine approval for beating out the brains of little children against the rocks, neither Welsey nor any other reformer has had significant success in editing the Psalter. Verses 1-6 of the bloody 137th psalm reach a peak of poetic power seldom surpassed in literature.

Corrupt Public Official

Corruption on the part of public officials did not develop as a result of special temptations placed in the way of United States congressmen and senators. The Horites, who developed an elaborate culture northeast of the Persian Gulf, left records of a civic swindle that took place about 1500 B.C.

At the site of the city of Nuzu, Edward Chiera found ancient villas stuffed with clay tablets. Beginning about 1925, he worked until he had recovered more than twenty thousand of them. Translation of the Babylonian texts has thrown a great deal of light upon life in the period roughly contemporaneous with the emergence of the Israelites as a distinct people.

Some of the Nuzu tablets are legal documents—"court records" of the period. One of them deals specifically with the activities of the city's mayor. According to it, Kushshiharbe was so flagrant in his abuse of office that citizens brought charges against him and secured his conviction.

Clay documents prepared about five hundred years before the time of Solomon show that Kushshiharbe used civic workers for his personal projects, had close ties with an organized band of kidnappers, indulged in immoral conduct, and accepted bribes.

Devastation by Locusts

Present-day studies suggest that the locusts or "multipliers" which constituted the eighth plague visited upon Egypt in the time of Moses actually may have been so thick that they "covered the face of the whole earth" and ate so voraciously that "there remained not any green thing" (Exod. 10:15).

There are numerous biblical allusions to devastation worked by hordes of insects which invaded in "bands" (Prov. 30:27) so dense they looked like smoke (Rev. 9:3). Their menace was so great that John of Patmos compared them with horses "prepared unto battle," whose wings sounded like a company of chariots moving at full speed (Rev. 9:7-9).

Such poetic passages, and more prosaic ones describing the plague of locusts that helped free the Israelites from Egyptian bondage, were long regarded as highly exaggerated. Generations of Bible readers who had no firsthand knowledge of the Near East considered an invasion by locusts to be relatively minor in impact.

Thanks to a six-year United Nations project much more is known about the insects today. To fight them, forty-two nations pooled resources in a military-like campaign that covered eleven million square miles. During one locust invasion it was found that an average swarm weighs about as much as the ocean liner *Queen Elizabeth*—more than eighty thousand tons. Each insect daily consumes its own weight in green stuff—the swarm thus accounting for about three tons per day per square mile in areas of reasonably thick vegetation.

Invasions of special force tend to occur about every ten to fifteen years; occasionally a built-up of locust populations creates conditions for a mammoth assault. In the light of these factors commentators now generally agree that the vivid account in Exod. 10:12-15 is reasonable and plausible.

Barbecued Right Forelegs

Like their Hebrew counterparts, ancient Canaanite priests used elaborate sets of rituals that involved a great many burnt offerings. In both cultures most of the sacrificial animal was customarily consumed by the fire, but some of it was laid aside for the use of priests (see Lev. 7:32). Because of this practice there is good reason to think that priests of Baal preferred their barbecue made from the right forelegs of the young animals they offered up.

Digging at Lachish in a series of expeditions that began in 1933, J. L. Starkey found three Canaanite shrines that dated from the fifteenth to the thirteenth centuries B.C. Excavated, they yielded numerous small cult objects plus a great pile of bones from sheep, goats, oxen, and gazelles. Practically all these bones came from the right forelegs of sacrificial animals; since other bones were burned on the altars, it seems likely that these came from the best pieces reserved by priests for their own meals.

Human Sacrifice

Human sacrifice was an almost universal practice among peoples of the ancient Near East. Frequent biblical denunciations of it are usually taken to mean that even the chosen people were perpetually tempted to engage in rites that involved the shedding of human blood (Lev. 20:2; Deut. 12:30; II Kings 17:31; 23:10; Ps. 106:37-38; Jer. 7:30-32; 19:3-5; Ezek. 16:20-21).

After becoming king of Judah in the eighth century B.C., Ahaz made his son "pass through the fire, according to the abominations of the heathen" (II Kings 16:3). Here the language is apparently a deliberate euphemism to avoid naming the act of burning children as sacrifices to Molech. (See Lev. 18:21; II Kings 23:10; Jer. 32:35.)

The vehemence with which Ahaz was condemned and the vigor of prophetic warnings against such practices attest to the fact that in the mainstream of Hebrew faith human sacrifice was never tolerated. Early repudiation of such ways of exhibiting piety is indicated by the famous story of Abraham's willingness to sacrifice Isaac, willingness that was interrupted and redirected by a specific act of God.

A Crude Iron Plowpoint

In spite of the fact that iron is the most abundant metal found in the natural state, it does not lend itself to use by primitive tribesmen. Softer metals, notably gold and copper, were employed far earlier than iron even in regions where iron occurred naturally or could be secured as an item of commerce.

Peoples living in the ancient Near East lagged considerably behind those in some other regions in the adoption of iron-working techniques. The hard metal was known as a rare imported item with great value as a curiosity, but it was not widely used in Palestine before 1200 B.C. Though mentioned nearly one hundred times in the King James Version, in its earliest occurrences the word "iron" is either a late modification of an earlier term for bronze, a gross mistranslation, or an element introduced by tradition. Tubal-cain, reputed to be the ancestor of all blacksmiths and first maker of bronze and iron implements (Gen. 4:22), is clearly a folk hero rather than a historical person. At the time he was introduced into the story, Hebrews were still in a stone age culture.

So it was a notable step forward when the Hebrews first learned to fashion utensils and tools of iron for themselves. Precisely when this took place, it is impossible to determine. But the earliest datable iron implement ever found in Palestine—a crude plowpoint—comes from a period shortly before or after 1000 B.C. William F. Albright found it in Tell el-Ful on the site of ancient Gibeah and guessed it to be of Philistine origin since these people had an absolute monopoly in Palestinian iron during the century that began in 1200 B.C. (I Sam. 13:19).

Solomon's Banquet Table

More than any other man in the history of the Hebrews, King Solomon exemplifies the opulence and extravagance associated with Near Eastern rulers. For example, he had a corps of twelve thousand horsemen who spent at least part of their time providing food for the king's table.

In order to feed his wives, concubines, children, courtiers, and retainers Solomon each day required one hundred sheep, twenty oxen that had been pasture-fed, and ten more fat ones from open range. Though he must have used great numbers of them, Scripture does not specify a daily quota for the harts, gazelles, roebucks, and fattened fowls served at his table.

As described in I Kings 4:22-27, Solomon's banquet table loaded with meat and fowls drained the nation's supply of grain at the rate of thirty measures of fine flour plus sixty measures of meal each day. Precisely how much a measure of the period held, no one knows. This much is certain, however—the king and his retainers put away great quantities of choice food.

Asses an Index to Wealth

One of the most ostentatious displays of wealth mentioned in the Old Testament revolves about an animal for whom men in the Space Age have little use. Ancient Hebrews regarded the domesticated ass (whose disposition was quite unlike his unruly wild cousin, the onager) as one of the most useful of all animals. It was employed as a beast of burden by laboring men lucky enough to own it. As a riding animal it was valued by both men and women and was considered good enough for a king. So the minor judge, Abdon the son of Hillel, was putting on a vulgar exhibition of his wealth and power when he made arrangements for each of his forty sons and thirty nephews to have their own mounts. Riding "on threescore and ten ass colts"

(Judg. 12:14), they were the ancient prototypes of today's drag racers and sport-car crowd. In Abdon's day a well-bred ass was equal in value to two or three or more healthy slaves.

Flourishing Commerce in Cedar

Large-scale international commerce flourished at a much earlier period than was once thought. A prime example is the trade in cedars from the mountains of Lebanon, a district of Syria adjacent to Palestine.

Both David and Solomon imported great quantities of cedar. Since the Hebrews were relatively close to the source of supply, logs were made into rafts and then floated along the seashore to Joppa. By using this technique, huge timbers were transported. Solomon used some of the finest as pillars in a building that came to be known as "the house of the forest of Lebanon" (I Kings 7:2).

Ocean-going peoples came great distances to secure Lebanon's cedars, which they used as masts for their ships.

Some timbers were transported across country at enormous cost in labor. Nebuchadnezzar of Babylon, whose "hanging gardens" or elevated terraces formed one of the wonders of the world, used cedar for the beams of his palace. A document drawn up during his rule and recently recovered describes the rebuilding of the royal residence in the king's own words: "Great cedars I brought from Lebanon, the beautiful forest, to roof it."

Forced Draft Copper Furnaces

No modern metal workers had forced draft furnaces until late in the industrial revolution, but Solomon's engineers put them into service some time during the tenth century B.C.

Exploring the Wadi Arabah, archaeologist Nelson Glueck discovered that Phoenician mercenaries built a copper refinery there during the early years of Solomon's reign. Their biggest installation was at Ezion-geber—one of the spots where the Israelites camped on their journey from Egypt (Num. 33:35). Situated between Edom and the elevated region of Sinai, it is a place where strong winds blow steadily from the north.

Workmen constructed a series of air ducts inside the main wall of a big building, and then connected them with two horizontal rows of holes which served as flues. Under the forced draft created by windstorms that blew most seasons of the year, fuel burned very rapidly and created intense heat. Though wood from the surrounding area may have been used, some evidence suggests that charcoal was brought in from a distance.

Solomon's copper production reached such a peak that he exported large quantities of the metal, much of which he bartered for materials and labor used in building his temple.

Hebrew Worship of Pagan Gods

Though details are obscure, it is reasonably clear that the ancient Israelite culture included religious rebels who deliberately engaged in rites calculated to insult Jehovah while winning the favor of other gods. Their conduct in this respect was somewhat like that of medieval Christians who engaged in the black mass—a premeditated form of group sacrilege practiced in homage to Satan. Semi-magical effects, somewhat like those linked with voodoo, were probably sought.

Isaiah promises divine punishment for persons who engage in such conduct. Though his language is obscure, the basic message is clear. "They that sanctify themselves, and purify themselves in the gardens behind one tree in the midst, eating swine's flesh, and the abomination, and the mouse, shall be consumed together, saith the Lord." (66:17.)

Tree worship has a long and elaborate history among many primitives. To dabble in it would alone be enough to mark one as a rebel against the Lord. But the orgiastic rites denounced by Isaiah included the eating of pork (sternly forbidden), plus mice and "the abomination." No one knows precisely what the latter may have been; evidently the name was a general label for vermin or filth. Some translators render the perplexing word as "creeping things." Like swine, mice were forbidden (Lev. 11:29). Viewed collectively, the ingredients in this forbidden feast are seen to make up a demonic meal analogous to the witch's brew so vividly described centuries later by Shakespeare in *Macbeth* (Act IV). Most authorities think at least a few of Isaiah's contemporaries really ate this vile concoction, taking it as a sacramental meal consumed in honor of pagan deities or the power of evil.

Singers Expected to Play Loudly

Pictorial representations of musical instruments date from remote antiquity. Few of these, however, include any written descriptions or even the names of the instruments. Hence the company of players and singers assembled by David after he had established Jerusalem as his capital probably represents the earliest municipal orchestra about which written records have survived.

Pioneer translators had great difficulty with the names of instruments used by David's players. Recent progress in archaeology has made it possible to identify them more accurately. As listed in the Revised Standard Version (II Sam. 6:5; I Chron. 15:16), the king's music makers employed at least three percussion instruments: tambourines, castanets, and cymbals. Their string section was made up of players who plucked lyres and harps. And even at this early date an important role was reserved for one wind instrument—the "cornet" (KJV), or horn (I Chron. 15:28 RSV), originally formed from an animal's horn and later fashioned from both wood and metal. Though the trumpet was of special significance in civil as well as religious ceremonies, it is not mentioned as having been used with other instruments.

Precisely how this royal orchestra performed, the Bible does not say. But instead of having a special choral section, players of instruments seem to have been trained to sing to their own accompaniment: "David also commanded the chiefs of the Levites to appoint their brethren as the singers who should play loudly on musical instruments" (I Chron. 15:16 RSV).

Cosmetics Widely Used

Far from being modern in origin, cosmetics were important weapons in the ancient feminine arsenal.

Hearing that Jehu was on his way to confront her, the infamous Queen Jezebel took decisive action. "She painted her face, and tired her head, and looked out at a window" (II Kings 9:30). As translated by J. M. P. Smith, this line in the drama reads: "She painted her eyelashes and adorned her head and peered out at the window."

Cosmetics mentioned in the Bible include various kinds of ointment, eye paint, and perfume. At least as early as 800 B.C. artisans of Palestine had developed the art of making cosmetic palettes of limestone. These bowls, about four inches in diameter, held colors used in preparing the face. Bone, ivory, and metal spatulas and spoons were employed in handling the pigments.

While cosmetics were known and valued throughout most of the ancient Near East, the Hebrews first made wide use of them during their Egyptian sojourn. An ivory rouge pot, found in the 1479 B.C. level by archaeologists digging in Egypt, is now in the University Museum at Philadelphia. Other items in the collection include bronze razor blades four to six inches long for shaving facial hair; a hook for removing ear wax; an iron buckle holding a wooden stick for applying kohl (a mixture of soot and oil) to the eyelids; bone and ivory hairpins; and a little mill dating from about 3000 B.C. that was used to grind eye paint.

Early Use of Coins

Until comparatively recently it was taken for granted that coins were unknown to ancient Hebrews. In an account put into writing about five hundred years after his death, David is reported to have collected for the building of the temple 5,000 talents of gold, 10,000 of silver, 18,000 of brass, and 100,000 of iron (I Chron. 29:7). Scholars thought every early reference to a "talent" involved a unit of weight rather than a specific piece of money.

It is true that many commercial transactions involved barter. Solomon used wheat and olive oil to pay King Hiram for lumber used in building the temple (I Kings 5:11). Israelites frequently paid their taxes with commodities (or "in kind"). Grain, oil, sheep, and wine were used in this fashion (I Sam. 8:15; Ezek. 45:13-16).

Special tokens were made from a number of metals—whose values were not always reckoned by modern standards. When iron was first introduced into Palestine, it was more precious than gold. Various bars and ingots were produced; these probably figured in David's transactions. Other metal pieces were formed in the shape of bracelets, rings, and heads of animals.

But the Hebrews were using money of modern form at least 2,500 years ago. This surprisingly sophisticated state of affairs is attested by archaeological finds made during this century. Coins minted not long after the time of Jeremiah were inscribed with the title *Yehud* written in Hebrew characters. Scholars think these pieces were made as a result of Greek influence, for the drachma is known to have circulated in Palestine during this period.

Though barter was still common in New Testament times the production of even limited numbers of standard coins meant that economic concepts were not nearly so naïve as once assumed.

Temples First, Houses Later

Ancient houses of worship were usually more costly and elaborate than private dwellings. Practices that later entered general use were often introduced in connection with building and decorating shrines. That was the case with whitewash, which is definitely known to have been employed in a Babylonian ziggurat, or temple tower, long before use of it became standard with tidy housewives.

German archaeologists excavated the site of the biblical city of Erech

(Gen. 10:10) in three expeditions. The first of them, 1912-13, revealed this city of ancient Sumer (about 160 miles from modern Baghdad) to be much larger than anyone had thought it. At the height of its influence its city walls measured about six miles in circumference.

It was here that J. Jordan uncovered the first Babylonian ziggurat. Many others have been found subsequently; a particularly large one may have been the original tower of Babel (Gen. 11:1-9).

Erech's tower, believed to have been built toward the end of the third millennium B.C., measured about forty-five yards square at the base. Some of its mud bricks were decorated with whitewash, patches of which were still clearly visible when the ziggurat was uncovered.

Originally so rare and costly that it was not used in private homes, whitewash became cheaper and more abundant as techniques for manufacture and use were improved. Eventually it was a standard article for household use among the Hebrews as well as their foes. Experts consider it inferior to modern wall paints in every respect except one: its capacity to endure for centuries where shielded from water.

The Synagogue: A Fruit of Captivity

Now universally associated with Jewish life and worship, the institution of the synagogue is believed to have been developed comparatively late. There is only one Old Testament use of the name (Ps. 74:8), and many interpreters doubt that this reference applies to the type of house-gathering that later became common.

During the time of the Hebrew monarchy, worship centered in the temple. Here, and here alone, priests performed elaborate sacrifices that were vital to Hebrew religious life. If a man wished to pay homage to Jehovah, he put aside all other concerns and went to Jerusalem for the purpose.

Observance of this centuries-old custom became impossible during the captivity in Babylon. Conquerors had destroyed the temple, and Jerusalem could be visited only in the imagination.

In this unique situation worship assumed a new character. Since men could not go to the temple to gain divine favor by participation in sacrificial rites, they began to gather in their houses for worship without sacrifice. Boys and girls were formally instructed in the Law in a movement that antedated the Sunday school by centuries. Public prayer and confession were emphasized. Developing slowly over a period of generations, this radical new pattern of worship eventually produced the synagogue—never regarded as having the sacredness of the temple, but far more important than the temple in the everyday lives of persons who lived and died without setting foot in Jerusalem.

A Steady Year-round Supply of Water

One of the most familiar landmarks of the nineteenth-century American city was the water tank—a by-product of plumbing and the desire for an uninterrupted supply of water. Though iron containers projecting above the ground are modern, the idea of the city water tank is not. Scripture had it first. The "pool of Gibeon" (II Sam. 2:13; Jer. 41:12) was an elaborate long-range project built relatively soon after the Hebrews began using iron tools and designed to store sufficient water to assure the city a steady year-round supply.

Numerous cities of the Holy Land (notably Jerusalem, Gezer, and Megiddo) had water reservoirs, but no others are specifically mentioned in Scripture and none even approached the complexity of Gibeon's. Settled after the Israelites returned from their Babylonian exile in the sixth century B.C., Gibeon was about eight miles north of Jerusalem near the head of the valley of Aijalon. "A great city, as one of the royal cities" (Josh. 10:2), its walls enclosed an area greater than that of the fortified section of Jerusalem in the time of Canaanite occupation.

Instead of being built above ground, Gibeon's water tank was sunk into solid rock near the peak of a hill—well above the level of the city proper. Thirty-seven feet in diameter and eighty-two feet deep, it was equipped with a circular staircase whose seventy-nine rock-cut steps permitted workmen to descend into the tank when it was drained for cleaning. Far the largest reservoir known to have been executed anywhere in the world at so early a date, the pool of Gibeon held enough water to supply the needs of a present-day county seat town in rural America.

Balaam the Butt of Humor

In spite of the fact that Jesus rode one of the animals during his triumphal entry into Jerusalem, the most renowned donkey mentioned in Scripture is the ass who rebuked the uncircumcised seer Balaam.

Altogether, there are at least 130 references to the sure-footed little beast in Holy Writ. Some point clearly to the onager, or wild ass, while others deal with its domesticated cousin. Law prohibited the yoking of an ass with an ox for plowing, for sturdy as it was, an animal that stood about three feet high was no match for a bull.

Usually regarded as both the most common and most useful work animal known to the Hebrews, the ass is not known to have been worshiped in any culture. Hence the role of divine messenger that it plays in the adventures of Balaam is unique.

Perhaps ancient storytellers deliberately made the animal a central figure in order to belittle the man who had set out posthaste to curse the Hebrews before the king of Moab. By telling of an ass who saw an angel overlooked by Balaam, the story makes the prophet ludicrous. Many interpreters think the conversation between man and beast (Num. 22:28-30) represents a twelfth-century B.C. example of the deliberate use of humor to convey a point; if so, it is the oldest joke in the world.

Wine Cellars of Gibeah

Long before wealthy European wine connoisseurs began building cellars so their best wines could be kept at a constant temperature, wholesale dealers of biblical times had mastered this art. Vats that maintained a constant temperature of 65 degrees Fahrenheit at all seasons were discovered in 1956-57. Located at Gibeah, about six miles northwest of Jerusalem, they were found by an archaeological expedition. More than forty vats, each with a capacity of several thousand gallons, were cut in solid rock. Most were designed to hold wine in jars, but a few were plastered watertight so that they could be used for bulk storage.

Always famous for the quality of its grapes, Palestine produced wine so early that Noah was credited with inventing it (Gen. 9:20-21). Among the products of his own land that Solomon traded for the timber used to build his famous temple were 20,000 baths of wine or about 110,000 gallons (II Chron. 2:10). Wineskins were made from whole goat hides with the necks and feet tied, and openings for the escape of gases formed during fermentation. It was proverbial that new wine should not be put into skins hardened from use.

Jars of capacities up to twenty gallons were manufactured especially to hold the precious fluid which was widely used as a medicine as well as a beverage. Still, it wasn't until the vats of Gibeah were discovered that anyone knew ancient Palestine had facilities for the storage of wine in wholesale quantities.

Urban Renewal 2,500 Years Ago

Though it has many new aspects in its modern application, the basic concept of urban renewal is at least 2,500 years old. One fruit of such a project long before the time of Christ still survives in the biblical city of Damascus.

Uz, grandson of Shem, is credited with having been the founder of Damascus. In traveling from Ur to Canaan, Abraham passed near the city if he did not actually visit it. Captured by David and held briefly within the Hebrew empire, Damascus later became the capital of the Syrian state that was in frequent conflict with Israel and Judah before forming an alliance with the latter.

Because Damascus was symbolic of Israel's foreign foes, several Old Testament prophets called down destruction upon it (Isa. 8:4; 17:1; Amos 1:3; Jer. 49:23-27). Their visions were fulfilled in 732 B.C. when Tiglath-pileser III of Assyria conquered the whole surrounding region and virtually leveled Damascus.

Rebuilt in sprawling fashion under the Persians, it later came under Greek control. These people sent Hippodamus of Miletus, a noted architect of the fifth century B.C., to reconstruct the city. Already famous for his skill in devising broad, straight streets that intersected at right angles, Hippodamus regarded Damascus as a supreme opportunity. He designed the city in such fashion that its boundary was rectangular and its streets were laid out in patterns similar to modern city blocks. In the new Damascus the longest street ran entirely through the city along an east-west line. More than a mile long, it was later decorated with elaborate archways and costly colonnades; for centuries it was famous throughout the Near East as the street called Straight.

After his life-changing experience on the road to Damascus, Paul stayed in the house of Judas located on "the street which is called Straight" (Acts 9:11). Its course little changed from the time it was designed by Hippodamus, Straight Street is today known as Suk Midhat Pasha and is one of the world's oldest fruits of urban renewal.

Symbolic Significance of Biblical Names

Some widely circulated annual volumes of information, or almanacs, include several hundred biblical names. They aren't given for the sake of persons interested in the message of Scripture, though, for the names in these collections consist of those from Holy Writ which appear most frequently in crossword puzzles!

In order really to master the significance of an Old Testament passage that includes personal names, one must look beneath the surface. Many obscure names that are now used as raw material by the makers of crossword puzzles had deep symbolic significance in ancient times.

A few biblical names are taken from names of plants in the Holy

Land. Tamar is a direct equivalent for "palm tree." Elon (Hittite father-in-law of Esau who appears in Gen. 26:34) was named "oak tree." Many more names are those of running, flying, and crawling creatures. Caleb is the Hebrew name for "dog," while Deborah means "bee" and Rachel is equivalent to "sheep." David's wife Eglah (II Sam. 3:5) was named from "heifer," and the man known to his contemporaries as "serpent" entered the English Bible as Nahash (I Sam. 11:1).

Numerous biblical names are short stories in capsule form. Eve called her first child Cain to celebrate the fact that she had acquired (*qanah*), a future man (Gen. 4:1). Dying in childbirth, Rachel called her son Benoni or "son of my sorrow"; Jacob later altered this slightly to the familiar Benjamin or "son of my right hand." Gershom (stranger) was so named because he was born while his father Moses was a *ger* living in a strange land (Exod. 2:22). Both Hosea and Isaiah gave their children symbolic names (Hos. 1:4, 6, 9; Isa. 8:3-4). It wasn't until the close of the Old Testament period that the Hebrews adopted the custom of giving a child a family name; even then, it was usually the name of the grandfather rather than the father that was employed.

War and Conquest

Esdraelon: A Plain Bathed in Blood

Though it is a relatively small region, the triangular Plain of Esdraelon is one of the most fought-over strips of land in the world. Comprising most of the western portion of the Jezreel Valley, it gains its English name from Greek *esdraelon.* This, in turn, is a rather corrupt variant of an ancient tribute to the fertility of the region through its Hebrew name, Jezreel ("God sows").

Thutmose III, one of the greatest of Egyptian rulers, chose this region for a decisive encounter with Canaanites. In a battle named for the key fortress of Megiddo and fought about 1479 B.C., Egypt brought all Syria to her knees. Saul fought the Philistines in this area (I Samuel 28–30), and it was here that Gideon's decisive victory over the Midianites shaped the future course of Hebrew history (Judges 7). Followers of Barak fought a great battle with Canaanites on the plain and defeated Sisera (Judges 4–5). Here Josiah later met vastly superior Egyptian forces under Pharaoh-nechoh, who crushed his army and killed or assassinated the Judean king (II Kings 23:29-30).

But the bloodbath in this strategic area where ancient highways crossed did not end in Old Testament times. It was here that Saladin's Moslem hordes fought an army of Christian crusaders led by Richard I of England and Philip II of France, in the twelfth century. Esdraelon figured in the Napoleonic Wars and then once more emerged into world prominence when British and Turkish armies met there in 1917.

In Scripture it is termed "the great plain" (I Macc. 12:49) or simply "the valley" (Josh. 17:16; Judg. 1:19; 5:15; 7:1; etc.). Some interpreters believe John of Patmos envisioned this region as the site of the Battle of Armageddon.

High Cost of Chariots

Conservative voices among religious as well as military groups made the Hebrews comparatively slow to accept the only major war vehicle of ancient times: the chariot.

Since wooden chariots of vanquished armies were often burned, few relics have survived, but there are abundant drawings and pictures. These show the instrument of war to have been drawn by horses in the time of the patriarchs, though asses were used earlier in Mesopotamia. By 1700 B.C. the chariot was beginning to be relatively common in Egypt and Syria. Early vehicles used wheels with four or six spokes; after 800 B.C. eight were used. In the fourth century B.C. the Persians added scythes to the wheels of their chariots.

Partly because the Hebrews were comparatively late in adopting the use of iron (essential in building some types of chariots) but largely because of their reluctance to handle horses, they fought on foot long after their foes began riding into battle. Natural conservatism on this score was strengthened by the fact that Hebrew infantrymen won the Battle of Tabor near the site of the town of Taanach when the chariots of Sisera mired down after a heavy rain had caused the river Kishon to overflow (Judg. 5:21-22).

Once they began using them, though, the chosen people went all the way. From technical references in I Kings it is evident that each of Solomon's chariots employed a complement of three men—instead of the two customary in Egypt. At the height of his splendor Solomon claimed to have a ring of chariot cities among which 1,400 vehicles with 12,000 horsemen were distributed (I Kings 10:26). Assyrian records show that at the Battle of Karkar in 853 B.C. King Ahab had the biggest contingent of chariots among all the allies—two thousand of them. The prohibitive cost of maintaining such a force helped throw Israel into economic chaos. By New Testament times chariots were rarely seen anywhere in the Holy Land.

Loot Brought Home by Raiding Parties

War trophies captured by ancient kings and sometimes transported for considerable distances are among the most important relics that supplement and confirm Old Testament accounts of political and military events. Two of the most unusual of these "keepsakes" were found at the site of a single city—Susa, once a royal residence of the Persians.

They were brought there about 1200 B.C. by marauding Elamites —citizens of the territory east and northeast of the Tigris-Euphrates valley. Urban communities flourished in this fertile region as early as 3500 B.C.; these were attacked and often conquered by various groups of foes. During the third millennium the great King Sargon brought all Elam into his domain. Later the region was overrun by soldiers of Babylon's military genius, Hammurabi.

Sometime during the thirteenth century an Elamite leader, Shutruk-Nahhunte, became powerful enough to lead an expedition against Babylonia. Though he did not topple that mighty empire, he did penetrate deep into its territory. Everywhere he and his men went, they seized anything portable that seemed worth taking home. Their interests were not confined to objects made of precious metals; religious and civil trophies were also prized as loot.

Among the things they brought back with them was a copy of the now famous Code of Hammurabi—a six-foot slab of black granular rock with fifty-one columns of cuneiform engraving. Along with a *stele,* or memorial pillar created by subjects of the Babylonian king Naram-Sin, the big slab of rock was put on public display in the Elamite city of Susa. Eventually, though, the "Babylonian treasures" were covered with rubble. Rediscovered in 1902-3 by De Morgan's archaeological expedition, the loot transported from Babylonia by Elamite raiding parties proved to be among the most important and famous historical documents of the ancient Near East.

Circumcision as a Ruse in War

In all ages and cultures, strategems and ruses have been employed by military leaders. None in the whole history of strife is more bizarre than that devised by the sons of Jacob, for they deliberately used a religious rite as a way of incapacitating a group of foes—whom they then killed without mercy.

As recounted in Genesis 34, a young prince of the Hivite people (prominent in Canaan before Israelite settlement there) assaulted Dinah the daughter of Leah. Shechem's father, Hamor, learned of the boy's misdeed and tried to make amends by proposing a marriage settlement. Dinah's brothers pretended to go along with this idea. But as a precondition to establishing a blood relationship between themselves and the Hivite tribesmen they insisted that the latter should take Jehovah as their God. Once this stipulation was accepted, the next step was to point out that male followers of Jehovah must be circumcised.

Eager to patch up a quarrel and not especially reluctant to add Jehovah to their pantheon of deities, the Hivites agreed to all the conditions. They duly submitted to the sacred ceremony in which a flint knife was used to slice off the foreskins of "converts," and thought the matter had ended peaceably.

But the whole emphasis upon fidelity to Jehovah was a ruse. On the third day after their prospective in-laws had been circumcised, "when they were sore," Dinah's brothers Simeon and Levi "took each man his sword, and came upon the city boldly, and slew all the males" (Gen. 34:25). This feat accomplished, they took all the animals and agricultural products of their foes "and all their wealth, and all their little ones, and their wives took they captive, and spoiled even all that was in the house" (Gen. 34:29).

Every War a Holy War

Virtually every war fought by the Hebrews was a holy war—literally and not in a figurative or symbolic sense. For in addition to invoking Jehovah's aid in battle, the Hebrews practiced specific religious rites considered to be avenues toward divine favor—and consequent victory.

Mentioned in the Old Testament more than two hundred times under a score of different titles, the mystical ark of the covenant was frequently used in war. Considered to represent the physical presence of Jehovah, it was extremely potent. A source of protection to the children of Israel, it was also a source of danger to their enemies.

One of the longest and most detailed accounts of the way this religious symbol figured in conflict is found in I Samuel 4–5. Fighting against the Philistines, the Israelites were badly beaten the first day. In this dilemma they sent to Shiloh for the ark; "and when the ark of the covenant of the Lord came into the camp, all Israel shouted with a great shout" (4:5). Their optimism was premature; the Philistines rallied, captured the ark, and set it up as a trophy in the temple of their god Dagon. In the end the potency of the ark not only overthrew the image of Dagon but created such havoc that the Philistines were glad to get rid of it.

In addition to taking the ark of the covenant with them into battle, the Hebrews made formal use of consecrated trumpets. These were blown only by a priest, who used some long-lost pattern of sounds to create a signal to charge the enemy and kill in the name of the Lord (Num. 10:2, 9; 31:6; Josh. 6:5; Judg. 7:20-21; etc.).

Prototypes of Modern Artillery

"Love thy neighbour" is a dominant note in the Bible. Yet technical evidence embedded in Scripture gives strong support to the idea that the first major inventions devised by the Hebrews (or borrowed from their neighbors) were ancient versions of modern artillery. From the Hebrew verb for "to think, to devise," an invention was given a special name whose nearest English equivalent is "engine." One of the triumphs of Uzziah's reign was the fact that "he made in Jerusalem engines, invented by cunning men, to be on the towers and upon the bulwarks, to shoot arrows and great stones withal. And his name spread far abroad; for he was marvellously helped" (II Chron. 26:15).

The "engines of war" that are mentioned in Ezek. 26:9 were almost certainly battering rams. These devices were crucial to the capture of a walled city and achieved power and sophistication not ordinarily linked with ancient mechanical devices. By the time of the caesars, Romans customarily used rams at least 150 feet long. Josephus, first-century Jewish historian, described one battering ram (used in the siege of Jerusalem) that required the driving power of 300 oxen and 1,500 men.

Other inventions that appeared very early included both defensive and offensive gear. A kind of armored shelter to protect men and animals who worked battering rams was in use centuries before the time of Christ and remained a basic military item as late as the Crusades in the twelfth century A.D. Uzziah's eighth century B.C. engines for shooting arrows and great stones were far in advance of those developed in the Greek world; apparently such products of cunning minds and skilled hands played no major role in Greek combat before the time of Dionysius the Elder of Syracuse (430-367 B.C.). "Artillery" employed by Alexander the Great was little if any more powerful than the "engines" used five hundred years earlier by Hebrew military commanders.

David's Character Maligned

Faulty understanding of ancient languages on the part of early translators led to a widespread notion that David, traditional author of many of the greatest psalms, had no mercy upon his enemies. This mistaken view turns upon the shades of meaning of a single Hebrew word in I Chron. 20:3.

After capturing Rabbah (modern Amman) which was the capital of the ancient Ammonite kingdom and situated just twenty-three miles from Jerusalem, the Hebrew king "brought out the people that were in it, and cut them with saws, and with harrows of iron, and with axes." Generations of Bible readers who pondered this account in the King James Version may have found justification for the merciless treatment of witches and other offenders in the precedent supposingly set by the shepherd king.

Modern scholars are unanimous in rejecting the view that David actually engaged in the barbaric torture of war prisoners. In the Revised Standard Version he is reported to have "brought forth the people" from Rabbah. But instead of sending them to slow death, he "set them to labor with saws and iron picks and axes."

George M. Lamsa, first linguist to render the Bible into English from the Peshitta, or authorized Bible of the Church of the East, is even more explicit. In his 1957 translation he reports that after David captured the enemy stronghold he "brought out the people who were in it, and bound them with chains, iron bands, locks and fetters . . . and did likewise to all men who were found in the cities of the children of Ammon; but he did not kill any one of them; and he brought them and settled them in the villages of the land of Israel."

Even allowing for the possibility that centuries of transmission led to editorial changes in the text of the Peshitta that were favorable to David, modern scholarship rejects the sadistic interpretation of the King James Version.

Jephthah's Bloody Vow

Jephthah the Gileadite, "a mighty man of valour" (Judg. 11:1), is best known for having burned his own daughter on a sacrificial altar as a result of a bargain he made with the Lord.

Son of a harlot, Jephthah was driven away from home by his half brothers. After a period as an outlaw he gained a reputation for cunning in battle and in time of national emergency was persuaded to head Israel's fighting forces. He won several victories, and then found himself confronted by an overwhelming force of Ammonites who constituted an independent state on the fringe of the Syrian Desert.

Fully persuaded that he was inspired by the spirit of the Lord, Jephthah took the offensive and "vowed a vow unto the Lord, and said, If thou shalt without fail deliver the children of Ammon into mine hands, Then it shall be, that whatsoever cometh forth of the doors of my house to meet me, when I return in peace from the children of Ammon, shall surely be the Lord's, and I will offer it up for a burnt offering" (Judg. 11:30-31).

As he anticipated, the Lord delivered his enemies into his hands. He smashed their military machine and conquered twenty cities. On his return in triumph his only child, a daughter, "came out to meet him with timbrels and with dances" (11:34). Though he tore his clothes as a sign of sorrow, he told the girl that he couldn't go back on his word to the Lord. She asked for a reprieve of two months in which to mourn. When her period of grace ran out, "she returned unto her father, who did with her according to his vow which he had vowed" (11:39).

Humiliation of Captives

Adoni-bezek, Canaanite ruler of the city of Berek, may have died of humiliation because Joshua subjected him to the punishment he had meted out to his own captive princes: the amputation of thumbs and great toes.

Most scholars think he was identical with Adoni-zedec, who was king of Jerusalem at the time of the Hebrew conquest (Josh. 10:1, 3). Whether that was the case or not, he had won many victories in war and seemed to delight in making his captives grovel. "Threescore and ten kings, having their thumbs and their great toes cut off, gathered their meat under my table," he boasted (Judg. 1:7).

Defeated and taken prisoner by motley invaders under Joshua, he was given a dose of his own medicine. Joshua inflicted on him the same punishment he had given his own royal captives and then sent him as a living war trophy to be exhibited in Jerusalem. Though the amputation of thumbs and great toes was seldom fatal, the wounds may have become infected. If that was not the case, there is a good chance that the once proud captive starved himself to death in embarrassment at having been mutilated.

Enemies Given Speech Test

According to the account in Judges 12, a tendency on the part of ancient Ephraimites to speak with a slight lisp cost these people 42,000 casualties in a time of civil war.

Fighting against the forces of Gilead under the leadership of Jephthah, famous for having made a sacrificial offering of his own daughter, the warriors of Ephraim found themselves outnumbered and outclassed. They suffered a decisive defeat, broke ranks, and tried to ford the Jordan to return to their own territory and safety.

His enemies couldn't be distinguished by their physical appearance, insignia, or weapons so Jephthah resorted to a strategem based on regional differences in speech. Men of Ephraim traditionally had trouble sounding the Hebrew consonant *shin,* functionally equivalent to the English *s.* This tendency to lisp was especially obvious when they tried to pronounce "shibboleth"—Hebrew *sibboleth*—the common name for an ear of grain.

Jephthah's border patrols seized all stragglers and tested them by demanding that they say the crucial word. Those who "could not frame to pronounce it right" were executed on the spot (Judg. 12:6).

Ahab's Gallant Death

Ahab, king of Israel from about 870 to 850 B.C., is best known as the husband of Jezebel. As a result of having chosen the daughter of the king of Tyre to be his queen, Ahab, who was often under Jezebel's thumb, is usually depicted as cowardly and self-centered. But Ahab's vivid career ended in an act of military bravery that antedated by centuries the exploits credited to El Cid and other European heroes.

During his reign tension between Israel and her powerful neighbor Damascus had much in common with that between the United States and Russia at the midpoint of the twentieth century. There were ceaseless charges and countercharges, plus periods of outright war.

For both economic and military reasons, late in life Ahab set out to recover the captured city of Ramoth-gilead, located somewhere on the present border between Syria and Jordan. This campaign takes up most of I Kings 22, where it is described in greater detail than most others that figure in the biblical story.

Ahab persuaded the fighting men of Judah to join him, and then assembled four hundred holy men ("prophets") and consulted them about whether or not to attack Ramoth-gilead. In an apparently unanimous decision they assured him that divine strength would support him. Only Micaiah, "a prophet of the Lord," voiced a negative opinion. For his pains he was thrown in prison and put on a diet of bread and water.

Knowing that his foes would make him their first target, Ahab disguised himself before going into battle. Though the thirty-two captains of the Syrian horde failed to recognize him, a random shot by an archer hit Israel's king "between the joints of the harness." In spite of the fact that he was badly wounded he refused to retire from the field of battle. Propped up in his chariot so his troops would not panic at seeing him fall, Ahab bled to death.

During the 1930's a Harvard archaeological expedition excavating the site of ancient Samaria uncovered a huge pool, once watertight, that many think served as the chariot-wash in which the blood of the valiant king was scrubbed from his vehicle (I Kings 22:38).

Hebrew Chronology from Military Records

Until recent decades the problem of assigning specific dates to events in ancient Hebrew history seemed insuperable. For the most part Scripture makes no reference more exact than "the fifteenth year of the reign of Asa" (II Chron. 15:10) or "the third year of the reign of Jehoiakim" (Dan. 1:1). Even these clues aren't very helpful until one knows precisely when a particular king's reign began.

Today, however, many events that took place nearly three thousand years ago have been precisely pinpointed. This development was made possible by the fact that ancient foes and conquerors of the Hebrews often made precise records of their conquests. Military accounts, written on clay tablets or engraved upon stone markers, were particularly important in the eyes of both the Assyrians and the Babylonians.

As a result of archaeological discoveries that stem from the tendency of conquerors to leave permanent memorials commemorating their victories, many dates in Hebrew history are now known through the records of their foes. Some such dates and the events and persons who figured in them are as follows:

853 B.C. Battle of Qarqar; Ahab repulsed Shalmaneser III of Assyria

738 B.C. Menahem, king of Israel, paid tribute to Tiglath-pileser III of Assyria

609 B.C. Josiah, king of Judah, died in the year that Egyptian forces marched to the aid of Assyrian troops who were hard pressed by Nabopolassar of Babylon.

Once a skeleton of firmly fixed dates is developed in this fashion, the biblical account enables historians to fill in details of some periods in almost year-to-year fashion.

Amaziah Exterminates His Foes

After successful military campaigns typical kings and conquerors in the ancient Near East executed enemy leaders and men who were in positions to head a revolt. Then they usually deported large numbers of common people, who frequently were assimilated into the culture of their former foes.

But one Judean king, Amaziah, anticipated the modern scorched earth policy by many centuries and refused to settle for anything less than the extermination of his enemies. According to the account in II Chronicles 25, he ascended the throne at age twenty-five (about 800 B.C.). Once he had firm control, he drafted all male citizens over twenty and formed an army of 300,000. Then he strengthened his forces with 100,000 mercenaries from neighboring Israel. Warned in a vision that these hired troops might not prove loyal in a crisis, he sent them home.

Then he led his men in an attack upon the Edomites, who lived on and about Mt. Seir. He killed ten thousand in the Valley of Salt; except for the number of casualties reported, this was not unusual. But once victory was his, "ten thousand left alive did the children of Judah carry away captive, and brought them unto the top of the rock, and cast them down from the top of the rock, that they all were broken in pieces" (II Chron. 25:12).

There is no textual evidence in ancient manuscripts to support the view that this passage may have been mistranslated. In *The Interpreter's Bible* (1954) W. A. L. Elmslie contents himself with a single line of commentary in which he expresses the hope that the account of the savage treatment of the Edomites may have been "due to some old tradition and not to the Chronicler's own invention." Regardless of whether or not Amaziah pushed precisely ten thousand captives off a cliff to their death, the bloodthirsty ruler was given a dose of his own medicine. Victim of a court conspiracy, he became a fugitive and escaped to Lachish, where he was tracked down and murdered.

Cannibalism in Scripture

Few Bible dictionaries or encyclopedias include an entry under the topic "cannibalism," but the grisly practice was vividly remembered if not actually practiced as late as the sixth century B.C.

One detailed report comes from a much earlier period when Samaria was besieged by Syrians. Attacking forces, probably led by Benhadad, cut off all food supplies sometime during the life of Elisha late in the ninth century. Matters grew so bad that starving folk resorted to desperate measures; "an ass's head was sold for fourscore pieces of silver, and the fourth part of a cab of dove's dung for five pieces of silver" (II Kings 6:25).

A ruse by Israel's leader, probably but not certainly Jehoahaz, drew invaders away from the city and the siege was lifted. As he rode through Samaria in a victory parade, the liberator was challenged by a woman who complained that her neighbor had failed to keep her bargain. They had agreed to eat their two sons, she said, one after the other. But when one had been boiled and consumed by the voracious women, the other mother hid her boy. This story caused the Israelite ruler to tear his clothing in shame, but instead of punishing the cannibals he blamed the famine upon Elisha. (II Kings 6:26-31.)

Nearly three centuries later, at the time the book of Lamentations was written, cannibalism required no explanation. "Shall the women eat their fruit, and children of a span long?" the prophet demands in accusing the Lord of sending famine (Lam. 2:20). Another reference, perhaps made deliberately obscure by horrified translators, refers to the fact that "the hands of the pitiful women have sodden their own children" (Lam. 4:10). Here "sodden" refers to boiling in a pot.

Love in a Climate of Hate

Jesus' entire life was spent in a region occupied by troops of a foreign conqueror. Hence his message was delivered in an occupied country. Still, the Gospel records indicate that he never gave the slightest support to any movement aimed at a military revolution that might bring national freedom.

Pompey the Great, a war-hardened Roman general, took command of the empire's eastern armies in 66 B.C. He quickly defeated forces of the Scythian king Mithridates VI despite the fact that the latter had great military ability and was one of the most formidable opponents Rome ever faced. After the defeat Mithridates committed suicide in 63 B.C., and Pompey not only reclaimed all of Rome's old territory but also annexed Syria and Palestine.

Hence for approximately sixty years before the birth of Jesus and for decades after his death, the hated Roman standard appeared in streets and on public buildings throughout Judea. It consisted of a laurel wreath to signify victory, an eagle to signify power, and the letters SPQR—an abbreviation for *senatus populusque Romanus* (the senate and the people of Rome). No token occupation, Roman control was absolute.

To a degree unmatched by any other people whom the legions of the caesars conquered before or after this time, the Hebrews resisted imperial control. Much of their implacable hatred for the Romans centered in the cult of emperor worship which ran directly counter to the Hebrew worship of one God.

Yet Jesus exhorted his followers to love their enemies. He even went so far as to say that they should voluntarily give twice as much service as required of them under the Roman law that compelled a person without citizenship to carry the baggage or equipment of a Roman official or soldier for a mile along the road. The full force of Jesus' edict at this point does not emerge in the older translations; in Today's English Version of the New Testament it reads: "If one of the occupation troops forces you to carry his pack one mile, carry it another mile" (Matt. 5:41).

Military Prelude to Missionary Expansion

By a quirk of fate—or the purposeful operation of divine providence—Roman military successes created a situation in which the rapid spread of Christianity was possible. For a comparatively brief period before the birth of Jesus and for a few generations after his death, the *pax Romana* (peace of Rome) permitted free travel and communication throughout the western world in a fashion unknown before or since.

Wherever the Roman armies went, they imposed the authority of the senate and the citizens of Rome—and later, that of the emperor. All national boundaries were erased. Both citizens and subjects could travel freely wherever they wished, without passports or visas. Great highways were built so sturdily that some of them are still in use.

Rome's sway extended around the whole Mediterranean, and her rule prevailed in regions as distant as Britain and Cappadocia. A man on foot could travel the imperial highways at a rate of fifteen to twenty miles a day. Even when he left the great trunk roads, he was likely to make fast progress along lesser highways such as Britain's Icknield Street. The free flow of commerce was encouraged. Linguistic barriers fell; even in the most obscure provinces not simply scholars but also ordinary people knew enough Greek and Latin to converse with almost anyone else in the Roman Empire.

Had this unique and comparatively brief period of peace gained through military conquest been lacking, the missionary journeys of Paul and the subsequent explosion of Christianity into the Greco-Roman world would have been impossible. Had Jesus lived, taught, died, and inspired near fanatical zeal among his followers at any time other than the era in which the *pax Romana* prevailed, it is possible that Christianity would have remained an obscure and little-known Jewish sect confined to a portion of Palestine.

Suicide in Preference to Slavery

Masada, whose name is derived from the Hebrew for "mountain stronghold," was long considered the strongest fortress in the Holy Land. For centuries it was heralded as being literally impregnable, able to withstand any attack launched against it. Today the high place is best known as the site of one of the largest mass suicides on record.

According to the famous Jewish historian Josephus, this gaunt rock was first fortified by the high priest Jonathan about the middle of the second century B.C. This places its beginning squarely in the middle of the intertestamental period. That is, Old Testament records terminated somewhat earlier, and the New Testament had not yet begun to take shape. So in spite of its vital significance to the Jews, the citadel is not mentioned by name in Scripture.

During the reign of Herod the Great (King of Judea under the Romans from 37 to 34 B.C. and grandfather of the Herod who figures in the Acts of the Apostles), Masada became a complex and luxurious system of palaces and fortifications. The Romans occupied it shortly after the birth of Jesus and held it until A.D. 66.

That year a group of fanatical warriors who called themselves the Sicarii used a strategem to gain possession of the great rock towering 1,300 feet above the sands of the Judean desert. Soon the Romans launched a counterattack. They failed to dent the network of defenses and so from A.D. 70 to 73 kept Masada under constant siege. A company of less than one thousand Hebrews held off an estimated fifteen thousand Roman legionnaires for month after month. When surrender became inevitable, the defenders along with their wives and their children committed mass suicide rather than live as the slaves of their conquerors. Vivid details concerning the years in which they conducted one of the most brilliant military operations of all history became known only when Masada was excavated in 1963-65.

Special Prayers to Peter

The conversion to Christianity of a fifth-century king not only made possible the vast missionary enterprises of the Middle Ages, but also resulted in the mistaken transformation of the character of the apostle Peter.

Clovis I, who became king of the Salian Franks at the age of fifteen, won a series of major victories and greatly extended his empire. In A.D. 493 he married the princess Clotilda, a Christian who earnestly desired the conversion of her husband. Clovis permitted their children to be baptized but set up a major condition which had to be met before he would accept his wife's faith. He would become a Christian, he vowed, if God would give him victory over the Alamanni—then threatening to overrun the Frankish empire.

When his enemies were defeated, Clovis kept his promise and embraced Christianity. As a result, Gaul was hospitable to missionaries who used its highways to reach Germany, Britain, and Scandinavia. Had it not been for this turn of events, it would have been difficult or impossible to evangelize northwestern Europe.

But the royal convert who learned to fight almost as soon as he learned to walk brought many pagan ideas into Christianity. Because a follower of Jesus had used his sword to slice off an ear of the high priest's servant (Matt. 26:51; Luke 22:50), Clovis took this as a religious omen. Following the account as preserved in John 18:10, the king of the Franks viewed Peter as a military champion. For generations the people of Gaul frequently offered special prayers asking Peter to bring them victory in battle.

Psalms Versus the Manual of Arms

Oliver Cromwell, often referred to as "the uncrowned king of England," was obsessed with Scripture. He not only read it habitually himself and quoted from it in his public speeches, but he also insisted that everyone associated with him be steeped in it.

When civil war broke out in 1642, Cromwell gathered a band of followers and set out to become master of England. He had no military training and no experience as a leader until he was forty, but he picked men for their religious enthusiasm as well as their physical might. Then he drilled them relentlessly in the standard cavalry maneuvers of the day and taught them to sing psalms as battle hymns.

With metrical versions of the psalms pouring from their lips, his men won an easy victory over a supposedly stronger force at the Battle of Marston Moor in 1644. This led to the nickname "Ironsides" for the troops he commanded. They moved on to one victory after another, and for a period Cromwell was the ruler of England. Strangely, the man who knew the Bible so much better than the manual of arms is one of the few great military leaders in all history who never lost a battle.

Transition at Bethlehem, Pennsylvania

Through an ironic series of events a city named in honor of Jesus' birthplace has become one of the world's major centers for the production of armaments.

Bethlehem, Pennsylvania, was in wild back country when founded in 1741 by Moravians under Count Zinzendorf. On the first Christmas observed by members of the settlement a service of Holy Communion included the use of a hymn with the lines:

> Not Jerusalem, but Bethlehem—
> Of thee cometh what me rejoiceth.

German settlers in the United States were notable for their enthusiasm about biblical names, so it was typical rather than unusual that Zinzendorf's colonists should decide to commemorate the Saviour's birthplace by bestowing its title on their young community. In its literal meaning the Hebrew name meant "house of bread"; some scholars think the biblical Bethlehem was an early center of commercial baking.

Bethlehem in the New World remained obscure until the discovery of coal fields and iron ore deposits in the region brought it to the attention of financiers. Charles M. Schwab helped to found the Bethlehem Steel Corporation, which began producing steel in 1905. Huge profits made during World War I brought it to second place among the world's steel corporations. During both World War I and World War II, armor plate, cannon, ammunition, and heavy-duty combat equipment poured from Bethlehem's ovens at the rate of hundreds of tons per day.

The Mutineers' Bible

Sailing from Tahiti in 1789 under the command of Captain William Bligh, *H.M.S. Bounty* carried a cargo of young breadfruit trees. It was hoped that they could be made to thrive in the West Indies. Bligh's merciless treatment of the ship's company drove his men to mutiny. Put to sea in an open boat with eighteen crew members who remained loyal, Bligh managed to take his tiny craft across 3,600 miles of open water to the island of Timor.

Meanwhile, the mutineers fled to Tahiti and then to desolate Pitcairn Island. They reached this haven in 1790, bringing with them a few tools, limited amounts of food and clothing, and one copy of the Bible. When Great Britain took formal possession of Pitcairn Island in 1838, it proved to be the only spot on earth where everyone attended church regularly. Through the influence of the mutineers' Bible a tiny house of worship had been built, and every person on the island was a professing Christian.

Shiloh Battleground

Frontier circuit riders inadvertently named one of the bloodiest battles of modern times, from which more than 23,000 casualties were reported.

It was a common practice for open-air preachers to gather a few settlers and expound on the text: "And the whole congregation of the children of Israel assembled together at Shiloh, and set up the tabernacle of the congregation there" (Josh. 18:1). Frequently this biblical precedent was cited as an urgent reason for establishing a congregation and starting to build a church—or at least a brush arbor—on the spot. As a result of this practice, the name Shiloh was attached to scores if not hundreds of early American churches.

One of them was built in Hardin County, Tennessee, near Pittsburgh Landing on the Tennessee River. Though it never had more than a few dozen members, Shiloh church was the only prominent institution in the region. Hence by extension its name came to be used for the surrounding countryside.

Here Confederate Generals Johnston and Beauregard, commanding about 45,000 men, attacked Grant's force of about 32,000. In the epic battle of April 6-7, 1862, Grant fought off his foes long enough to get reinforcements and to reform his lines. Testifying under oath, Sherman later said that at least 10,000 Union soldiers ran from the battlefield. In spite of staggering losses on both sides, the engagement was inconclusive. Partly for that reason the battle that was named as a result of enthusiasm for church building is still a focus of keen interest by military strategists and historians.

Korean Scripture in Pickle Crocks

During many centuries Bibles and Testaments have been smuggled across borders, treated as contraband merchandise, and concealed to prevent confiscation. In the entire history of Holy Writ perhaps the strangest hiding place ever chosen was a set of pickle crocks.

When Korea won its political independence from Japan in 1945, the government quickly introduced a new system of spelling. This change in the Korean language created an imperative demand for a revision of the Bible. Sponsored by the Korean Bible Society, this project was headed by Im Young Bin of Seoul.

It was completed only a few weeks before Communist armies in North Korea launched their 1950 attack upon South Korea. Too bulky to be carried away by fleeing refugees and too easily burned to leave behind, the manuscript created a dilemma.

Im considered several hiding places but rejected all of them as being insecure. Then he remembered that his wife had a set of big crocks in which she made pickles. Stuffed with the only existing copy of the Bible in the new Korean tongue, the crocks were buried in Im's own yard. Once United Nations forces had freed the city from the threat of Communist attack, the Korean scholar dug up his crocks and retrieved the manuscript. It was used to print what has now become the standard Korean Bible.

Worldwide Bible Reading Launched

Within this century an American started a global program of Bible reading, but it got off to such an inconspicuous start that his name has been lost.

Toward the end of World War II, a marine wrote his parents and suggested that they join him in simultaneous reading from the Bible. He enclosed a list of suggested passages, one of which was to be read each day. Neighbors and friends of his family heard about this novel way of maintaining ties and asked to be included in the experiment too.

Eventually the idea led to the establishment of a worldwide Bible reading program observed annually between Thanksgiving and Christmas by millions of persons. As in the case of the original plan, all participants read the same passages each day.

But the name and serial number of the man who thought of it are unknown. All that's established with certainty is that he was a lonely marine then stationed on Guadalcanal.

Rickenbacker's New Testament

As a result of the fervent testimony of one man, Scripture became a standard emergency item issued for use by men adrift at sea.

On October 21, 1942, Captain Eddie Rickenbacker's big bombing plane ran out of gas and was forced down somewhere in the South Pacific. Members of the crew were separated; three soon found refuge on a tiny island. But along with two of his men, Rickenbacker spent twenty-four days on a life raft drifting on the open sea. Alternately attacked by blistering sun and drenching rain, the men were forced to eat raw fish in order to survive.

A New Testament, swollen to approximately twice normal size, was found in a compartment of the raft. Rickenbacker thumbed the tiny book in search of passages that would give comfort and encouragement. In this situation he and his comrades found life-saving strength in two verses: "Take no thought, saying, What shall we eat? or, What shall we drink? or, Wherewithal shall we be clothed? (For after all these things do the Gentiles seek:) for your heavenly Father knoweth that ye have need of all these things" (Matt. 6:31-32).

Picked up in open seas six hundred miles north of Samoa, Rickenbacker was in surprisingly good condition. He credited the survival of the trio to the New Testament to which they had turned for strength.

As a result of this experience the American Bible Society developed a New Testament with waterproof covers, wrapped in lead foil and cellophane and then stored in a waterproof package that would float indefinitely. Twelve thousand copies were produced in the first printing. By March, 1943, this special item was included in survival kits stowed along with food and first aid supplies in lifeboats of the Merchant Marine as well as planes and ships of the armed forces.

The Book of Books and the Fine Arts

Hebrew Art Actually Elaborate

Early warnings against making graven images were extended to cover all the arts: "Thou shalt not make thee any graven image, or any likeness of any thing that is in heaven above, or that is in the earth beneath, or that is in the waters beneath the earth" (Deut. 5:8; see also Exod. 20:4; Lev. 26:1).

Scriptural codes were one thing, however, and actual practices quite another. Scholars of the eighteenth and most of the nineteenth century thought ancient Jews practiced neither painting nor carving, in obedience to the Law of Moses. But archaeological finds in recent generations have shown that they often interpreted the law to suit themselves.

Even the biblical record in I Kings and II Chronicles indicates that Solomon's temple was a breath-taking artistic showplace. Sculptured panels of wood were decorated with gold inlays or gold foil; gourds, palm trees, pomegranates, and other plants were carved in profusion. Figures of oxen adorned the base of the huge vat known as the "molten sea" (I Kings 7:25; II Chron. 4:4). Cherubim, lions, and other animal figures were executed in bronze, wood, gold, and ivory.

So historical sections of Scripture as well as archaeology show that Moses' followers abstained from depicting deity—but violated the law that if taken literally would have stifled all art whatsoever.

Role of the Pomegranate in Early Art

Curiously, the pomegranate figured largely in Old Testament art. The best guess as to the reason why connects it with early notions about its power to increase sexual fertility. Even today, pomegranates have a special role in weddings among the bedouins of rural Palestine. Whenever possible, a fine specimen is secured and split open by the groom as he and his bride open the flap of their tent or enter the door of their house. Because this fruit has many jewel-like seeds, its abundant grains are considered to assure the couple who eat it that they will have many, many children.

Whether or not this shade of meaning was linked with the fruit in ancient times, the pomegranate evoked sufficient emotional response to lead the Israelites to conclude that it was not covered by laws prohibiting the making of images. Even the sacred "robe of the ephod," prescribed for wear by priests on occasions when lots were cast to determine the will of Jehovah, was adorned with blue, purple, and scarlet representations of the potent fruit (Exod. 28:33). Pillars of cast bronze erected by Solomon at the entrance to his temple and named Jachin and Boaz were adorned with two hundred metal pomegranates (I Kings 7:18, 20, 42). Scriptural references are so precise that the production of metal pomegranates in large numbers cannot be questioned.

The fruit is mentioned in describing the bride in the Song of Solomon (4:3, 13). In non-Hebrew cultures the pomegranate was sometimes depicted as the tree of life. Hence conjecture that ancient artistic representations had sexual symbolism is greatly strengthened.

Egyptian Art Strangely Modernistic

So-called modern art employs many different techniques and is based on a variety of ideas about the nature and function of art. Basic to all such ideas is the view that art should not attempt to portray reality as it is observed by the human eye. Rather, reality is often deliberately submerged or altered in order to produce a mood, an impression, or an emotion.

Such treatment of canvas, marble, and other raw materials is in complete contrast with realism, which prevailed in centuries when many now priceless masterpieces were produced. During the great age of realism in European art, painters and sculptors went to great pains to produce works that looked completely natural. This marked contrast points to the swing of the pendulum by which nonrepresentational art is now termed modern.

Moses and the Israelites were exposed to many paintings and other works of art executed with no attempt at depicting "things as they are." Whether the abundance of Egyptian art played a decisive role in scriptural edicts forbidding the manufacture of "graven images" is uncertain.

Many of the beautiful works seen in the land of the pharaohs twenty-five centuries ago were strangely modern in tone. That is, they did not mirror visual experience but modified it. Reasons for some of their practices are not known. For example, the human torso and legs are nearly always shown in profile—but with shoulders "full face." Artists always showed the insides of both feet—and never the outsides. Tables were shown in profile, but objects lying on tops of them were represented as suspended in the air above. As a result, paintings and works of sculpture seen and later prohibited by Hebrews who had spent centuries in captivity had many features that are today linked with surrealism and impressionism.

Only Portrait of a Hebrew King

Because of the long-standing Hebrew prohibition of carved figures, Palestine is barren of royal memorials like those that abound in many parts of the world. Unlike the rulers of Egypt, Babylon, Assyria, and other surrounding nations, the kings of Israel and Judah left behind no monuments or statues or mosaics or paintings that bore their own images. Centuries of exploration have uncovered only one picture of an Israelite king—and it was made by his conqueror.

Jehu was the son of Jehoshaphat. With the support of prophetic religious leaders, among whom Elisha may have been numbered, he led a rebellion against the royal family of Omri. This phase of his career is recorded in II Kings 9:1–10:28. Jehu is famous—or infamous—for the ruthless slaying of King Joram and for having ordered Queen Jezebel to be thrown from her palace window. He drove his war chariot with such dash and fervor that a sport who takes too many chances is still said "to drive like Jehu."

But in Shalmaneser III of Assyria he more than met his match. Attacked by the vastly superior forces of their foes in 842 B.C., the Israelites didn't have a chance. Though Jehu continued to boast about "all his might" (II Kings 10:34), he actually surrendered with little resistance and paid tribute in the form of gold and silver vessels and wooden objects whose nature is unknown. Historians who compiled Hebrew chronicles that became part of the Bible had little to say about all these matters. But the victorious Assyrians erected a famous black obelisk that shows a man (probably King Jehu) doing obeisance to his conqueror and actually presenting the tokens of his submission. This pictorial record of war and conquest includes the only known "portrait" of an ancient Hebrew ruler.

The Tree of Life

Artists in the Eastern Roman Empire, whose capital city was Constantinople (modern Istanbul), developed highly stylized methods of treating religious subjects. Influenced by the splendor of the Far East, they produced richly ornamented and decorated works. At the same time they typically combined two or more biblical motifs to produce symbolic works conveying messages rooted in Scripture but quite different from anything found there.

Ivory carvers of the ninth or tenth century showed Christ crucified not upon an ordinary Roman cross, but on the tree of life described in the Genesis story. They also accepted the tradition according to which the cross itself was erected in a cleft of the boulder which marked the graves of Adam and Eve. So an exquisite icon of the period shows Christ crucified upon the tree of life and bears the inscription: "The cross grafted in the bowels of Adam."

Brother Benedict's Cup

Jesus' use of a cup for the Last Supper with his disciples led to great veneration of any vessel employed for the same rite. At least as early as the second century some of the wealthier Christian churches began to use silver and gold chalices for the celebration of Holy Communion. Later many individual vessels were adorned with diamonds, rubies, and other jewels.

Artisans of northern France, where the stories of the Grail originated, developed such absorbing interest in the biblical cup that it was considered to be all but living. It was natural then for local custom to dictate that the maker of a chalice should enable the vessel to speak by means of an inscription upon it.

A serpent-decorated chalice from this region, now preserved as a priceless work of art, "speaks" in this fashion: *AD . HONOREM . B. MARIE . VIRGINIS . F. BERTINUS . ME. FECIT . A° . MCCXXII* —"Brother Benedict made me in the year of our Lord 1222 to honor the Blessed Virgin Mary."

Twenty Years with a Walrus Tooth

True ivory comes only from the tusks of elephants. Since ancient times artists and craftsmen have recognized that African tusks are larger and superior in quality to those from India, but ivory has for centuries been an important item of commerce in both lands.

Transportation and communication lines often failed during the Middle Ages, producing an acute scarcity of ivory. As a substitute for the exotic material, many artisans turned to comparatively abundant supplies of walrus teeth. Though it usually has coarser grain than ivory and hence does not so readily lend itself to miniature carving, such "walrus ivory" can be worked if one has patience.

An artisan who worked in or near Bury St. Edmonds, Suffolk, England, achieved more than local fame as an ivory sculptor of the twelfth century. He is believed to have spent at least twenty years working on two pieces of walrus ivory. From them he fashioned a delicate cross that is illustrated with eight scenes from the Old and

New Testaments, symbols of three of the evangelists, figures of twenty-one prophets, and scores of brief biblical quotations or allusions to Scripture in Greek and Latin. Experts don't agree as to precisely how many heroes of Scripture are portrayed, but the usual count is 108—plus more than sixty inscriptions.

Artistic Restraint Abandoned

A consistent theme that runs throughout the Old Testament warns that any attempt to represent God constitutes an open door to idolatry. God is wholly beyond man's capacity to depict; indeed, he cannot be known except in the most incomplete fashion. Even his name is holy and hidden; it must not be spoken or written except in roundabout fashion.

Though they were thoroughly aware of this absolute prohibition, Christian artists never took it as seriously as did the Jews. Grasping at the freedom involved in the concept of the New Covenant, they began by depicting the Son of God in various art forms. Then on the rather flimsy basis of argument that restrictions concerning "graven images" (Exod. 20:4; Lev. 26:1; Deut. 5:8; etc.) applied only to sculpture, all caution was abandoned. For more than one thousand years God himself has been depicted through a great variety of art forms.

One of the earliest great works depicting God was executed as a panel for a bronze door. Cast about A.D. 1015 and designed for the Church of St. Michel at Hildesheim, Germany, it depicts Almighty God (complete with bronze halo) rebuking Adam and Eve after they had succumbed to the wiles of the serpent. A French miniature believed to have been executed in the thirteenth century shows God in the form of an architect who holds divider points used by masons; bending over the still-unformed world, the Great Architect is in the process of dividing it much as a medieval builder would divide stone or timber before incorporating it in a structure.

Michelangelo not only painted a portrait of God, he placed it on the ceiling of the Sistine Chapel in the Vatican. William Blake's drawings, watercolors, and engravings include many representations of a rugged God with white hair and a flowing beard.

Readers of the Bible who insist that every word of it must be taken exactly as it is written seldom take seriously Scripture's edict that flatly forbids every attempt to make "any likeness of anything that is in heaven above, or that is in the earth beneath, or that is in the waters beneath the earth" (Deut. 5:8).

Michelangelo's "Pietà"

Christendom's most highly acclaimed statue owes its existence to a strange set of motives including piety, pride, and penny-pinching.

Michelangelo Buonarroti very early showed extraordinary artistic ability. He was just fourteen years old when his work caught the eye of Lorenzo de' Medici, who encouraged him and guided him in his studies. But for several years after the death of his patron in the year Columbus discovered America, the man known to history as Michelangelo found few customers. At twenty-one he went to Rome in the hope of receiving some commissions.

Two years later he received one from the French cardinal of St. Denis. Jacopo Galli, a wealthy Roman banker, handled the arrangements and guaranteed that the youthful sculptor would furnish a statue "that shall be more beautiful than any work in marble to be seen in Rome." But the businessman wanted a cut-rate price that he couldn't get from sculptors with well established reputations. For this reason he agreed that it should be executed by Michelangelo.

The young sculptor out to make a name for himself carved a pietà, or representation of Mary lamenting over the body of Jesus. He placed his own name on it (on the band across Mary's breast), making it the only one of his works he ever signed. Critics of the period protested that he had made Mary too youthful; they taunted Galli for having wasted his money. Art lovers of later generations have rejected that verdict and generally agree that Michelangelo's "Pietà" is one of the world's finest works of sculpture.

Angels: Male or Female?

Though many of the divine messengers mentioned in the Bible are male, no passage suggests that all angels are of one sex. Largely through the influence of art, angels have been depicted in recent centuries as predominantly feminine. In this paradoxical situation the United States government used a feminine form for the angel Gabriel on its 1965 Christmas stamp and drew a flood of protests from indignant Bible readers. The controversial Christmas stamp was not fashioned after an Old Master, however. It was inspired by Lucille Chabot's watercolor of a weathervane made about 1840 and placed on top of People's Methodist Church, Newburyport, Massachusetts.

In Holy Writ "angel" is the English form of the Latin word *angelus*. This in turn is from the Greek word *angelos*, used in the Septuagint Bible to render Hebrew *mal'akh*—or "messenger." Many references to such a divine messenger include no descriptive details at all. Often there is nothing in the context to suggest that this bearer of divine tidings was conceived in any form other than human.

Winged angels—actually more like biblical seraphim than the messengers who are described in Scripture—came into vogue during periods when painters and sculptors were trying desperately to convey the sense of the supernatural. Once firmly established in art, they have proved highly resistant to change in spite of the fact that they obviously have little in common with angels such as those who accepted Abraham's hospitality without revealing their identity (Gen. 18).

In the controversial motion picture *The Gospel According to St. Matthew,* the part of the unnamed angel who brings messages to Joseph and to Mary is played by an adolescent girl.

The name Gabriel, a transliteration of the Hebrew *gabri'el* ("El [the Lord] is strong"), appears in the book of Daniel and in the Gospel of Luke. Though Gabriel really is masculine in Luke 1:29, this doesn't close the door to the possibility that artists are right and most angels are feminine.

Everyday Utensils Decorated

Practically all utensils used in medieval churches were decorated with biblical scenes. A plain, unadorned piece of gear was virtually unknown; some craftsman was sure to take the existence of such a bit of raw material as a challenge and use it to display his handiwork. This was largely but not entirely the result of piety. Artisans couldn't keep their hands still; in the same fashion that whaling men of later generations carved scrimshaw from the teeth of whales just to keep themselves occupied, men translated Scripture into art, especially in the periods of the Crusades, partly because they had to be doing something.

Unknown artisans of Düsseldorf spent years with what was then a very common piece of ecclesiastical ware—a bucket for holy water made of ivory. Around the whole outer surface of the vessel men whose lives centered on the message of Scripture carved miniature but intricate scenes illustrating events in the life of Christ. Then they enriched it with inlays of copper-gilt and added a gilded metal rim and handle. When they finished, it was of no monetary value to persons of their day, but now it is displayed in New York's Metropolitan Museum.

Unique Role of Stained Glass

One of the most distinctive art forms ever developed—stained glass—was a product of medieval eagerness to tell the Bible story to persons unable to read. Though bits of colored glass were arranged into patterns much earlier, it was not until the great era of cathedral building that stained glass windows were deliberately executed as works of art. Requiring enormous quantities of skilled labor, many of them were extremely expensive, even in an era when workmen were paid just enough to afford them a bare living. Only a culture whose members erected Gothic cathedrals and whose wealth was concentrated among royal families and religious institutions could have launched a movement as elaborate as the creation of stained glass windows.

Glassmakers did not produce big sheets; instead they aimed at gemlike chunks that imitated the colors of the ruby, the sapphire, the emerald, and other precious stones. Strips of lead, whose cross sections were like the letter H, were used to hold colored particles. At each point of junction, leading was soldered together, with cement or putty pushed into the crevices between metal and glass. By means of copper wires soldered to leads, each window was attached to an iron saddle bar inserted into masonry.

Some famous windows, such as those of Chartres and Reims in France, York and Tewkesbury in England, and others in Germany, Spain, and Italy contain thousands of components—each meticulously set by hand. Scriptural scenes already made famous by painters were interpreted afresh in this new medium. Outside medieval Christendom, no other culture has produced even close counterparts to the crucifixions, annunciations, creations, ascensions, and other biblical events portrayed in cathedral windows executed during the thirteenth, fourteenth, and fifteenth centuries.

Michelangelo Compelled to Paint

Working for the most part flat on his back, a man who considered himself a sculptor rather than a painter reluctantly produced the world's largest masterpiece of biblical art.

After having lived for a time in the palace of Lorenzo de' Medici and studying under great masters of his day, Michelangelo was summoned to Rome by Pope Julius II in 1505. Under strict orders from the pope, and frequently reprimanded for attempting to divert his energies into other channels, the artist decorated the ceiling of the Sistine Chapel.

He spent four years on the job he didn't want to start. Painting prone on scaffolding within arm's reach of the ceiling, he executed mighty scenes interpreting the creation, the fall of man, the flood, and other key stories of the Bible. Before he quit, he covered ten thousand square feet with what admirers came to regard as the most splendid set of paintings in Christendom. Critics and connoisseurs of later centuries have agreed that the scenes created by the man who yearned to be working with hammer and chisel have a place in art comparable to that of Dante's *Divine Comedy* in literature.

Leonardo Painted in the Wrong Place

Judged by almost any standard, the most famous biblical painting in the world is Leonardo da Vinci's "Last Supper." Prodded into painting it by a prior with whom he bickered, Leonardo broke with artistic conventions of the Middle Ages and moved Judas to the same side of the table as Jesus. This arrangement has since been followed by scores of other artists. Yet the original work of Leonardo is for practical purposes lost.

Leonardo was a many-sided man. His achievements in science and engineering have caused some biographers to wonder how he succeeded in overcoming the hurdles of logic in order to free his imagination when he turned from mathematical exercises to depicting biblical personalities and events. Contemporaries regarded him as "extraordinarily accomplished" with the favorite musical instrument of the period, the lute.

Late in the turbulent closing decade of the fifteen century, this many-sided virtuoso determined to depict the Last Supper in such fashion that it would cause viewers to stand at the door of the Upper Room, in their imagination. He employed daring new techniques and succeeded even better than he had hoped.

Unfortunately, though, he chose the wrong place for his masterpiece. Painted on the wall of a convent refectory in Milan, it began to deteriorate within a few years after it was completed. Time, moisture, and the gradual settling of the building have virtually destroyed the original. It has been repaired and touched up so many times that the existing work retains few spots actually painted by Leonardo.

Reality Deliberately Distorted

During the Middle Ages artists who worked in a variety of media tried to convey biblical concepts that cannot be depicted literally. To do so they developed an elaborate "visual symbolism" in which reality as we know it was deliberately distorted in the interest of communication.

One of the most unusual of such devices came to be known as the stem of Jesse. Several New Testament passages emphasize the importance of the fact that Jesus was a blood descendant of David; even Paul refers to the Saviour as having been "made of the seed of David according to the flesh" (Rom. 1:3). David was the son of Jesse, a patriarch of the tribe of Judah who resided in Jerusalem. Little is known about Jesse; what details we have of his life center in I Samuel 16–17.

Though he was unimportant or even insignificant in his own right, Jesse was elevated to a major place in Hebrew thought because it was he who sired David. As a result, Isaiah's prophesy concerning the coming Messiah stressed that "there shall come forth a rod out of the stem of Jesse" (Isa. 11:1).

Seeking to visualize the concepts involved in a genealogy beginning with Jesse and ending with Jesus, medieval artists evolved Jesse's stem. It appears on canvas, in ivory, and in stained glass. A typical example depicts a tree growing from the chest of a reclining Jesse. Each branch of this tree ends with one or more of his descendants who became kings and rulers. At the top is Jesus (or Jesus and Mary), portrayed for all the world as though literally growing from the stem of Jesse. This popular biblical representation may have given rise to the term "family tree" as a synonym for "genealogy."

Raphael's Bible

Raphael's Bible is largely the work of men other than Raphael and was prepared partly with secondhand material, yet it is universally regarded as one of the most suggestive of all interpretations of Scripture.

Raffaello Santi was a world-renowned artist by the time he was twenty-five. At the request of Pope Julius II he became a citizen of Rome in 1508 and began executing a series of artistic and architectural triumphs that occupied the rest of his brief life.

Julius conceived the idea of having his brilliant young protégé execute a "living Bible" by painting the major scenes of both the Old Testament and the New in a single collection. For this project he chose the loggia, an apartment inside the Vatican. With its many arcades, it offered wall space in abundance. Unfortunately, though, much of the area was already occupied by the work of the then renowned painters Signorelli and Piero della Francesca. No matter.

Upon orders from the pope himself earlier works were plastered over to make room for Raphael's Bible.

Working frequently on resurfaced walls that hid earlier masterpieces, Raphael outlined scenes like the building of the ark, Abraham about to sacrifice Isaac, Jacob wrestling with the angels, and dozens of others that ranged all the way to the birth of Christ and the Last Supper. In fact, he sketched so many that the actual execution of his designs was largely relegated to Perino del Vaga and a group of other students attached to Raphael's staff. Virtually all present-day volumes on art inspired by Scripture include one or more reproductions from Raphael's Bible, and the display is so important that it rates an entry in many general reference works.

Worthless Strips Salvaged

Seven Bible-inspired "cartoons" not intended for lasting use are among the greatest art treasures in the world. Preserved only by virtue of the reluctance of working men to throw good cardboard away, they were produced by Raphael about 1514.

Pope Leo X wanted a new set of tapestries to adorn the lower part of the walls of the Sistine Chapel in the Vatican. Already the roof and east end bore paintings by Michelangelo. He commissioned Raphael to make paper patterns that could be used by weavers. Drawn in chalk on *carton* (or cardboard) and tinted in distemper, each working drawing measured about twelve feet in height and fourteen to eighteen feet in length.

For convenience in using them, artisans cut these patterns into strips which they tossed aside as sections of the tapestry were finished. As pieces of art they seemed worthless; holes had been made in them for the weavers to transfer their outlines, and in places they were almost cut through by tracing. But some thrifty workman salvaged many strips and packed them in boxes. As a result, seven of Raphael's original ten cartoons were eventually discovered and restored. The tapestries made from Raphael's cartoons were executed at Arras, Flanders, in silk, wool, and gold. Each piece cost $3,500. Because these and copies made for display in Berlin and Dresden were cataloged very early (and many have been preserved), all Raphael's subjects are known in spite of the fact that three original sketches perished.

Now priceless, the "worthless" patterns for tapestry makers are the only works of Raphael that do not seem physically small when compared with Michelangelo's frescoes in the Sistine Chapel.

Contemporary Figures in Biblical Paintings

Numerous pieces of biblical art take Scripture as a starting point and then become strangely mixed. During several centuries it was commonplace for a king, emperor, or other wealthy patron to commission an artist to execute a biblical scene that included the proud owner of the work.

William II, king of England and ruler of Normandy, extended his empire as far south as Sicily. There in the majestic Cappella Palatina, Palermo's most beautiful church, his loyal subjects found a place to express their admiration for him. Artists were hired to paint two elaborate panels. One of them centers upon the Virgin Mary, who is depicted in the act of accepting a model of the church from the hand of King William. In the second, the biblical figure is Christ himself. But instead of being occupied with multiplying loaves and fishes or eating with his disciples in the Upper Room, in this work of art he is shown placing his hand on the crowned head of William II. The irony of these paintings is heightened by the fact that when William was killed by an arrow while hunting in New Forest, the clergy of nearby Winchester Cathedral refused religious rites to his body.

The church of San Vitale in Ravenna, Italy, preserves a memorial to the vanity of a religious leader. A mosaic executed in the sixth century depicts Christ handing the martyr's crown to Saint Vitale. But just to the right of the angel who flanks the Saviour stands a representation of Bishop Ecclesius, founder of the church in which the work of art still reposes.

Impetus to Audio-Visual Aids

Audio-visual aids, regarded as essential to modern education in fields ranging from biology to computer programming, were given great impetus as a result of zeal for the communication of the Bible's message.

No precise date can be assigned to the world's first visual teaching device. Greeks of the pre-Christian era probably used this technique. Late in the second or early in the third century, Christians definitely used mosaics and crude paintings in their instruction of converts. Words of Scripture were reinforced and supplemented by these visual devices.

By the early Middle Ages churchmen were consistently and habitually using a variety of nonverbal teaching aids. Art, sculpture, and architecture were deliberately employed as media of communication. So were music and drama; the latter, born in the church, developed into miracle plays and morality plays that prepared the way for the rise of the modern theater.

Tape recorders and motion picture projectors are more sophisticated devices than those developed by churchmen intoxicated with communicating the good news in every possible way. But the basic principle of educating through the eye and ear, with words made subordinate or eliminated entirely, was thoroughly established in the monasteries, convents, and cathedrals of medieval Christendom.

Epilepsy Treated with Art

Psychological conditioning as a means of treating illness was practiced by monks of the early sixteenth century. The tools used in their pioneer attempts to devise a system of mental therapy were masterpieces of Christian art.

Matthias Grünewald executed a series of panels and great altarpieces depicting biblical characters and events. His largest and finest, completed about 1516, was done for the cathedral at Issenheim, Germany. It consists of eleven hinged panels, a carved central shrine covered with a double set of wings, and two side pieces. Among the most noteworthy of these individual works are the temptation of St. Anthony, the Crucifixion, the Marys wailing over the body of Jesus, and the Resurrection.

A common malady of the period was known locally as *mal des ardents* or St. Anthony's sickness. Descriptions lead modern analysts to think it was related to epilepsy. A person afflicted and taken to Issenheim for treatment was placed before the altar and required to stare at Grünewald's visual interpretations of Scripture for three days. Without parallel in the history of art, the Crucifixion (now in the museum of Colmar, France) omits no gruesome detail. A contemporary critic concludes that it blends the mystical and the macabre in such fashion that it "dwells, almost hysterically, on horror"—without losing an overwhelming sense of reverence and triumph. After long exposure to it and other paintings, a sufferer or *ardent* turned his gaze to the triumphant Resurrection and let its message soak into his brain through his eyes. Then and only then was he formally admitted to the hospital for additional treatment that often led to cure.

Centuries earlier the Greeks had employed the same basic approach—that is, the treatment of emotional-mental disturbances by means of art—at Epidaurus and probably at other cities as well. Specific details of their methods of treatment are not as well established, however, as are those that were employed in sixteenth-century Germany.

Controversial Christmas Stamp

Numerous pieces of religious art have stirred up controversy. In some instances, painters and sculptors have violated accepted traditions with the hope of creating turmoil that would make their works the center of debate. That was not the case with the most talked-about work of art reproduced in the United States during 1966.

"Madonna and Child with Angels" is a relatively obscure painting by a minor Flemish master. Hans Memling (or Memlinc) spent much of his life in Bruges and achieved a distinguished reputation among fifteenth-century art collectors. About one hundred of his works have survived. Among these the most important are the "The Marriage of St. Catherine," the "Last Judgment," and the "Legend of St. Ursula." His portraits of St. John the Baptist, St. Lawrence, and other notable figures in Christian history appear in many anthologies of art.

But his "Madonna and Child with Angels" seldom rates an entry in an encyclopedia. Precisely how it came to be chosen as the subject for a special 1966 Christmas stamp issued by the United States Post Office Department, officials of that service have not revealed. But chosen it was. Presses at the Bureau of Printing and Engraving had hardly stopped rolling before the uproar began.

Arthur J. Lelyveld, president of the American Jewish Congress, condemned the stamp as violating the principle of church-state separation becaue the masterpiece it reproduced "is plainly both religious and sectarian." Other opponents of even token ties between church and state raised their voices in a chorus of protest, but the stamp was made available at post offices throughout the nation. Special Postal Assistant Ira Kapenstein issued a blunt explanation. No one was in any way put under pressure to buy the stamp, he explained. And "Madonna and Child with Angels" was chosen as a piece of art rather than for any sectarian emphasis that may be linked with it.

William Blake's *Book of Job*

Though he was obsessed with all Scripture in a fashion seldom matched, William Blake was particularly fascinated by the book of Job. He read it and pondered it for more than forty years—always considering it to be the key that would unlock mysteries in his own personality and experience.

He made at least four different sets of drawings and a series of engravings before he was satisfied with his illustrations of the book of Job that he specifically indicated to have been "invented" rather than painted by him. Because there are twenty-two letters in the Hebrew alphabet, he limited himself to twenty-two plates. In the absence of explanatory notes or commentaries, Bible readers presented with a reproduction of Blake's book might not grasp its dependence upon the story of Job. But the artist himself considered it to contain the distilled essence of all Scripture plus his own wisdom.

Blake had openly clashed with the great Sir Joshua Reynolds and made no attempt to follow the conventional practices of other artists. His *Book of Job* was for a time regarded as so insignificant that it was a waste of time for anyone of taste to look at it. Now its twenty-two plates, produced over a period of forty years, are considered a landmark in the history of European art.

Literature and Letters

Specialization in Music and Poetry

Biblical injunctions against the visual representation of God, persons, creatures, or things are frequently considered to have been framed as reactions to the gross practices of surrounding peoples among whom a great variety of idols were worshiped as divine or semidivine. Though flagrantly disregarded by Solomon, scriptural edicts are considered responsible for the fact that Hebrews produced comparatively few works of art in the form of paintings and sculptures.

But their creative energy could not be suppressed. Diverted from channels commonly used by many of their contemporaries, worshipers of Jehovah specialized in two art forms: music and literature. Since it was never transcribed but transmitted orally from one generation of players to the next, all ancient Hebrew music has been lost.

That was not the case with their great poems—which ranged from hymns of national rejoicing at victory in battle to tender love songs to carefully executed lines of praise to the Lord. In the whole of ancient literature—Oriental, European, African, and Near Eastern—there is nothing quite like the poetry of the Hebrews. From the brief victory song of Deborah (Judg. 5:2-31) to the psalms of David and the Song of Solomon, makers of sweet sounds weighed every syllable and considered each shade of meaning in the metaphors they employed.

Hence, there is considerable evidence to support the theory that lacking divine prohibition of representational arts, the Bible would be quite different. Men who could not depict Jehovah in stone or by means of paintings diverted much of their energy into a single channel: the representation of his greatness by means of words, many of which eventually became venerated as Scripture.

Dives Not Likely to Be Dislodged

Many of the greatest writers in the western world have included Dives as a character in their tales or have made references to him. Despite this wide coverage, it is an error to refer to him as a man identified in Scripture.

In Luke 16:19-31 there is a vivid tale of a poor man named Lazarus (meaning "without help") and an unidentified rich man. But since the Latin term for rich was *dives,* the descriptive title crept into popular speech through the influence of the Vulgate, and common folk as well as literary notables treated it as the name of the man who went to hell and in his torment begged Abraham to send Lazarus "that he may dip the tip of his finger in water, and cool my tongue" (vs. 24).

In his "Summoner's Tale," Geoffrey Chaucer treats Dives as a name drawn from Scripture in the same fashion as Lazarus. Shakespeare puts on the lips of Falstaff (*Henry IV,* Part I) a memorable line concerning the tendency to "think upon Hell-fire and Dives that lived in purple."

Though the name emerged through the popular retelling of a New Testament story, Dives is so firmly entrenched in literature that no amount of explanation is likely to dislodge it.

Charlemagne's Biggest Defeat

Charlemagne overthrew one enemy after another in order to become king of the Franks and emperor of the West. But he was defeated in his attempt to improve the language of his subjects by requiring priests to use better grammar when they read the Scriptures and delivered sermons.

No one knows precisely what motivated the emperor to issue his famous encyclical of A.D. 786. His own deep reverence for the Scriptures was doubtless a major factor in his decision. At any rate, he ordered all the bishops and priests in his realm to employ correct grammar—measured by classical standards—in their public reading of the Bible and exposition of its message. This move was made in an attempt to stop the spread of Vulgar Latin, already well entrenched among the masses.

But his prowess on the battlefield did Charlemagne no good in the struggle to control speech. Instead of accepting classical Latin as he had expected, the king's subjects quickly modified their spoken language, and this stabilized as Old French. This development—considered by some linguists to be the most specific of all historical examples illustrating the close relationship between religion and speech—could not be ignored. In A.D. 813 the king who had overcome the Saxons, Lombards, Arabs, and Avars himself admitted defeat. He issued a new proclamation ordering churchmen to employ the French language in lieu of classical speech, *lingua latina,* whose attempted imposition had spurred the rise of the new tongue, *lingua romana rustica.*

Beowulf Transformed by Scripture

Wherever the Bible has gone, its adherents have used it as a weapon with which to overthrow "heathen" practices and systems of thought. Frequently the process of conquest by assimilation has been more significant than victories gained by frontal assault. Where pre-Christian literature could not be supplanted by Scripture, missionaries have deliberately or unconsciously engaged in reshaping native tales.

A classic case is that of *Beowulf,* Anglo-Saxon epic poem of 3183 lines dating from the eighth century or earlier. It deals with the adventures of a folk hero who successively overcomes the monster Grendel, Grendel's dreadful mother, and a dragon. Most of the action takes place in Seeland—opposite Gothland. Thoroughly pagan in both its outlook and details, the ancient poem was gradually transformed under the impact of the Bible.

Late versions of it include songs based upon Genesis, incidents involving the use of twig crosses, and the repetition of the Lord's Prayer as a semimagical incantation. So great was the impact of Scripture that this most important relic of Anglo-Saxon thought came to portray Beowulf's arch foe Grendel as a descendant of Abel's murderer, who was therefore marked with the mark of Cain.

Our Bible-shaped Alphabet

Reading and writing developed in Great Britain very early, though the severe climate of the island kingdom caused documents to rot more rapidly than in the dry Near East, where Dead Sea Scrolls survived for two thousand years. Britons used old Teutonic runes, utterly different from the letters of the English alphabet, to spell out their words. But pioneer Christian missionaries to England brought the Scriptures with them in Latin.

According to the most ancient account, the supply of sacred writings consisted of a two-volume Bible, two copies of the psalms, and copies of two of the four Gospels. Avidly read, copied, and translated into Anglo-Saxon, these six books had an impact so great that the Latin alphabet eventually supplanted the Teutonic system of writing.

Only one trace of the pattern made obsolete by Latin Scripture remains in the English alphabet—the modern *y.* It is based on the Teutonic rune for *th,* which is why it frequently appears in "Ye Olde Antique Shoppe" and other signs that seek to preserve an aura of antiquity.

Old Testament Books Listed in Verse

Until high-speed printing presses made great quantities of literature available at low cost, many persons stored lists in their brains instead of relying on reference books. To facilitate memorization of the order of the books of the Bible, several jingles—all hopeless as poetry but functionally useful—were composed. As refined over a period of generations in which it was transmitted orally, one such list of Old Testament books runs:

The Great Jehovah speaks to us
In Genesis and Exodus;
Leviticus and Numbers see
Followed by Deuteronomy.
Joshua and Judges sway the land,
Ruth gleans the sheaves with trembling hand;
Samuel and numerous Kings appear
Whose Chronicles we wondering hear.
Ezra and Nehemiah, now,
Esther the beauteous mourner show.
Job speaks in sighs, David in Psalms,
The Proverbs teach to scatter alms;
Ecclesiastes then comes on,
And the sweet Song of Solomon.
Isaiah, Jeremiah then
With Lamentations takes his pen,
Ezekiel, Daniel, Hosea, lyres,
Swell Joel, Amos, Obadiah's.
Next Jonah, Micah, Nahum come,
And lofty Habakkuk finds room—
While Zephaniah, Haggai calls,
Wrapt Zechariah builds his walls;
And Malachi, with garments rent,
Concludes the ancient Testament!

The New England Primer

A sketch showing prominent blotches on the skin of Job identifies a book that had a circulation of two million copies in early America but is now so rare that collectors pay astronomical prices for it. Benjamin Harris, an amateur poet and professional printer, established a nondescript shop in Boston during the reign of King James II. There he issued *The Protestant Tutor,* quickly abridged to form *The New England Primer*.

His first edition came off the press about 1690; only fragments of it have been preserved. During the following century there were at least forty large printings, but by 1900 libraries and collectors estimated that only about fifty copies of the little book had been preserved intact.

Alphabet rhymes illustrated with woodcuts as crude as the verses are its best-known features. But like the English primer (or "first book," from the Latin *primus*) that it supplanted, the New England teaching aid was full of scriptural material. Hence, it was commonly called "the Little Bible." Puritans saw in it a device by which to preserve and spread sectarian views and so put their full support behind it. Spots representing Job's sores were just a few of many graphic devices used to cram Scripture into the heads of boys and girls in the process of learning their letters. Once children mastered the primer, they were set to reading from the Bible itself—usually Psalms and the New Testament.

Milton's Incorrect Quotes

John Milton won lasting fame with *Paradise Lost*. Yet after exhaustive study University of Illinois scholar H. F. Fletcher concluded that Milton didn't go to the trouble of looking up Bible passages when he wanted to quote them. As a result more than half of his quotations used in prose works before 1652 depart from the accepted text.

All this changed when he lost his sight at the age of forty-four. From that time until his death, all of his Scripture quotations are letter perfect. Presumably this is due to the fact that the blind writer's secretary took time to check each verse and phrase to which Milton referred before incorporating it in a manuscript.

Pilgrim's Progress

Though *Pilgrim's Progress* is intensely biblical, the famous book contains few direct quotations from Scripture. Author John Bunyan, a tinker whom some critics have labeled semiliterate, didn't need to quote. He had so steeped himself in the thought, imagery, and literary style of the King James Version that he could not write or speak in any fashion except biblically.

Like many other classics, Bunyan's work is now admired everywhere and seldom read—except as a required book in courses on religion or English literature. But for at least 150 years after it appeared in 1678 the story of a man named Christian who made progress in his spiritual life against great obstacles was the most influential tale in the western world. The London *Times* once called it "the world's best supplement to the Bible."

Before Bunyan died in 1688, the book he wrote in jail while serving time as a promoter of seditious assemblies had sold at least 100,000 copies. During the first century of its existence *Pilgrim's Progress* went through nearly one hundred separate editions; by the time of the second centennial of its publication, it had been translated into at least ninety languages. Though immensely popular in many of them, its most profound impact was upon the English-speaking world.

Tens of thousands of persons who had read no other book except the Bible were intimately acquainted with this book inspired by the Bible. Part of its popularity stemmed from the fact that *Pilgrim's Progress* might be considered the first soap opera. For the central character who gave the book its name went through one hair-raising adventure after another, and alternately endured defeat and enjoyed victory in his progress toward his goal of eternal life.

Sir Walter Scott and the Bible

Sir Walter Scott wrote reams of material about violence and death, intrigue and murder. But this supreme master of characterization and storytelling repeatedly stressed the fact that he learned more from the Bible than from all other books combined.

On the flyleaf of his personal copy of the Scriptures, Scott penned with his own hand a set of lines especially written for this spot:

> Within that awful volume lies
> The mystery of mysteries!
> Happiest they of human race,
> To whom God has granted grace
> To read, to fear, to hope, to pray,
> To lift the latch, and force the way,
> And better had they ne'er been born,
> Who read to doubt, or read to scorn.

Numerous biographers and students of English literature have amassed abundant evidence that his tribute was not perfunctory. Scott really did "lift the latch"—for numerous plots, subplots, and characters in his novels are drawn directly from the Bible. It takes only a cursory reading to discover Leah and Rachel in *The Abbot,* his first novel published after he was made a baronet in 1820. Abraham and Sarah are as readily identified in *Kenilworth* (1821). A casual acquaintance with Scripture enables one to find Ruth and Naomi in *Guy Mannering* (1815), but the less familiar story of Elijah and the widow of Zarephath (I Kings 17:8-24) is not quite so readily identified in *The Monastery* (1820). A complete list of characters and situations drawn directly from Holy Writ by the still popular teller of tales would run to many pages.

William Blake's Strange Proverbs

Only one man in history is known to have deliberately taken key ideas of Scripture and turned them inside out in order to make them into diabolic maxims for pious purposes. About seventy such sayings are included in the central section of William Blake's *The Marriage of Heaven and Hell.* According to his own account, in a visionary state he himself visited hell. He became acquainted with some of the devil's agents and from them collected his proverbs. They are quite different in style and content from the material in Ambrose Bierce's *Devil's Dictionary* of a later period (1906).

Convinced that the unrest which produced the French and American revolutions indicated the second coming of Christ and the end of the world, Blake so titled his book because the Revelation frequently refers to cosmic destruction as a wedding in which Christ takes the church as his bride. Some of Blake's distilled satanic wisdom, deliberately framed to express views opposite to those of the book of Proverbs, form capsule philosophies of life.

> Drive your cart and your plow over the bones of the dead.
> Prudence is a rich ugly old maid courted by Incapacity.
> The cut worm forgives the plow.
> Prisons are built with stones of Law,
>   Brothels with bricks of Religion.
> The lust of the goat is the bounty of God.
> The nakedness of woman is the work of God.
> As the caterpillar chooses the fairest leaves to lay her eggs on,
>   so the priest lays his curse on the fairest joys.

Blake Branded a Lunatic

William Blake, one of the few men in history to be recognized as a creator of the first rank in two separate fields—painting and poetry—was considered by many in his own day to be mad. As late as 1809 Robert Hunt described him in *The Examiner* as "an unfortunate lunatic, whose personal inoffensiveness secures him from confinement."

Wordsworth concurred in the general verdict that Blake was insane, but added to his judgment a footnote: "There is something in the madness of this man which interests me more than the sanity of Lord Byron and Walter Scott."

From childhood Blake was so saturated with the words, images, and central ideas of Scripture that he never fit comfortably into the culture that included him. His pictures and verses, long brushed aside as incoherent or meaningless, are now so highly prized that a whole literature has grown up to interpret the man and his works. Without a thorough knowledge of both the Old Testament and the New, however, it is all but impossible to make sense of anything William Blake wrote or painted.

Big Boost for the English Language

When the King James Version was published, English was still a remarkably polyglot language. Many words and phrases came from Anglo-Saxon by way of Old English. Others were borrowed directly from Latin, French, German, and Dutch—or modeled after words in those tongues. Common nouns and verbs were spelled in six or ten or a score of different ways; it seemed that every county had its own dialect.

Partly because it was so far from being standardized and partly because its roots extended deep into the guttural speech of barbarians, English was regarded as inferior to classical languages. As late as 1516 when Sir Thomas More wrote his famous *Utopia,* he chose to give it to the world in Latin. It was translated into German, Italian, and French before it was finally rendered into English. Francis Bacon used Latin for what he considered his important scholarly works and English for casual essays—but was careful to translate one edition of his essays into Latin so that they might survive after English ceased to be spoken!

Mass distribution of the King James Version of the Bible served as a catalytic and crystallizing force in English speech. Gradually the spellings used in it made all competitors obsolete. Figures of speech and colloquial expressions—"clear as crystal," "fat of the land," "salt of the earth," and scores of others—became organic components of the developing language. Technical words from the biblical vocabulary entered common speech with changed meanings as did the word "talent." Used in Jesus' parable to name a unit of money, it quickly came to stand for a special aptitude or skill.

The impact of the King James Version upon English was one of the greatest forces ever to affect it.

James Fenimore Cooper's Favorite Book

James Fenimore Cooper, author of the famous Leatherstocking series that constituted the first cycle of successful novels about the American frontier, had no personal knowledge of exploration and Indian fighting. A prosperous country gentleman who tried his hand at fiction in response to a chance challenge by his wife, Cooper found many of the ingredients for his action-packed stories in the book that he read more often than any other—the Bible.

He was especially interested in the poetic and prophetic sections of the Old Testament, plus the New Testament books of Hebrews and Revelation. After experimenting with a variety of patterns of reading, he and his wife settled upon a plan that they followed for many years. Each morning they sat down together and read one hundred verses of Scripture before eating breakfast.

One of the founders of the American Bible Society, Cooper was as full of action as some of the fictional characters he created. Editors of many religious journals attacked him because he opposed the practice of kneeling in public. When newspapers smeared him for his criticism of American culture, he filed a number of libel suits and won most of them. During the period of his most bitter controversy he completed two of his best-known books, *The Pathfinder* (1840) and *The Deerslayer* (1841). Though he never went so far as to call himself a modern David fighting against Goliath, notes in his journals suggest that he saw himself in that role.

Hundreds of biblical allusions appear in his tales about Indians and frontiersmen. One character in *The Last of the Mohicans,* Gamut, rode a mare that bore the name of Moses' sister Miriam. Gamut is so obviously based on King David, traditional author of the psalms, that Cooper openly labels him as "an instructor in the art of psalmody."

Washington Irving's Famous Ichabod

Though the connection between them is not immediately obvious, there is a close link between "The Legend of Sleepy Hollow" and an Old Testament incident. Washington Irving's central character, Ichabod Crane, gained his name as a result of the impact of the biblical story upon English speech.

One of the earliest catastrophes that befell the Hebrews was the loss of the ark of the covenant to the Philistines. This symbol of Israel's glory was captured in battle, and news of the disaster stunned members of all the Hebrew tribes. One expectant mother was so shaken by the tragedy (plus the loss of both her husband and father-in-law in battle) that she gave birth to a son and then died in a state of shock (I Sam. 4:19-21). Her child was given a symbolic name—"inglorious," or "dishonor." Rendered into English, the Hebrew original became Ichabod.

Obscure as he was, Ichabod was important to generations of persons who prided themselves on knowing the Bible from cover to cover. Hence his name entered general speech as a title for any foolish, inept person. Irving created a character whose background as a teacher should have made him alert but didn't. Then he turned to the frontier taunt that was born of an all-but-forgotten biblical incident and employed the name Ichabod to symbolize the dim wit of his main character.

John Greenleaf Whittier's once famous but now little known poem entitled "Ichabod" hangs that label on Daniel Webster for softening in his support of the cause of abolition.

Biblical Impact upon World Literature

More than any other single force, the Bible has been responsible for the production of Oriental dictionaries and books of grammar. Though many Oriental countries have had fairly high levels of literacy for centuries, early missionaries found word books and manuals of style nonexistent.

Dr. Hepburn produced the first Japanese dictionary in 1867—as an essential tool in his work of translating Scripture. William Carey published dictionaries in both Sanskrit and Bengali. Judson issued the first Burmese dictionary, Morrison the first Chinese, Jaeschke the first Tibetan, Gale and Underwood the first Korean.

Men obsessed with the Book didn't stop with the preparation of verbal tools. Sometimes against great opposition they also introduced western printing practices. The Bible-oriented Shanghai Mission Press led the way in quantity production of movable Chinese type. By his work in preparing the Arabic Bible at the American Press in Beirut, the missionary printer Hallock practically determined the standard of Arabic type faces. So it has been throughout most of Asia—and in Africa and South America.

Kipling's Scriptural Hammer

Rudyard Kipling took an almost superstitious view of the writing materials with which he produced his world-famous stories. For his *Plain Tales* he used a slim eight-sided pen with a special nib; later he switched to a silver penholder with a quill-like curve. He used a pewter inkpot on which he scratched the names of the books he dipped out of it.

His most unusual gesture took place in Jerusalem. Stopping briefly in the holy city during one of his world tours, he found a "slim, smooth, black treasure"—a pen that to him seemed potent with a capacity to pour out fresh and more powerful words. Kipling formally named his pen Jael—in honor of the woman who admitted an enemy king into her tent and then drove a nail through his temple with one blow of a hammer (Judg. 5:26).

He gleefully promised that with this modern-day Jael he would smite the Philistines mercilessly. Using it, he actually did turn out stories and poems which, in contrast with those of his youth, challenged vested interests and disturbed a comfortable society clinging to the fading glory of the British Empire.

Biblical Impetus to Growth of English

Though England was comparatively late in getting a printed Bible, the rapid production and distribution of it has helped make English the fastest-growing language in the modern world.

Just four centuries ago English was spoken by only five million persons. Many who used it as their native tongue regarded it as inferior for scientific and scholarly works. Measured in terms of the number of persons who used it, English was then surpassed by German, French, Spanish, Italian, and Dutch.

Partly through its commercial-industrial impact and partly because the earliest and biggest Bible societies were rooted in English-speaking cultures, the once minor language is now second only to Chinese (in the number of users). In terms of worldwide influence it has no close contender for first place.

More Bibles have been printed in it than in any other language. Today more persons use English as their native tongue or as a second language than do those who speak German, French, Spanish, Italian, and Dutch combined. Estimates of the world total of those using the language shaped by Scripture and Shakespeare range at about the 400,000,000 level—eighty times that of the sixteenth century.

Lew Wallace and *Ben Hur*

An agnostic, who publicly doubted that there is anything men can really believe, inspired the writing of one of the most famous biblical novels of all time.

One evening in September, 1870, two men riding across Indiana on a train struck up a conversation. Soon they began to argue about the inspiration of the Bible and the message of Jesus Christ. Robert G. Ingersoll, already internationally famous as a challenger of Scripture's message, was trying to make a convert of General Lewis Wallace.

Better known as Lew, the Indiana-born officer fought through the whole of the Civil War. He participated in many lesser engagements and then took part in the bloody Battle of Shiloh. Later he prepared the defenses for Cincinnati and was made commander of the Eighth Army Corps. After hostilities ceased he resumed his legal practice.

But the lawyer and veteran of many battles was unable to cope with Robert G. Ingersoll. He felt frustrated and defeated when he parted company with the noted agnostic, having failed to make any dent in the network of arguments with which Ingersoll defended himself from the challenge of faith.

As a result, Lew Wallace went home determined to write a novel that would serve as a powerful argument for the divinity of Christ. Finished while he was serving as governor of the Territory of New Mexico, it was entitled *Ben Hur; A Tale of the Christ.* One of the most popular books of modern times, it presents the message of the New Testament within a framework of vigorous action that involves believable characters. Ingersoll didn't live to realize it, but the story whose writing he inspired became widely read even in regions of the United States where all novels had previously been frowned upon as immoral.

Ecclesiastes: Source Book for Novels

H. Rider Haggard is best known to contemporary Americans as the author of the novel *King Solomon's Mines,* which became a hit in movie form. His own adventurous life included a hitch in the British Foreign Service that took him to the Transvaal during the Boer War. Some of his novels not quite so well known today as during the last century are filled with fantasy, blood, and action. Titles such as *Ayesha* (or *The Return of She*) and *The Witch's Head* hint at the basic style he employed in his writing.

Questioned about the textbook from which he had learned, the author of these superthrillers named the book of Ecclesiastes—often skipped by modern Bible readers who consider it dull. Haggard described Ecclesiastes as a book that "utters all the world's yearning anguish and disillusionment in one sorrow-laden and bitter cry, whose stately music thrills like the voice of pines heard in the darkness of a midnight gale."

Most Widely Quoted Book

Practically everyone in the western world either owns a Bible or has access to a copy of it. In spite of this near total accessibility, many dictionaries of quotations devote enormous space to the Book of Books.

In its thirteenth and centennial edition, John Bartlett's famous *Familiar Quotations* puts succinct sayings from Holy Writ in a special section that runs to forty-six pages. In the *New Dictionary of Thoughts* column after column is filled with familiar expressions from the Bible. These range all the way from "weighed in the balances, and found wanting" (Dan. 5:27) to "we see through a glass, darkly" (I Cor. 13:12) and "eat, drink, and be merry" (Luke 12:19).

In *The Penguin Dictionary of Quotations* Old Testament quotations occupy fifteen pages; one page is devoted to books of the Apocrypha, and sayings from the New Testament fill twelve pages. Editors of the monumental 2812-page *Home Book of Quotations* include so many quotations from Scripture that they make no attempt to enumerate them in the list of sources. In the case of less ambitious books, more space is devoted to Holy Writ than to any other collection of writings. For example, the paperback revised edition of *Best Quotations for All Occasions* (1966) gives the Bible about 50 percent more space than all the works of Shakespeare combined.

Though no one can be absolutely sure how much or how little modern man reads his Bible, this much is clear: in the English-speaking world it has no close competitor for first place as the most quoted book.

Ba'al, "Lord of the Flies"

Somewhat clumsy rendering of a biblical word into Greek, and mistranslation of the Greek term into English, furnished the title for the best-selling novel *Lord of the Flies.*

William Golding published the book in 1955. It won immediate critical acclaim around the world and within five years had sold more than two million copies. Though on the surface it seems a simple adventure story of boys who degenerate into savagery when marooned on a desert island, the novel is actually a symbolic analysis of human nature. Its name is taken from one of the many titles given to the devil.

Hebrew *Ba'al Zebhubh,* a comparatively late term, was formed on the base *Ba'al*—long considered the personal name of the pagan deity worshiped by the Canaanites in Old Testament times. Today it is generally believed that Baal was a title with an approximate meaning of "lord" or "master." Each local Baal was likely to be designated by means of a qualifying adjective that named the place of his shrine or some special feature in his worship.

Long before archaeological study revealed these details about the ancient Canaanite religion and speech, the pagan god whom worshipers called *Ba'al Zebhubh* came into special prominence. Greek-speaking Hebrews transliterated the title into *Beelzeboub,* which was adopted into English (Beelzebub) as a particularly vivid name for Satan. It was so used in the King James Version (Matt. 10:25; 12:24; Mark 3:22; Luke 11:15, 18-19), apparently through influence of Baalzebub (II Kings 1:2-16).

Nobody knows for sure what the title originally meant, but it was translated as "lord of the flies" and used to personify forces of decay and demoralization. Though Golding's novel is in no sense biblical, he chose the Scripture-rooted title to symbolize the theme of depravity and futility that runs through the best seller.

The Bible—by Christopher Fry

Under twentieth-century United States copyright laws there is no way to restrict a person from printing his own copies of a book issued more than fifty-six years ago. Even in the case of volumes still covered by copyright it is difficult and often impossible to protect a title alone. Still, it was something of a shock to discover on the spine of a 1966 paperback volume the title *The Bible,* followed by the author's name: Christopher Fry.

Title to the contrary, the book is neither a revision of the Bible nor a retelling of its story. Instead it is the screenplay written for a motion picture of the same title, which deals with central events in the opening chapters of the Bible. A more descriptive and far more appropriate title for the work would have been, simply, *Genesis,* for the story begins with the creation and ends with Abraham's journey to Mt. Moriah to offer up his son Isaac in sacrifice (Gen. 22).

In his preface to the screenplay Christopher Fry stresses some of the problems faced in dealing with even this brief segment of the biblical story. Cain's wife had to be taken into consideration—but where did she come from? Was the serpent inherently evil, or did he become evil only after he tempted Eve and as a consequence was sentenced to crawl upon his belly? Should the incest foisted upon Lot by his daughters (Gen. 19:31-35) be included as an integral part of the story or omitted as morally degrading?

Fry reports, tongue in cheek, that while some of the other issues are insoluble, the question of the serpent "took care of itself when the real snake slept through the whole proceedings."

The Gospel According to St. Matthew

Since the time of *Ben Hur* and other pioneer literary works of its type, it has been taken for granted that only a strong believer can produce a persuasive biblical novel or play. This point of view was rudely shattered by the fact that a 1965 film directed by an avowed Communist won acclaim as "the greatest biblical movie ever made."

Produced on a low budget with little hope of commercial success, *The Gospel According to St. Matthew* became a box-office sensation in Europe. Shown in America with English subtitles, it made such a hit that voices of English actors were dubbed into the original Italian film.

Few motion pictures—religious or secular—have achieved such quick and fervent critical acclaim. Many big-name reviewers reported that the film moved them as no other interpretation of Scripture ever has.

Part of the power of *The Gospel According to St. Matthew* stems from the fact that it had to be kept simple because the producer didn't have money for elaborate effects associated with Hollywood versions of biblical epics. But many analysts think its impact stems chiefly from a simple but profound factor: approached by a creative mind not consistently exposed to the story from childhood, the Bible story was seen in a fresh and provocative way.

According to this view, many persons who have had an incidental but not life-shaping acquaintance with the Bible all their lives develop spiritual-emotional cataracts and are unable to see the gospel story in its raw grandeur. Director Pier Paola Pasolini opened a New Testament by chance, read the first pages of the first Gospel, and was immediately gripped by what he called "an irrational movement or experience" that drove him to put Matthew's account upon film.

Whatever the explanation for its power may be, the story of Jesus Christ as seen and filmed through the eyes of a nonbeliever has an emotional and persuasive impact often missing from the works of many fervent evangelists, missionaries, and proponents of the faith.

Enthusiasm Unlimited

Waiting for Jehovah at Qumran

So many ancient documents have been discovered in the vicinity of the monastery of Qumran that it will be years before all of them are deciphered and translated. Yet almost from the beginning of the international excitement over the Dead Sea Scrolls one thing was clear. The men who produced these writings, which became the biggest biblical treasure trove yet uncovered, were zealous to the point of fanaticism.

Their community was a strict fellowship that required renunciation of self-interest. Both priests and "laymen" were accepted as members, but all followed a communal pattern that was rooted in Scripture and dedicated to the glory of God. Hence, the basic features of the Christian monastery were anticipated by centuries.

Only a person wholeheartedly dedicated to the goals of the group could find peace at Qumran. Under the leadership of elders and priests, all members of the fellowship devoted at least one half of their waking hours to Bible study and worship. Hymns were sung at regular intervals each day; most of them emphasized thanksgiving to God for his goodness. No full-fledged member of the community had anything he could call his own; his time, his labor, his clothing, and even the pen and inkwell he used for making copies of Scripture belonged to the fellowship rather than to him.

At Qumran a substantial number of men regarded themselves as the true Israel and devoted themselves to prayer, study, and work while waiting for the physical reign of Jehovah. Small wonder, therefore, that in a comparatively brief period they produced the greatest hoard of Scriptures and other writings yet recovered from an institution close to Jesus in time and space.

St. Francis Versus Simeon Stylites

Inordinate passion for ordering one's life by the Scriptures has produced both the greatest saints and the weirdest pathological figures in Christian history. Let enthusiasm for God and his Word pass the level of ordinary decorum, and a person is likely either to make a permanent contribution to civilized life and thought or to be branded as a crackpot by future generations.

Francis of Assisi stands at one extreme. His absorption with the Bible and its message made him incapable of living a conventional life, so he renounced his family and his future inheritance in order to "marry" poverty and faith. Strangely stirred by the account of Jesus' commissioning of the twelve disciples, he founded the order of Barefoot Friars. In obedience to the letter of the scriptural injunction (Matt. 10:9-10) he and his followers went out with empty purses, no shoes, and a single cloak each. Details concerning his life are colored by tradition, but there is no escaping the recognition that this man so filled with zeal inspired his contemporaries as well as persons of every succeeding generation.

Opposite results stemmed from an explosive meeting between the Word of God and Simeon Stylites. Early in the fifth century he spent so much time with his Bible that it became the dominant influence in his life. But instead of causing him to turn his energies into creative channels, his sense of mission led the Syrian to condemn all that men consider normal as "the work of Satan." As a result of pondering Holy Writ, Simeon persuaded a band of his followers to erect in an isolated place a pillar about sixty feet high. Then he climbed on top of it and perched there for the last thirty years of his life—refusing to climb down even for the necessities of nature. Simeon was the first and most widely known of the pillar saints or *stylites*. Analysts of later centuries have concluded his influence to be pathological and negative—derived from the same source as that of Francis, but opposite in impact.

Concordances to Scripture

Bible study produced the world's first tool enabling a reader to find a passage by means of any word included in it. Since then the basic idea has been extended to many other bodies of literature both ancient and modern. As a result it is now possible to get concordances not only to Scripture but also to the works of Plato, Cicero, Dante, Milton, Shakespeare, Browning, and many other writers.

The late Latin word *concordantia* ("harmony") gave rise to the title for word lists whose original purpose was that of showing the whole of the Bible to be "harmonious." Use of a concordance as an index to find a verse or phrase was a secondary development, but it quickly became the most important function of such a book.

Tradition credits Anthony of Padua (1195-1231) with making the world's first concordance—based upon the Latin Vulgate. His work was brief and inadequate but demonstrated the importance of such a tool. Hugh of St. Cher issued a far more comprehensive concordance to the Scriptures. He is said to have been assisted by five hundred of his fellow monks.

A Hebrew concordance was compiled in 1437-45 by Isaac Nathan. And the first Greek concordance to the New Testament was published at Basel in 1546 by a Lutheran minister, Sixt Birck. Thomas Gybson, first to publish in English, labeled his work: "The Concordance of the New Testament, most necessary to be had in the hands of all soche as delyte in the communication of any place contayned in ye New Testament" (1535). Dozens of Bible concordances have been published since; each required five to thirty years of work by the compiler. James Strong's *Exhaustive Concordance* occupies more than 1,800 oversize pages with three to six columns of fine print per page. Alexander Cruden devoted most of his life to the preparation and revision of the famous concordance that bears his name.

A Period of Concentrated Zeal

During a period of about three centuries intensive study—centered principally in Scripture and works about it—was the hallmark of an Englishman who strongly wanted to succeed. Many modern success goals did not exist; others were minimized. This period of concentrated zeal can be explained only by the fact that the mood of the times made heaven the ultimate goal of life—with the Bible regarded as the surest highway to that goal.

John Morton (1420-1500) typically rose at 4:00 A.M. to begin his day of study, refusing to modify that pattern until far past eighty. That he became Archbishop of Canterbury was not nearly so significant in his own eyes as the fact that he "truly knew the Scriptures, yea, from beginning to end."

Matthew Poole (1624-79) was equally ardent. For years he spent every waking moment upon the manuscript of his book *Synopsis Criticorum Biblicorum,* an abridgment of "all the writings and labours of former Biblical scholars of all ages and countries." His five-volume work was published in 1669. Poole often rose at 3:00, studied for five or six hours, and then allowed himself the luxury of eating one raw egg. After another four or five hours spent with the Scriptures and books about them, he ate another raw egg for lunch.

One pastor of this period set out to write an exhaustive commentary on the book of Hosea—which has just thirteen chapters. He filled four thick volumes before he died with his commentary unfinished. Another zealot was absorbed with the book of Job; he pored over it for decades and wrote more than five thousand pages of explanation and comments. Though produced at the cost of "blood, sweat, and tears," few such books attracted more than passing interest from other men absorbed with the Book of Books and none at all from the general public.

Six Thousand Miles for a Bible

In the days of sailing vessels a physician-clergyman traveled almost six thousand miles to rescue his Bible.

Scotland, divided by religious quarrels that stretched over a period of several centuries, saw a particularly violent outburst when King Charles II ascended the throne in 1661. A few months after assuming power, the "Merry Monarch" issued a proclamation that substituted the Episcopal for the Presbyterian form of church government. Three hundred ministers who refused to take loyalty oaths were forcibly removed from their manses and replaced by the king's appointees.

In this situation the Rev. Robert Hemphill decided to seek freedom of religion in the New World, but he couldn't take his personal copy of the King James Bible with him. At that time Bible burning was an almost daily occurrence. So Hemphill put his little Bible in his medicine kit with a razor and razor hone and hid them in a hollow log on the bank of Loch Neigh.

After two years in America he returned to his homeland to retrieve the Book left behind. He succeeded in getting it across the Atlantic and left it as a legacy to his heirs. Today it is a prized possession of one of his descendants, Earl Hemphill of Freeport, Texas.

In order to continue the tradition of passing the Bible along to the youngest child of the next generation, Mr. Hemphill keeps it in a fireproof bank vault. Issued in 1648 by Roger Daniel, printer to Cambridge University, the Bible is bound in wood and sheathed in rawhide. Corner guards are made of hand-beaten brass.

John Wesley's Reliance on the Book

John Wesley, founder of Methodism, was regarded by some churchmen of his day to be intoxicated with Scripture. He usually turned to the Book six to ten times a day, read, and meditated upon a passage. Frequently he recorded in his journal the location of the section that occupied him and noted the time spent with it.

As a young man he was far from robust—at twenty-seven he was spitting blood and eleven years later considered himself to be "in the third stage of consumption." Yet in order to have more time for Bible reading and his devotional exercises that accompanied it, he limited himself to five hours of sleep. As a college student he formed the habit of rising at four in the morning so he could spend a quiet period with the Book.

Most of his life he refused to rest or to remain more than a few days in one place. Once he broke his rule and treated himself to a two-week outing in Holland—just after he had turned eighty.

He occasionally took "the machine" (as the stagecoach was then commonly called) for emergency trips, but he preferred to ride horseback because he could read better in the saddle. He claimed to have ridden over 100,000 miles, spent more time with the Bible than most men devote to their wives and children, and preached more than 40,000 sermons. Sustained by the Book and by inner enthusiasm, he remained vigorous in old age, but at eighty-five he protested that "his eyes were very dim and his strength had quite forsaken him."

Alexander Cruden's Concordance

An eighteenth-century eccentric who spent several terms in lunatic asylums devoted more than thirty years to the preparation of a Bible concordance still used by multitudes of students and readers.

Alexander Cruden, born at Aberdeen in May, 1701, began to show signs of instability soon after being rejected by his sweetheart. This led to the first of several terms of involuntary confinement. Released, he worked for years on an improved and enlarged English-language concordance to the Scriptures. Published at a financial loss in 1737, the elaborate book was dedicated to the queen in the hope that she would bestow a gift on the author. Though she accepted a presentation copy and expressed her intentions of sending Cruden a substantial gift, she died sixteen days later without acting on the promise.

In spite of the disappointment, Cruden devoted the rest of his life to enlarging and correcting his monumental volume. In 1761 he personally presented a copy of the second edition to King George III (to whom it was dedicated) and is said to have received a gift of £100. Eight years later he issued a third and final edition on which he realized a profit of about £300.

Though the book was reprinted several times, editions remained comparatively small until the copyright expired. Since then, it has been published many times in both England and the United States in large editions. One American publisher made facsimile plates from an early copy and issued a trial printing in May, 1953. Since then nearly 200,000 copies of this edition alone have been sold. Cruden's *Concordance,* still recognized as a work of outstanding importance in the history of Bible-study aids, runs to seven hundred pages of microscopic print, three columns to a page.

Mary Jones Gets a Bible

Many persons have yearned for Bibles they could call their own. Few even approached the zeal of a semiliterate Welsh girl—or the consequences that stemmed from her burning desire to own a copy of Scripture.

Mary Jones lived in a village with the improbable-sounding name of Llanfihangel. A daughter of a weaver, she had no formal schooling, for in the 1790's Wales had few schools and they were reserved for the wealthy. After she had learned her letters, the girl developed a great yearning for a Bible, but her poverty-stricken parents couldn't afford to buy one for her.

So Mary ran errands and did household work in order to save money for the precious Book. At the end of a year, she had accumulated precisely one shilling. That had to be sacrificed to buy medicine for her sick father. But she refused to abandon her dream. For at least five years she worked, scrimped, and saved. Finally she had about twenty shillings—enough to purchase a Bible. But no one in her village had a Welsh Bible for sale. She heard of a minister twenty-five miles away in the town of Bela who was reputed to have an extra copy. She walked the entire distance, found Thomas Charles and told her story. He refused to take her money and insisted on giving her the Bible. She scrawled on the flyleaf the notice that "Mary Jones His the True Onour of this Bible."

Charles told her story many times. It fired the imagination of religious leaders from all Britain and was a major factor in creating the climate that led to the organization of the British and Foreign Bible Society in 1804. Mary Jones' Bible is now a prize item in the historical collection of the Society.

He Counted Letters

Thomas Hartwell Horne (1780-1862) devoted most of his life to the study of the Bible. Especially among other English clergyman, he made quite a reputation as a scholar. But for some reason he never explained, he spent three years of his life counting not only the chapters, verses, and words, but also the letters of the Bible in the King James Version.

According to him there are 2,728,100 letters in the Old Testament and 838,380 in the New Testament, making a total of 3,566,480. Other enthusiasts for numbers have disputed his tally. One reported a total of 3,567,180 and another 3,586,489 letters. In spite of the fact that the good doctor may have accidentally left out the results of a month or two of counting, it is Horne's total that appears in the *Guinness Book of Superlatives.*

Bible Produced with One Finger

Samuel Isaac Joseph Schereschewsky, a Lithuanian Jew trained as a rabbi who emigrated to the United States in the nineteenth century and was converted to Christianity, became a leading Bible translator. He eventually came to speak thirteen languages and read seven more.

As a missionary-translator in China, he produced a version of Scripture in Easy Wenli, a form of the nation's literary language. This version is famous as the one-finger Bible because before he even began work on it Schereschewsky became too badly paralyzed to continue touch typing. As a result, he pecked out the entire translation with the middle finger of one hand.

Evangelistic Zeal Launches Annuities

Several hundred charitable, religious, and philanthropic organizations in the United States now operate gift annuity programs—from an idea born as a result of concern for distributing the Bible.

Early in 1843 a Mr. Keith of Boston, Massachusetts, persuaded his minister to tender an offer to the then youthful American Bible Society. He would like to make the Society a gift of $500 for use in its program of producing and distributing the Scriptures, said Mr. Keith, on the condition that the Society pay him interest during his lifetime.

After considerable debate, officers agreed to accept his money—the principal of which would belong to the Society upon his death—and to pay him 6 per cent interest as long as he lived. Launched in this fashion, the first of all gift investment programs is now the world's largest. It offers important tax benefits and instead of the fixed rate paid in 1843 operates on a sliding scale with interest up to 8 percent depending upon the age of donor-investors.

"Hallelujah!" as an Outlet for Enthusiasm

Members of the corps that launched an 1880 "invasion" of the United States used "Hallelujah!" as their battle cry. It was shouted repeatedly by the seven women and one man who made up the first unit of the Salvation Army sent to "conquer" this country. Their ship, the *Australia,* docked at Castle Garden in New York on March 10, 1880.

Members of the salvationist task force were dressed in vivid uniforms and black derby-like hats that quickly attracted a crowd of spectators. When the gangplank was lowered, the invaders marched down it shouting and carrying a red, yellow, and blue silk banner. On reaching the shore they knelt in a circle to pray and claim America for Jesus.

As used by ancient Hebrews, hallelujah probably meant "praise be to Yahweh!" Especially prominent in some of the psalms, the exclamation is linked with the expression of gratitude for the mighty works of the Lord. Because the word occurs so frequently in translations of them, psalms 146–150 are often called the hallelujah psalms. Here the King James Version employs "Praise ye the Lord" and transmits "Alleluia!" only in Revelation 19.

Early Christians probably used hallelujah both in worship and as a symbolic greeting. Popular throughout the Middle Ages, the ancient shout was endorsed as acceptable by Martin Luther in 1523; three years later he tried to prohibit its use but did not succeed. Prominent in both Catholic and Protestant music—especially that linked with Easter—the initial *h* of the word is frequently dropped for use in singing. But in its spoken form it remains very close to the cry already old in the time of David.

Passionate Absorption with Hades

Were it not for his passionate absorption with the subject of Hades, the name of S. F. Pell would be unknown. Because of it, he is remembered as one of the most ardent (though misguided) modern champions of the Greek-language Septuagint Bible.

Hades (comparable to Hebrew *Sheol*) was the underworld—or abode of the dead—in classical Greek mythology. Early Christians who used the term gave it special associations so that gradually it came to name a place of testing or torment.

Pell devoted years to his study of Sheol, Gehenna, and Hades. No scholar, he nevertheless discovered that a majority of New Testament quotations from the Old Testament (in manuscripts that have survived the centuries) are not taken directly from the Hebrew original. About 70 percent of them are drawn, instead, from the Septuagint. This accounts for the fact that the Greek *Hades* appears more frequently in the New Testament than does the Hebrew *Sheol;* even so, references are sparse.

After having completed a rambling analysis of the use of the word "Hades," Pell stumbled across a treasure in a secondhand bookstore. It was a battered copy of the Bible as translated by Charles Thomson, who was forced to work from the Septuagint because he knew no Hebrew. Pell took his discovery as a sign from heaven; he added the text of the Thomson Bible to his own work and in 1904 persuaded Skeffington and Son of London to issue the massive volume.

Pell subsidized the project with the whole of his fortune, but it proved a complete failure. According to many scholars, its only merit was that of making available thousands of fresh copies of the Thomson Bible which was then virtually unobtainable but interesting for historical purposes.

Nineteenth-Century Children's Crusade

By the mass purchase of ten-cent shares, juvenile "stockholders" of two lands outfitted a special Bible boat just before the outbreak of the Civil War. More than 150,000 schoolchildren in this country and the Hawaiian Islands invested their dimes in *The Morning Star*—a sloop built especially for the purpose of taking the Scriptures to the Marquesas Islands and little-visited regions of Micronesia.

On her first voyage the vessel logged more than 10,000 miles. Receptions accorded Bible distributors by various groups of islands were so cordial that when *The Star* was wrecked she was replaced by a two-masted vessel bearing the same name. Before the saga of distribution by sailboat came to an end, three other ships named in honor of the children's original *Morning Star* were worn out taking Bibles to coral atolls and volcanic islands of Oceania in the western Pacific.

Gospels Carried to Korea

Though the concept of the iron curtain was not originated until after World War II, practices associated with that term are much older. Korea was sealed off from the west until 1882. Not only was there no commercial contact or travel, but the importation of western books was forbidden.

In spite of this situation, smugglers succeeded in getting two Gospels across the Manchurian border and through the curtain of isolation. When missionaries were finally admitted into the land, they found a considerable number of persons in Seoul asking for baptism, having been converted to Christianity by reading the story of Jesus from a forbidden book.

Ronald Knox, Modern Translator

During the entire history of the Bible only a handful of men have translated both the Old Testament and the New Testament from Genesis to Revelation. One who succeeded at this prodigious task is better known in some circles as a writer of mystery stories than as a linguist and scholar.

Born in a rectory of the Church of England, Ronald Knox became a convert to Catholicism in 1917. As early as 1911 he had begun writing papers about Shcrlock Holmcs and G. K. Chesterton's fictional sleuth, Father Brown. But it wasn't until 1925 that Knox published his own first novel: *The Viaduct Murder.* It was followed by such volumes as *The Three Taps, The Footsteps at the Lock, The Body in the Silo, Still Dead* and *Double Cross Purposes.*

With his reputation as a mystery writer firmly established, Knox suddenly announced his intention of translating the Latin Vulgate into contemporary English. He won somewhat grudging permission to start on the New Testament in 1939 and completed it in time for publication in April, 1944. The first printing of 1,500 copies was not available in bookstores.

It proved, however, an immediate success with the author's circle of friends. As a result Knox started work on the Old Testament, laboriously working through the whole of it at the rate of about twenty-four verses per day. An irrepressible wit, he later quipped that his period of translation had involved a sentence of nine years at hard labor. During most of those years Scripture was his sole preoccupation; he "ate, lived, and breathed the Bible." Generally considered to be the most vigorous of all private translations accomplished by modern Catholics, the Knox translation has been highly successful throughout the British Commonwealth and in the United States as well.

Digging at the Site of Nineveh

Since the Crusades amateur and professional searchers for biblical relics have plundered the Holy Land. Especially in regions where Christians conquered, were mastered by Moslems, attacked successfully again, but were once more defeated and driven out, churches and other old buildings have been systematically looted time after time.

Beginning about the middle of the nineteenth century, a new approach developed. Ancient relics, always interesting and sometimes valuable, were sought underground. Tombs were broken open and rifled; some half-buried ruins were uncovered, and at points where searchers thought they were on the trail of a valuable cache, they sometimes dug several feet into the ground.

It wasn't until recent decades, however, that anyone thought of exploring the rounded hills and truncated cones that dot Palestine and much of the Near East. Such a mound, it was learned, is practically certain to be man-made and to contain debris from a long-buried city. From a Semitic label that distinguishes this kind of structure from a natural hill, it is commonly called a tell.

Once the basic nature of the tell was generally understood, archaeologists launched a frontal attack. Many teams of scholars, who usually hired native workmen to help them, uncovered twenty, thirty, or forty feet of earth. By many standards, however, the most zealous digger of the lot was M. E. L. Mallowan. At the site of ancient Nineveh he became convinced that earlier searchers had stopped too soon and as a result had overlooked the most important area. Mallowan dug more than ninety feet into the Nineveh tell before he was satisfied that he had reached the lowest stratum. Archaeologists now generally concede that the man who refused to stop digging pointed the way to the exploration of the site of one of the world's oldest cities.

Present-day Vendors of Scripture

Around the world several hundred persons still make their livings by selling low-cost Scriptures provided by subsidized programs of western Bible societies. Named from a French term for "one who carries from the neck," such a *colporteur* may visit as many as 150 villages on his annual sales route. In isolated regions where there is little money he often barters Holy Writ for coconut oil, fish, eggs, salt, or lodging for the night.

First Long Book Recorded

The commercial recording of books was not launched until long after a variety of musical records were widely available. Approximately the same length as *Gone with the Wind,* the Bible was the first lengthy body of literature to be made available for ears of listeners rather than eyes of readers.

An LP recording of the Book runs to 169 double-faced records which play for eighty-four hours. Now the Old Testament and the New are also available on tape. Only eight reels are required for the Revised Standard Version New Testament.

Records and tapes have special appeal to men and women whose vision fails after middle life, for such persons often find it difficult or impossible to learn braille. There is an additional advantage in terms of production, for no effective low-cost method has ever been devised for printing Scripture in braille. As a result, in 1968 a braille Bible in grade 1½ (twenty volumes) cost $90 to produce. On 16⅔ rpm records the Old Testament occupies fifty-two records which cost $23.40 from the American Bible Society. The fifteen-record New Testament is available at just $6.75.

Biblical Names Dominant with American Presidents

Enthusiasm for biblical names accounts for the fact that two thirds of the presidents of the United States and half of their wives have borne names taken directly from Scripture or adapted from it.

John, James, Thomas, and Peter are the most common masculine names drawn from the King James Version. Mary has no close contender for first place among feminine names that derive from the same source. Elizabeth is next in order, but Ruth and Lois are very popular.

Many widely used surnames were also formed from slight or drastic modifications of biblical originals. Noyes betrays its indebtedness to Noah, and Cobb exhibits the imprint made by Jacob. But except for specialists in linguistics, few persons today would recognize Atkinson as having been formed from Adam or Perkins as a variant of Peter.

A Bible-reading Marathon

Villagers of Scranton, Kansas, read the entire New Testament aloud on Universal Bible Sunday, 1938. In order to mark the twentieth anniversary of the launching of this special day in the church calendar, all six hundred persons living in Scranton began gathering at the Methodist church in the early hours of the morning.

Reading began at 3:00 A.M. and continued without a break until 9:00 P.M. When one reader became hoarse or tired, he handed the Book to a successor waiting to take up at the spot marked by his thumb. Such nonstop reading from cover to cover was later practiced at Philadelphia's Baptist Temple and in other American congregations.

Scripture's Impact upon Emotions

Though Scripture produces joy and serenity in many persons, it is also potent enough to precipitate states ranging from depression to schizophrenia. This effect is so marked that many psychiatric clinics forbid patients to have possession of even brief excerpts.

Most analysts hold that Holy Writ doesn't produce abnormal states;

it is simply seized as a tool or a crutch by persons already somewhat unbalanced. But the effects can be devastating.

A typical case was the 1959 hatchet slaying of Mrs. Valada McHugh. After being attacked with a three-inch, single-bladed weapon, she ran screaming from her home and died within two hours.

Investigators discovered that friends considered her husband a religious fanatic. Questioned, he said, "The Lord made me do it." Evidence introduced at his trial included several tablets filled with hand-copied Bible verses. Witnesses said McHugh read the Bible avidly for two years before the slaying.

Committed to a hospital for the criminally insane, he died there six years later with murder charges against him still pending in the courts of Evansville, Indiana.

World Record in Bible Reading

Frank Tripplett, of Coeur d'Alene, Idaho, is believed to have set a world record in Bible reading. During the first six months of 1965 he read the entire Bible six times.

A resident of Pinewood Manor nursing home, Tripplett was once blind. When his vision was restored, he determined to spend the rest of his life with Scripture and performed his marathon reading in partial fulfillment of that resolution. Confined to a wheel chair and forced to use a steel hook in lieu of the left hand he had lost earlier, the Bible reader was eighty-one years old at the time he established his all-time record.

Finger-powered Phonograph

The world's only finger-powered phonograph was developed to play Scripture records for Navaho Indians whose hogans are without electricity. Made of lightweight plastic, the sound-producing device is now distributed globally by the American Bible Society.

Though the quality of sound production is not uniform, brief practice enables most persons to develop sufficient skill to spin records so that they are intelligible. There is no power other than the whirling finger of the person who operates the finger-fono.

Workers with illiterate tribesmen on reservations in the American Southwest first saw the need for such a device. Once perfected, it caught the imagination of missionaries in various remote regions. So in India, Africa and South America, villagers can now spin records with their fingers in order to hear the Word of God in their own languages.

Handwritten Production of Holy Writ

Adventures of a Manuscript

Though the odds against its preservation were great, a major manuscript of the Bible escaped damage when religious wars led to pillage of the city where it was kept.

Lyons, France, about 315 miles south southeast of Paris, has been a center of controversy for centuries. Built where the Rhone and the Saône rivers converge, it was a key military post under the caesars. Augustus made it the starting point of four great roads. Burned in A.D. 59, it was rebuilt by Nero.

In later centuries the city was successively ravaged by barbarians, Franks, and Saracens. Each time it recovered, and in the thirteenth century it became a major ecclesiastical center. Partly because it had earlier entertained a convocation of five hundred Catholic bishops, Protestant revolutionaries set out to level the city to the ground when they seized control of it in 1562.

They actually did kill, burn, and loot on a large scale. But they kept whatever they considered interesting or valuable. Among the loot from the monastery of St. Irenaeus was a fifth-century copy of Scripture. How it reached Lyons originally and where it was produced no one knows with certainty. But when Protestants turned their backs on the burning city to leave, the ancient codex (or book) went with them. Eventually it came into the possession of Théodore de Bèze, French-born successor to John Calvin in the leadership of the church of Geneva, Switzerland.

In 1581 Bèze gave the manuscript to the University of Cambridge; from the Latin form of his name scholars call it the *Codex Beza*. Particularly important in establishing the original text of the book of Acts, the much traveled piece of war booty was published in facsimile about 1,500 years after it was originally produced by hand.

Lengthy Scrolls Made Very Early

The manufacture of paper in continuous rolls rather than small individual sheets played an important part in the formation of the Bible. Papyrus plants, abundant in Egypt, were cut into strips and laid side by side with a second layer superimposed at right angles. When beaten and smoothed, papyrus (which later gave its name to all paper) formed a writing material less durable than leather but much lighter. Artisans knew how to make it into long rolls at least as early as the time of Egypt's King Wedimu, for a blank roll has been found in the tomb of his chancellor, buried about 3000 B.C.

From their conquerors, Abraham's descendants learned the art of preparing papyrus rolls. As a result, all the earliest Bibles were transcribed on them. Writing from right to left (because Hebrew runs in that direction), a prophet or scribe could put an immense number of words on a roll and be sure that they would be preserved in the proper order. There was no possibility of getting pages mixed; the nature of the roll eliminated that problem.

Isaiah's "great roll" (Isa. 8:1) may have been fashioned of leather rather than papyrus. But the scroll prepared by Baruch the scribe at the dictation of Jeremiah (Jer. 36:2) was almost certainly papyrus —because the stench would have been intolerable had a leather roll been burned bit by bit (Jer. 36:23). Some of the Dead Sea Scrolls were written on papyrus rolls, and this was doubtless the material used for the letters of Paul. But arts associated with paper making declined during the centuries that followed the fall of Rome. Craftsmen ordinarily produced only individual sheets of paper (often made from flax) and so it was hailed as a triumph of the industrial revolution when inventors perfected machines that once more made paper in long, unbroken rolls.

Documents Deposited for Safekeeping

Long before the entire Bible or even the Old Testament as we know it had been assembled, scribes regarded copies of sacred writings as the most valuable possessions of a synagogue or community. In order to keep these precious documents from being damaged, the earliest forerunner of the modern safety deposit box was devised. It consisted of a heavy earthen jar especially made for the purpose, in which a scroll could be placed and protected by a movable lid or fixed seal.

This earliest repository for valuable papers—reserved at first for copies of the Law of Moses and writings of the prophets but later extended to legal documents—is described in Scripture itself. In a period when most of his countrymen felt that the Lord had deserted them, Jeremiah was given a divine commission. As a symbol of his faith in God's ability to assure the nation a future, the prophet bought a parcel of real estate. Then he took the "evidences" that corresponded with a modern deed, delivered them to Baruch the scribe, and instructed him to deposit them for safekeeping: "Take these evidences, . . . and put them in an earthen vessel, that they may continue many days" (Jer. 32:14).

An ancient account called The Assumption of Moses includes instructions that indicate some specific practices associated with storing Holy Writ and other scrolls produced through countless hours of laborious work. "Receive thou this writing that thou mayest know how to preserve the books which I shall deliver unto thee," a subordinate was told. "And thou shalt set these in order and anoint them with oil of cedar and put them away in earthen vessels." (1:17.) Though essentially a religious rite, the act of anointing with oil of cedar before depositing scrolls contributed substantially to their capacity to resist mold and moisture.

"Bible" Originally a Name for Any Book

Ever since the printing press made big business out of book production, publishers have consistently devoted great attention to the matter of getting good titles for their volumes. But the title of the all-time best seller was bestowed by persons unknown. Actually it's simply a modified version of the ancient Greek *biblion,* a word used to name any collection of writings put down for posterity on the inner pith of papyrus. Along with hundreds or thousands of other works, volumes of Scripture were long called books. There isn't a shred of evidence to suggest who first had the inspiration of calling the collected Judeo-Christian sacred writings *ta biblia—the* Book (s).

Biblia is applied to Holy Scripture in the Second Epistle to Clement of Rome, written about A.D. 170, but this was not the first appearance. It had already been used as a title in I Maccabees (about 104 B.C.). So this special name was current sometime early in the second century. Perhaps the label developed independently in numerous centers at various times. Regardless of how it started, it was soon so well established that there was no other contender for the title, and Holy Writ came to be universally known as the Bible.

Still, as late as the time of Chaucer in the fourteenth century, the immortal storyteller clung to the original Greek sense of the term and applied the name to any book.

Additions to the Book of Esther

The book of Esther is essentially a patriotic rather than a religious work. Nowhere in it is there any mention of God. Largely in order to repair this omission and partly because he wished to heighten the strong anti-Gentile character of the book, an unknown Jewish scribe made a series of additions shortly before or after 100 B.C.

Since scrolls were comparatively rare and communication was slow, it was impossible for all persons engaged in copying the Old Testament to compare notes with one another. As a result, the six insertions (now divided into 105 verses) made by an ardent Hebrew nationalist were copied and then recopied. Eventually they came to be considered by many persons as part of the original.

By chance, the Hebrew text used by scholars who prepared the Greek-language Septuagint followed the "expanded" version of Esther. In later centuries editors of the Latin Vulgate identified the passages that appear in the Greek but not the Hebrew Old Testament. They collected them into one body of material and faithfully copied them word for word—but placed them at the end of the book of Esther.

Protestant editions of the Apocrypha, or collection of holy books whose authority is not fully accepted, include a brief one entitled the Additions to the Book of Esther. As printed in many pulpit editions of the King James Version, this brief tract—whose chief appeal lies in the fact that it repairs the omission by which a book of the Bible doesn't mention God—stipulates that the additional verses "are found neither in the Hebrew, nor in the Chaldee." The Peshitta, or simple Syriac version, largely bypassed Greek influence and was drawn directly from Hebrew; as a result this version ignores the Additions to Esther and leaves that book without any mention of deity.

The Codex Vaticanus

Widely believed to be the oldest complete Bible in existence and therefore of unmatched importance to translators, the Codex Vaticanus was for centuries the most jealously guarded of all handwritten copies of Scripture.

A great deal of evidence indicates that it was produced about A.D. 350. Scribes who worked on it followed the text of the Greek-language Septuagint and arranged the holy message on pages with three columns. Each column was precisely forty-two lines long; this physical pattern, comparatively common in handwritten Bibles, determined the arrangement of the first printed Bible that was produced by Gutenberg.

Partly as a result of Protestant-Catholic attacks and counterattacks that began during the time of Martin Luther, keepers of the archives at the Vatican refused to give scholars access to their ancient book. No one knows when it was acquired by the Vatican library, or how it got there. It was first listed in a catalog prepared in 1481. Since a similar catalog of 1475 doesn't include it, some scholars have concluded that it was acquired between those years. This is pure conjecture; it is equally possible that it rested in Rome for decades or even centuries before finding a place on an official list.

Once recognized as old and rare, it was put under lock and key. Only one obscure specialist, J. L. Hug, managed to get a look at it—and that was during the brief period Napoleon held it as war booty after taking it from Rome in 1809. Armed with credentials from the Czar of Russia, Count Tischendorf saw it briefly in 1842 and again in 1866. But it wasn't until 1889/90 when Vatican scholars issued a photographic reproduction that the treasured codex became generally available to persons seeking to get as close as possible to the original text of Holy Writ.

Scripture Erased in Favor of Sermons

Ephraem of Syria lived during the first three quarters of the turbulent fourth century. A scholar who wrote theological works, hymns, and commentaries on Scripture, he was highly appreciated by his contemporaries.

Copies of his sermons were in such great demand and such short supply that sometime in the fifth century an unknown scribe had an inspiration. A rather battered handwritten New Testament was lying about the monastery; why not erase the sacred text and produce a fine blank book on which to copy some of Ephraem's great sermons? Once conceived, the idea was slowly executed.

Late in the seventeenth century a keen-eyed scholar doing research on Ephraem noticed the queer feel of the pages he turned. Scrutiny showed the parchment in his hand to hold not one but two manuscripts. Attempts to decipher the original proved fruitless; the work of erasure had been done so well that only a few lines could be recovered. During the 1840's, Count Tischendorf spent two years with the codex and then published what he thought he found.

More than a century later the vexatious problem was finally solved by new techniques. Using infrared light, photographers succeeded in recovering the original text of what is now valued as one of our oldest New Testament manuscripts. Entitled Codex Ephraemi Rescriptus (Rewritten Book of Ephraem), it is stored in the French National Library.

Development of Illuminated Scriptures

Old Testament statutes forbade the making of visual representations or idols. These laws, which if strictly obeyed would have inhibited the rise of Christian art, guided those who produced copies of Scripture for centuries. Egyptians of the fifteenth century B.C. illustrated their *Book of the Dead.* But in the great Mediterranean region that served as the "cradle of the Bible," scribes long considered it improper to include works of art within copies of Holy Writ. As a result, early development of now famous "illumination" of the Bible took place chiefly in regions far removed from Hebrew influence.

Latin *illuminare* ("to throw light upon," "to brighten") named the process of putting "little windows" into the pages of Scripture. At first these were confined chiefly to the elaboration of initial letters. Then the use of complex geometrical designs was added. Finally, tiny paintings or miniatures were included, depicting persons and events described in the sacred text. At its ultimate the movement produced numerous copies of the Bible in which concern for design, color, and overall beauty outweighed the aim of communicating the time-hallowed message.

As early as the seventh century Irish monks developed great skill in making elaborate borders, interlaced ribbons, intricate knots, spirals, zigzag patterns and delicate interwoven designs. These were painted with thick, bright pigments. A famous illuminated copy of the Gospels written in Celtic, the *Book of Kells,* is unbelievably intricate and brilliant. The *St. Gall Gospels,* also produced under Irish influence, took form about A.D. 750. During the next six centuries the art of illumination—including frequent use of gold leaf—flourished in Britain, France, Germany, and Italy.

No Bible produced south of the Alps ever quite matched the brilliant colors and endless variety of designs executed by Celtic penmen. But the popularity of illuminated Bibles increased throughout the Middle Ages. Today many individual sketches from such works are held by museums and libraries as valuable works of art.

A Famous German Book of Psalms

Even in the case of elaborately ornamented copies of Scripture, few of the many produced during the Middle Ages can be traced to individual scribes. An important exception is the case of a man whom his colleagues derided under the nickname of Big Lip, or Labeo.

Born about 952, Labeo Notker grew up in northern Switzerland and received an unusually good education. Much of his adult life was spent as an official, or magister, of the school at St. Gall. In cooperation with students who worked under him, he translated and transcribed many ancient works of literature. Each letter was carefully and precisely formed. But one important job he reserved for himself.

Using a Latin Bible as his guide, he rendered the psalms into Old High German. History does not say whether he was born with a protruding underlip or gained it during years of meticulous work while bent over sheets of parchment. Whatever the case, Big Lip fashioned a Bible portion so beautifully inscribed that it is famous in the history of bookmaking. Some admirers declare that calligraphy, or the art of hand-lettering, reached its zenith under his deft hand and that his Psalms is the most nearly perfect book ever produced. Mechanical limitations make it impossible for any printer to achieve the grace, symmetry, and sheer beauty of pages penned by the skilled hand of the tenth-century Swiss calligrapher.

Irish St. John with Pen and Ink

Just when men learned to make the first of modern writing instruments—the quill pen—no one knows. It greatly extended human capacity to transmit ideas across time and space by means of those abstract symbols that we today take for granted: letters, numerals, and words.

No fowl that was abundant in the ancient Mediterranean region provided a substantial quantity of stiff feathers with hornlike roots, so an informed guess links the gray goose of northern Europe with the biggest forward step in the preservation of ideas that was taken before the invention of the printing press. A sturdy old goose has many thick quills whose bases are firm, yet easily trimmed. The natural shape of the feather makes it a splendid container for a drop of ink.

We may not know whether or not it actually was the gray goose rather than some other fowl that helped boost man up the communication ladder or where the first quills were used, but there is no argument on one score. The world's oldest drawing of a scribe holding a quill pen and inkpot grew out of absorption with Scripture. An Irish Gospel produced about A.D. 800 is illustrated (or "illuminated") with a sketch showing the apostle John holding then-new writing instruments.

Two hundred years older than any other drawing in pen and ink, this rare sketch supports the view that monks who devoted great time and energy to copying Scripture discovered that goose feathers make writing instruments surpassed only by the products of modern technology.

Adoption of Lowercase Letters

Charlemagne became king of the Franks in A.D. 768 and emperor of the West in 800. He is best remembered for his brilliant military campaigns and for the skill with which he administered a vast and complex empire.

But his most lasting contribution to western civilization stemmed from his interest in Scripture and the manner in which copies of it were produced. Chiefly for the sake of encouraging and developing scribes who would fashion more and better Holy Books, the emperor founded a formal school in his palace at Aix-la-Chapelle. There was no study of penmanship, as such. Nor was there anything approaching a systematic attack upon the problems of communication by means of the written word. But the school that enjoyed royal patronage flourished and began to encourage experimentation. Until this time manuscripts (biblical and secular) were written in capital letters only—without spaces between words and with little or no punctuation. In this respect early medieval works were a great deal like the most ancient Hebrew scrolls that we know anything about. TOMODERNS APASSAGEWRITTENINTHISFASHIONISALMOSTILLEGIBLE. Charlemagne's scribes invented, or adopted and gave status to, the radical practice of also using small or lowercase letters. When they added to this the practice of leaving spaces between words and sentences, our modern form of writing was practically completed.

Though sizes and vogues in penmanship come and go and styles of type have changed considerably, no subsequent innovation in the manner of writing (and hence of printing) has been as sweeping as that fostered by scribes in the palace school of Charlemagne.

Medieval Libraries

Copies of the Bible, devotional manuals, lives of saints, and the works of great classical writers were the most common volumes found in medieval libraries. Some had substantial collections.

Working under a direct commission from the Emperor Charlemagne during the eighth century, the monk Alcuin copied the Latin Bible, or Vulgate, in such fashion that it became a famous museum piece. Like many others of his period, Alcuin divided each page into two columns—usually called rubrics because the first capital letter in each column was colored with *ruber,* a red pigment then highly prized.

Centuries earlier, monks in northern Italy had produced a copy of the Holy Book written in letters of silver (with an occasional letter of gold included) on crimson parchment. This noted Codex Argenteus, or Silver Book, was never intended to be used as a guide to the ways and will of God. Rather, it was one of the first exhibition Bibles —a remote ancestor of the ornate and expensive family Bible that is placed on display but seldom read.

Beginning in 1146 the library of Fleury, France, was financed partly by an imposed contribution—one of the earliest examples of tax support for the purchase of books. At Fulda, Germany, Abbot Sturmius (a protégé of Charlemagne) had funds enough to employ four hundred monks as copyists. Though such mammoth enterprises were rare, few monasteries or cathedral schools neglected the continuous production of the Bible in forms so elaborate that a man might spend his entire life working on a single copy.

Adventures of the Codex Aleppo

Early copies of the Scriptures were subject to all the accidents that now happen to printed books, plus a host of special perils. Many books were deliberately burned. Some were treated as booty of war. A few extravagantly expensive and beautiful ones were collected and hoarded not for their message but as objects of art.

In the entire history of the Bible, no individual copy is known to have experienced more adventures than the handwritten Codex Aleppo. Named because it was a treasure in the library of the synagogue in Aleppo, Turkey (modern Syria), from the fifteenth century until recent times, it is believed to date from about A.D. 900.

As in the case of other ancient Bibles, a definite date of production cannot be given. But it was already known and admired in the tenth century when Aaron ben Asher, a distinguished rabbi of the period, left a record of having read it from beginning to end. By now regarded as a treasure, it was purchased by a wealthy Jew who presented it to a synagogue in Jerusalem. Owners guarded it so jealously that the scroll was brought out for reading only three times a year—at the feasts of Passover, Pentecost, and Tabernacles.

In 1099 an army of Crusaders captured Jerusalem and seized many of its relics. Their leader was Baldwin I, Count of Flanders. He proclaimed himself king of Jerusalem—and took possession of the codex. Returned to the Jews seven years later, it somehow found its way to Cairo in the twelfth century. Three hundred years later it was a prized possession of the Jewish community of Aleppo, where it was reportedly lost when the synagogue was burned during a 1948 battle. Strangely rescued and smuggled into Israel, it now reposes in a vault in Jerusalem where accredited scholars may have access to it.

Wanted: A Mender of Psalms

Probably as a result of several separate sets of mechanical errors on the part of ancient scribes who copied Scripture by hand, not all present-day collections of the psalms are identical. Roman Catholic versions follow the division used in the oldest translation of the Old Testament—the Septuagint. Protestant versions follow the division used in Hebrew manuscripts of the ninth or tenth century A.D.

Hence, it's difficult for Protestants to follow Catholic citations of chapters and verses and clumsy for Catholics to trace Protestant references. No one knows just which psalms have been broken and which are whole, but the following table shows prevailing patterns:

Psalms as Divided in Catholic Bibles	Psalms as Divided in Protestant Bibles
1–8	1–8
9	9–10
10–112	11–113
113	114–15
114–15	116
116–45	117–46
146–47	147
148–50	148–50

Though the total is the same and numbers correspond for about two thirds of the individual psalms, the book itself is hopelessly scrambled. Due to the unmatched impact of the King James Version upon the English-speaking world, the psalm numbered twenty-two in most Catholic Bibles is all but universally called the twenty-third psalm.

Twelfth-Century Assembly Line

Principles basic to the modern assembly line were employed in Bible manufacture more than five hundred years before the industrial revolution.

Very early, heads of large religious institutions began including a scriptorium, or writing room, in each complex of buildings. By the middle of the twelfth century there were scores of them scattered over Europe. Though the number of workers varied from two or three in the case of a remote outpost of the church to as many as fifty or sixty in the case of a flourishing abbey, general practices were about the same everywhere. One monk read slowly and carefully from a copy of the Bible while his fellows transcribed the message word for word.

Any time a scribe was assigned to other duties or died, another took his place and started where he left off.

Mass-produced in this fashion, the Bible was more widely and generally accessible before the invention of printing than is commonly thought.

The Codex Alexandrinus

Early in his reign, King Charles I of England received a strange gift. Sent by Cyril Lucaris, patriarch of the Greek Church in Constantinople, it was calculated to cement friendship between his own people and those of Britain.

The Greek Bible, inscribed by hand in uncial fashion (using capital letters only), arrived too late; translators of the King James Version did not have access to it. Their interpretation was already in print and was in the process of becoming "frozen" as a result. Still the Codex Alexandrinus was quickly recognized to be five hundred to a thousand years older than any manuscript previously available to European scholars. Probably produced in or near Alexandria sometime during the fifth century, it varies from later copies in many respects. Twentieth-century translators have been influenced by its text at many points because it is the third oldest whole Bible in existence. Only the Codex Vaticanus and the Codex Sinaiticus antedate it. It remained the property of the British ruler until George II presented it to the nation.

Important as it has proved in the development of the modern Bible, the ancient book that King Charles couldn't read proved the undoing of Lucaris. Enemies who hadn't begun to catch the ecumenical spirit accused him of leaning toward Protestantism and persuaded their sultan to put him to death on charges of instigating rebellion among the Cossacks.

Wycliffe's Work Printed as a Monument

John Wycliffe's pioneer translation of the Bible launched a chain reaction that hasn't yet ended: the circulation of Scripture intended for use by common folk rather than students of classical languages. Yet the epoch-making version that appeared about 1380 circulated only in manuscript for more than four hundred years.

A great many handwritten copies of Wycliffe's translation were made. For long periods they were forbidden books which might cost a man his life, yet about two hundred copies, complete or partial, are still in existence.

It wasn't until 1850 that a printed edition of the entire Wycliffe Bible was issued—as a historical monument. For by the time admirers finally got around to setting the words and phrases of the great translator into print, the English language had changed so greatly that only specialists were able to decipher the old Book.

One factor that entered into the incredibly long delay was the spread of the printing industry itself. Progress on the continent of Europe was much more rapid than in England, where nothing was printed before 1477, when Wycliffe's Bible had been circulating for nearly a century. Tyndale and other followers of Wycliffe who got their Scripture translations into print did so by taking their manuscripts to publishing houses in Germany, Holland, and France.

By the time it got into print, Wycliffe's work was for practical purposes unintelligible. It is possible to get the meaning of Job 35:11, where he speaks of "the bestis of the erthe, the foulis of heuene." But a line such as Rom. 14:4 practically defies interpretation by the non-specialist; there Wycliffe reports Paul as saying: "And to hym that worchith mede is not arettid bi grace, but bi dette."

Oldest Known Copy of Isaiah

Until the present generation no biblical manuscript in Hebrew fully deserved to be called ancient. According to Werner Keller in *The Bible as History,* Greek manuscripts antedated the oldest known Hebrew one (the Codex Petropolitanus, dating from about A.D. 916) by about five hundred years. This strange absence of truly old copies can be explained partly by the ravages of time, and partly by the fact that Jews often buried worn copies of Scripture so that no profane eyes would chance to see the name of the Lord.

Time rolled backward in 1947. That year a leather scroll of Isaiah was found in a cave near the Dead Sea. Surprisingly well preserved, it measured about eighteen feet in length by one foot in width. Some of the first scholars who examined it dismissed it as a comparatively late copy; others insisted that it was so old that it made all other portions of Scripture seem modern by comparison.

After a heated debate linguists and archaeologists found more and more evidence pointing in the direction of the second conclusion. After years of study, it is now generally agreed that this copy of Isaiah is approximately a thousand years older than previously-known Hebrew manuscripts. This means that its ancient characters were carefully inscribed at least a century before the birth of Christ.

Almost completely legible after more than two thousand years, this recently found manuscript establishes beyond any question the fact that scribes who copied Scripture by hand were astonishingly accurate. They transmitted lengthy documents across periods of centuries with fewer errors than those made by a modern secretary in transcribing one day's correspondence by means of a dictating machine and an electric typewriter.

Trials and Triumphs of Translators

Scripture Used for Military Purposes

His identity is somewhat a mystery, but in the eleventh century a pioneer scholar-churchman of Britain retold many biblical stories in the language of his people with the hope that readers would become better warriors.

Aelfric, called the Grammarian, has been identified with three men known to have borne that name: the Archbishop of Canterbury, the Archbishop of York, and the Bishop of Crediton. Regardless of his exact office in the church, Aelfric was an ardent patriot.

Danish invaders had made a few coastal raids in the years from 978 to 991. They met little resistance. So in 991 a large fleet of Vikings came ashore in Essex and pillaged much of the district north of the Thames River. King Ethelred II made no effort to drive off the invaders; instead he paid them a bribe of ten thousand pounds of silver in exchange for their promise to leave his dominion. They kept their promise, but soon returned in larger numbers.

Alarmed and incensed, Aelfric set out to stir up a fighting spirit in the people of Britain. From the Old Testament and the Apocrypha he selected Joshua, Judith, Maccabees, and other warlike books. Then he rendered these stories into the language of his countrymen—not attempting exact translations, but shaping paraphrased versions that suited his purposes.

Manuscript copies of these rough Scripture portions were circulated for military motives, but they failed to achieve their purpose. In spite of the enthusiasm aroused by the patriotic stories of Scripture, many Englishmen gave up the struggle. Sweyn of Denmark was proclaimed king of England in 1012, and Ethelred fled to the continent for a brief period of refuge; he then returned and resumed the throne.

Ulfilas Among the Goths

Ulfilas, or Little Wolf, himself probably a Goth, served as a bishop to the Visigoths in the region beyond the Danube River from A.D. 341 to 348. With the permission of the Emperor Constantine he then settled near Nicopolis and made the earliest Bible translation into a north-European tongue. Using Greek letters and Gothic runes as raw materials, he is credited with being the first man in history deliberately to devise an entirely new alphabet for use by persons who had no written language.

Once his alphabet was completed, Ulfilas translated portions of

Scripture into Gothic. The remaining fragments of his translation are the oldest surviving literary work in any Teutonic language. Because he feared that accounts of ancient battles would stir his warlike readers to take up arms, he omitted I and II Kings from his work, which was finished in 380. Some copies made in the fifth and sixth centuries were lavishly elaborate; one of them, containing portions of all four Gospels, is written on purple vellum in large gold and silver letters.

As rendered by him into "the barbaric tongue of the north" (and altered to conform to modern ways of writing), the Lord's Prayer reads:

> Atta unsar thu in himinam. Weihnai namo thein. Quimai thiudinassus theins. Wairthai wilja theins. Swe in himina jah and airthai. Hlaif unsarana thana sinteinan gif uns himmadago. Jah aflet uns thatei skulans sijaima, swaswe jah weis afletam thaim skulam unsaraim. Jah ni briggais uns in fraistubujai. Ak lausei uns af thamma ubilin, unte theina ist thiudangardi, jah maths, jah wulthus in aiwins.

Ulfilas' language, itself greatly influenced by the grammatical structure of New Testament Greek, contributed mightily to later Teutonic tongues. But like many other early languages, in the form he used it Gothic has become obsolete and is no longer spoken or written.

Scripture Conquers Rome's Conquerors

Both professional and amateur historians have devoted a great deal of time to speculating about factors underlying the fall of the Roman Empire. Few of them have noticed that the conquerors from the north were themselves conquered—by Latin, the language then used for the Christian Scriptures.

In *The Story of Language,* Mario Pei underscores this paradox. Normally, says he, military victors impose their patterns of speech upon peoples whom they subdue. Why, then, did Germanic invaders who became masters of the Roman Empire adopt the language used by those whom they conquered?

According to the Italian-born linguist, "There is only one answer, one so obvious that it is often rejected." Moving into southern Europe in successive waves, the Germanic invaders became converts to Christianity. This meant that they adopted the Bible as their holy book, and the Bible then commonly circulated was written in Latin. "Adoption of the religion carried with it adoption of the language indissolubly bound with that religion," Pei concludes.

If this line of reasoning is correct, it means that the early translation of the Scriptures into Latin was the most important molding factor in the history of western speech. For when scriptural Latin conquered the conquerors of Rome, the future development of Spanish, French, German, English, and other European languages was profoundly affected.

Stalin's Bible-shaped Language

Though Joseph Stalin made it illegal to print the Bible in Russia, Scripture was the most potent single factor shaping the native language of the Communist leader.

Hundreds of tongues and dialects, some of them transmitted orally for centuries, had no corresponding written languages until such became necessary for the translation of the Bible. That was the case with the tongue Stalin learned as a child growing up in the shop of a shoemaker near Tiflis, Georgia.

An independent kingdom of Transcaucasia for more than two thousand years, Georgia was first called Karthili or Karthveli. Ancient Persians knew it as Gurjistan. Greeks and Romans called it Iberia. Alexander the Great conquered the vast, remote region but was unable to keep control of it. This pattern was repeated in the case of the Roman general Pompey (65 B.C.) and the emperor Trajan (A.D. 114). Today this region is the Soviet republic Georgia.

About the middle of the third century the son of a Persian king married the daughter of a Georgian ruler and gained control of the land. This man, Miriani, erected the first Christian church in Georgia on the site later occupied by the famous cathedral of Mtskhet. Christianity grew slowly at first, but by the fifth century it had so many adherents that missionaries reduced the Georgian language to writing and produced a Bible as its first document. Naturally the Book in turn affected the future development of Georgian. It was within the context of this Bible-guided tongue, comparatively stable as languages go, that Joseph Stalin grew up late in the nineteenth century.

The Lindisfarne Gospels

Bede, one of the earliest of English historians and theologians, is believed to have lived in the approximate period of A.D. 673 to 735. He is often referred to as "the Venerable Bede," not because he lived to old age but because his scholarly works deserve respect, or veneration.

Abundant evidence indicates that Bede succeeded in translating large portions of the Bible into his native tongue, Anglo-Saxon. References to this early work and quotations from it are so numerous that it clearly exerted a wide and important influence. But since long-lasting writing materials were scarce and early forms of paper didn't survive long in damp, cold Britain, no complete version of the Bible in Anglo-Saxon was ever made.

At Lindisfarne Abbey the monks—who probably borrowed heavily from Bede's translation without acknowledging their source—worked out a splendid shortcut. They took a beautifully written copy of the Gospels in Latin and scribbled Anglo-Saxon equivalents above the lines. Now in the British Museum, the Lindisfarne Gospels are the nearest surviving approach to a Bible penned by hand in Anglo-Saxon during centuries when writing materials were scarce and costly.

Scriptural "cribs" produced at Lindisfarne later proved invaluable in reconstructing the Anglo-Saxon vocabulary, for frugal monks put native terms just above the Latin originals in such fashion that many are matched almost as though in a deliberately planned lexicon. Lacking this vital set of clues, scholars would have found the task of deciphering secular Anglo-Saxon literature all but insuperable. As rendered into Anglo-Saxon, the brief injunction of John 6:23 reads: "Neh oaer stoue oaer zeeton baet bread"; with the exception of "bread" the words are as strange as though they came from a language having no connection with English.

Caedmon, Illiterate Poet

A herdsman of the seventh century with no formal education had a strange knack for rendering the prose of Scripture into verse. As a result of the Bible's impact upon his life, Caedmon produced the earliest surviving literary work known with certainty to have been composed on English soil.

According to the ancient account by Bede, Caedmon frequently visited an abbey at the time of Bible reading and hymn singing. He was so awkward he couldn't take his turn when the harp was passed to him and so sensitive that he often fled from the company in shame. Once when he had done this, he fell asleep in a stall nearby. In a vision he was commanded to sing; he objected that he could not and explained that he had left the table for that reason. "Sing for me though," came the command; "sing the creation." On the spot, Caedmon rendered part of the Genesis story into verse.

When he told his experience and recited his lines, the abbess Hilda and her learned men tested him and found that though he could not read he could spontaneously produce poetry from Scripture passages read to him. Educated men transcribed Caedmon's lines, sometimes using dialects that differed from his own. One notable early manuscript survives. It contains Genesis (2,935 lines); Exodus (589 lines); Daniel (765 lines); and Christ and Satan (733 lines).

Erasmus Wrestles with the Trinity

Gerhard Gerhards, better known to history as Erasmus, performed a notable work of scholarship by editing the text of the Greek New Testament. But in the process of seeing two editions through the press he also set off a controversy that has continued to the present.

In preparing the first edition of his Greek New Testament in 1516, the Dutch scholar used the best and oldest manuscripts available to him. For purposes of scholarship he compared Latin and Greek versions by printing them in parallel columns. Ancient copies did not include at I John 5:7 a reference to the Trinity, standard in medieval copies of the Latin Vulgate. Guided by the principle that the oldest copies of a work, frequently transcribed by hand, are likely to be closer to the original than later copies, Erasmus omitted from the Greek side of his New Testament the allusion familiar to readers of the Latin Bible. The use of parallel columns made the omission immediately obvious.

This created a great storm of protest. Dignitaries of the church threatened severe consequences if he did not reinstate the missing words. Erasmus promised that he would restore them if a Greek manuscript could be found which included them. The libraries of Europe were combed. As a result, not one but two Greek New Testaments were produced that conformed to the familiar Latin Version. Both of these manuscripts were very late; Erasmus yielded, however, and in his second edition of 1519 made the Greek text conform to the Latin known everywhere in that period.

In producing the first printed New Testament in English, William Tyndale relied upon the Greek text of Erasmus—and used the edition of 1519 rather than that of 1516. As a result, until recent times all English Bibles included a reference that scholars know was not a part of the earliest New Testaments. For the sake of accuracy the debated verse was dropped from the English Revised Version of 1881. Confronted with the dilemma of having no seventh verse, editors of that version solved the problem by splitting the sixth verse of I John 5 and numbering the second half of it as verse 7. As late as 1946 when the Revised Standard Version continued this practice, the editors were attacked for having taken liberties with Holy Writ.

Martin Luther, Fugitive

Martin Luther's initial work upon his epoch-making German New Testament was carried out in a setting that had many ingredients of a modern spy novel. Though some persons supported him in 1521, many others considered him the most dangerous man in Germany. With his life in danger, he became a fugitive—hiding from the soldiers of the emperor in the grim castle-fortress of Wartburg.

Luther's room was small and cold. It contained only a bed, chest, table, and chair. With him the reformer brought writing supplies and a musical instrument—his lute. He secured a copy of the Bible and began the formidable task of rendering it into the everyday language of his contemporaries.

During the period of long daily work on his translation, Luther occasionally wrote letters to his friends, but because there was danger that they might be intercepted, he always gave a false return address. Isle of Patmos and the Wilderness were two of his favorites.

News of his hiding place filtered out, however. In a bold attempt to deceive his enemies, the translator wrote a fraudulent letter and contrived to have it lost in such fashion that it would be found by the authorities. "I hear that people are saying that Luther is in the Wartburg near Eisenach," he began. "They probably think so because I was once captured in the woods thereabouts. But here I am, safe and sound! It is strange that no one thinks of looking for me in Bohemia"

Precisely what role this phony epistle played the meager records of the period do not say. But the whole world knows that despite popes, emperors, and kings, Luther not only completed his work of translation but lived to see his German Bible hailed as a landmark of literature and scholarship.

Luther's Vivid German Bible

Martin Luther's basic goal in translating the Bible into German was that of making God's word available in words men use every day. He succeeded so well that his book had the effect of making Germany the first heavily populated modern nation to adopt one dominant language in lieu of a cluster of regional dialects.

Greek came comparatively easy for the reformer; he succeeded in rendering the entire New Testament into vigorous and idiomatic German in just eleven weeks. This quickly produced first draft was later thoroughly revised; still, the entire task was accomplished with ease and speed. Hebrew was a different matter. He enlisted scholarly friends and worked nine years on the Old Testament. Once he considered giving up the job. "How hard it is to make these Hebrew writers talk German!" he exclaimed. But he stayed with the task. His complete German Bible of 1534 even included the books of the Apocrypha, placed between the Old and the New Testaments.

Luther did everything in his power to make his translation vivid and forceful. He visited the slaughter house and watched a butcher kill several rams so he could learn the names of the animal's parts for use in describing Old Testament ceremonies. He made notes about the effects of a thunderstorm so he could enter the mood of psalm 29. He rejected learned words in favor of those used in everyday speech.

His translation into High German (speech of the southern highlands) was so successful that it became used throughout the nation. For the first time in the story of mankind, most members of a large language group were simultaneously exposed to a single book in their native tongue. As a result, regional differences in spelling and grammatical style gradually diminished. Low German (speech of the northern lowlands) dwindled in importance along with Hessian, Westphalian, and Bavarian dialects. Luther's similes and metaphors became idiomatic phrases, not simply among a small circle of scholars but throughout Germany. East, west, north, and south, "Luther's German" became the national tongue. Friedrich Klopstock, celebrated eighteenth-century German poet, surveyed the literary influence of Luther through his New Testament and concluded that "among no people has one man done so much to create their language."

Luther Tampers with the Text

Scribal changes in handwritten manuscripts, whether accidental or intentional, affected the text of many ancient books and scrolls. It isn't so well known, however, that the advent of the printing press didn't stop the operation of this human factor. Even Luther knowingly inserted some words and dropped others in order to strengthen the support for his own theological views.

Though Luther made a great many such changes in the text of printed Scripture, the most notable of them involves a single word—"alone." Rendering Rom. 3:28, he deliberately lengthened the phrase "man is justified by faith" to make it read "man is justified by faith alone." This modification, trifling in terms of size, had monumental impact. Luther and his followers held justification by faith as one of their main tenants. This was a shorthand way of asserting that man is made just or holy not by his own effort, but by the redemptive work of Jesus Christ.

Challenged about his treatment of Holy Writ—which came very close to outright tampering—Luther was quick to defend himself. "We do not have to inquire of the literal Latin, how we are to speak German," he retorted. "Rather we must inquire about this of the mother in the home, the children in the street, and the common man in the marketplace so that they will read with understanding."

Present-day translators underscore Luther's principle of translating to meet the vocabulary and needs of readers rather than rendering Hebrew and Greek into another language in stilted word-for-word fashion. But from the King James Version through the New English Bible, no important English translation of Rom. 3:28 retains the language of Luther, exponent of justification by faith *alone*.

Luther's New Testament Breaks All Records

Today it is the dream of every author, editor, translator, and publisher to hit the best-seller list. Few who strive for it know that Martin Luther conceived and executed the first best seller—and didn't receive a penny for his work on it.

His translation of the New Testament into German rolled from the press of Melchior Lotther in September, 1522, and found a Bible-hungry nation waiting. At least eighteen earlier German-language editions of Scripture had been published; still, Luther's caught the imagination of the public. Within two months after it appeared, five thousand copies had been sold. The cost of the volume—illustrated with twenty-two woodcuts from the studio of Lucas Cranach—was 1½ guilders, about one month's salary for a university professor.

During the next ten years approximately eighty-five editions appeared. Before the middle of the century nearly five hundred whole or partial editions of his work were issued. In the city of Wittenberg alone, at least sixty editions of about two thousand copies each were issued before 1600. Using the slow hand-operated equipment of the time, one printer, Hans Lufft, achieved the dream of many modern publishers with high-speed automatic machinery: the production of about 100,000 copies of a single book.

With minor revisions the book is still in print. But before the death of Luther in 1546 authorized and pirated editions put at least 750,000 whole or partial copies on the market. This was in a period when a printer-publisher considered a book to be highly successful if sales reached a total of five or six thousand copies. Within a few decades, Luther's translation was rendered into Dutch, English, Swedish, Hungarian, Danish, Lithuanian, and Polish, as well as the dialects used in Rumania, Bohemia, and Slovenia.

Archaic Language in a Catholic Translation

Contrary to surface impressions, the famous Rheims-Douai Version does not report a case in which men starved but women did not. In 1578 when Gregory Martin began translating the Old Testament at the rate of two chapters a day, the language he used was radically different from that of modern America and England.

"The bread is spent in our males," he wrote in I Kings 9:7. But in doing so he was not referring to the stomachs of men. Rather, he employed the current term for a leather bag or pouch used for storing and transporting provisions. As late as 1654 English law required a postman always "to have in readiness one good Horse or Mare to receive and carry the Male of Letters." Numbered I Sam. 9:7 in the King James Version, the reference reads "vessels" rather than "males."

Striving to render the story of Saul's long search for his father's lost asses into modern English for Catholic readers, Ronald Knox discarded both "male" and its later form "mail" and has the once perplexing sentence read: "No bread left in our wallets, not even a basket of food to offer!"

Punctuation of the King James Version

Acts 21 is the only major section of the Bible that ends with a comma. In the King James Version the long chapter about Paul's arrival in Jerusalem concludes with a dangling comma: "And when there was made a great silence, he spake unto them in the Hebrew tongue, saying,"

Numerous individual verses end with commas and some with colons. Exclamation points and question marks are abundant as indicators that verses are concluded, but are infrequent at the ends of chapters, yet the book of Jonah ends with a question mark.

Practically all twentieth-century translations and versions depart from the earlier pattern of Acts 21 in order to close the chapter with a period.

John Eliot's Bible for the Indians

John Eliot is famous as the translator who issued a Bible no living person can read. Working with tribesmen who spoke a Massachusetts dialect of the Algonquian Indian tongue, he published a New Testament for them in 1661. Two years later he brought out the Old Testament in their language. Several natives, among whom Cockenoe the interpreter was most important, assisted in the work.

This became the first Bible printed anywhere in the western hemisphere and was issued from the press of Samuel Green, Cambridge, Massachusetts, in an edition of about one thousand copies, of which twenty were formally dedicated to King Charles II. Approximately fifty copies of Eliot's Bible have been preserved, but no one can read it because tribesmen who spoke the language it employs have become extinct. A few words have been identified by scholars, however. Eliot rendered the phrase "kneeling down to him" (Mark 1:40) by a thirty-four letter word: Wutteppesittukgussunnoowehtunkquoh.

Though that word didn't survive, at least one of Eliot's is still in use. For the title "duke" (chief) that appears in Gen. 36:40-43 he substituted the native title "mugwump." Used as a slogan in several famous political campaigns, it is still included in the English dictionary as a label for a chieftain or person of importance.

Eliot placed Psalms after the New Testament under the title "Wame Ketoohomae Uketoohomaongash David," or "All the Singing Songs of David." In 1966 one copy of his Bible sold at auction for $43,000—more money than the missionary-translator made in his entire life.

Nonliteral Translation

One of the greatest obstacles encountered by Bible translators centers in the fact that some languages have no equivalents for words in others. Martin Luther was unable to avoid this issue when he rendered the Bible from Hebrew, Greek, and Latin into German. Many names of animals in the older languages were obscure or confusing: tragelaphus, oryx, mygale, pygargus, and camelopardus, for example. In some instances he deliberately substituted the name of a familiar creature for one with which he was not acquainted; since neither he nor other sixteenth-century Germans knew anything about the chameleon, he substituted the name of a familiar animal—the weasel.

Among the Bulu of Africa, there is no term for trust or holy, while righteousness can only be rendered as "straightness" and grace as "kindness." Valiente tribesmen of Panama know nothing of a Holy Spirit; the only varieties that they can name in their language are the tree spirit, house spirit, and long-armed monkey spirit.

Oceania's Ponape tongue has no word for father, but includes four or five different ways of saying brother. And because Barrow Eskimos do not keep sheep, this central animal of the Bible cannot be named in versions for their use. As a result, Ps. 100:3 in the Barrow Bible reads: "We are his people, and the woolly goats of his pasture." Instead of following familiar English usage and calling Jesus Christ "the lamb of God," among these people early missionaries referred to the Saviour as a seal pup.

Complexities of Primitive Languages

Missionaries and translators, chiefly working as agents of Bible societies, have taken the Scriptures to many cultural groups whose members had no written language or even alphabets. The reduction of a spoken language to writing is an extremely complex task—especially in the case of tongues where tonal values affect meaning.

"Ma ma ma ma ma" can be pronounced so that it is a complete sentence in the Shan language of Burma. With a different tone on each syllable it means: "Help the horse! A mad dog comes!"

Among the Valiente tribesmen of Panama changes in emphasis upon the *o* in *ko* can make the word mean: time, place, year, name, line, oil, or tied string. In the Red Bobo language of Upper Volta, *la* indicates take, deer, lion, together, or eat—depending upon the tone used.

Attempts to reduce tonal variations to writing create all but insurmountable problems for printers and proofreaders. In Quechua, the native tongue of vast numbers of Indians in the Andes of South America, *ca* means grind-stone; *c'a* indicates better, *ka* stands for if, and *k'a* means boys.

Sequoya's System of Writing

Though portions of the Bible have been translated into more than 1,200 languages, only one New Testament has been printed in a system of writing devised by a member of a primitive tribe. Sequoya, a Cherokee known to white men as George Gist or George Guess, was troubled by the fact that his people had no way to put their words into writing. About 1821 he completed work on a set of eighty-six characters that represented all the sounds in the Cherokee tongue.

Many of his symbols were borrowed directly from the English alphabet and others were adapted from it. Grateful tribesmen of the Cherokee General Council presented him with a silver medal in 1823. His "alphabet" (actually a syllabary) was quickly adopted and proved very successful. Used for printing the Cherokee constitution and briefly for a weekly newspaper, *The Phoenix,* it was later employed—unchanged—by translators who wished to make the gospel story available to Cherokees who read no English.

Tribal Customs Modify Text

A famous and much quoted promise attributed to Jesus has been deliberately mistranslated in Bibles designed for use by the Zanaki people of Tanganyika. Among these tribesmen honest men attract attention by standing outside doors and calling the names of those inside. Only thieves knock—so if they hear movement in response to their sounds they can run before they are seen.

This cultural context created problems in the case of Rev. 3:20: "Behold, I stand at the door, and knock." Translators finally resolved the difficulty by revising language to fit tribal customs: "Behold, I stand at the door, and call."

Those Troublesome Maritime Terms

Maritime terms in the Bible—numerous, vivid, and varied—have had tremendous effect upon the thought of most western nations. Many of the great hymns of Christendom are based upon nautical metaphors which in turn are rooted in Scripture. In landlocked cultures without experience with ships and seas, great difficulties have been faced by missionary-translators who have tried to render passages such as John 21:6. "And he said unto them, Cast the net on the right side of the ship, and ye shall find."

In the case of the Mossi people, who live on the fringes of the Sahara Desert, white men quickly found that they were not communicating when they talked about "an anchor of the soul, both sure and stedfast" (Heb. 6:19). So it was necessary to find an appropriate cultural substitute. The tribal practice of staking out horses and cattle at night, securing them by means of picketing pegs, offered such a substitute. Hence, they grasped meanings that go deeper than words when translators discarded maritime terms and wrote of "a sure and steadfast picketing peg for the soul."

Some Monumental Boners

Italian translators of Scripture have coined a phrase they use so often it has become proverbial. *"Traduttore—traditore,"* they say: "A translator is a traitor." The significance of this verdict is most dramatically underscored when rendering Holy Writ into a non-European tongue. An error of a single letter or one trifling mark above or below the line can transform an entire phrase or sentence.

A missionary to central Africa thought he was urging his readers to "enter the kingdom of heaven," but he actually insisted: "Go sit on a stick!" In an early Solomon Island translation of Ps. 104:11, the phrase "the wild asses quench their thirst" ended up meaning "the cannibal pigs drink water to stop hiccoughs." Translating the Beatitudes into an Indian dialect of South America, the scholar who pondered the word *bienaventurados* (blessed, fortunate, lucky) missed subtle shades of meaning. As a result, his version of this scriptural passage promises: "Lucky in gambling are the poor in spirit . . . ; Lucky in gambling are those who mourn. . . ."

A translator into an Eskimo dialect did his best with "nation shall rise against nation" (Mark 13:8) but later found he'd made an error of one letter in a seventeen-letter word so that his readers were actually being told that "a pair of snowshoes shall rise up against a pair of snowshoes."

Rendering Mark 1:7 into the Maquiritare language of Venezuela, a translator couldn't discover an exact equivalent for "worthy." So he chose the closest synonym he knew—a common term for "greater." But he failed to reckon with connotations of the term, and as a result tribesmen took his words to mean that Jesus was so huge that John couldn't remove his shoes. Yet the biggest of all boners in translation is probably that of the missionary to the Congo who thought he was referring to "five loaves and two fishes" but actually wrote "five loaves and two elephants"—enough food, the delighted natives concluded, to provide a feast for an entire tribe.

Deliberate Departure from Literal Meaning

It would be futile for some language versions to urge readers, "Thou shalt love the Lord thy God with all thy heart" (Luke 10:27). Natives of the Marshall Islands in the West Pacific, for example, love with their throats. Kanhobels of Guatemala declare that a person loves with his abdomen, and the Karrés of equatorial Africa love with their livers.

To tribesmen of Amazon jungles, where rain is a curse and not a blessing, it is impossible to be literal and still make sense of the promise that God "sendeth rain on the just and on the unjust" (Matt. 5:45). Bano'o people of Cameroun in west Africa left early missionaries speechless by insisting that they *wanted* to go to hell if it is a hot place, for they spend their lives in dread of chilling winds that bring suffering and sickness.

European readers seldom notice the phrase "taste of death" (Matt. 16:28; Mark 9:1; Luke 9:27; John 8:52; Heb. 2:9), but the Cashibo of Peru, only a few decades removed from cannibalism, would take this as a reference to eating human flesh if it were translated for them in literal fashion. Congo tribesmen who learned of Paul's suggestion that a Christian should heap coals of fire upon the head of his enemy (Rom. 12:20) were delighted. "What a marvelous way to torture people to death!" they exclaimed.

Hebrew and English Compared

The transcription of Hebrew letters into English ones is a cumbersome and awkward job. To make matters worse, two out of the twenty-two letters originally used in writing the Old Testament have no English equivalents.

Aleph, the first letter of the Hebrew alphabet, is a visual symbol that signifies a complicated form of glottal stop involving the glottis, or space between the human vocal fold and cartilage of the larynx. Children who hear that sound from infancy find it easy to imitate. But persons reared in cultures that do not employ it in speech find *aleph* difficult or impossible to form. *Ayin,* the sixteenth letter of the Hebrew alphabet, indicates a sound that is a bit closer to one employed in present-day speech—a guttural *g*.

Typographical barriers are equally high. Instead of being represented by a letter of the English alphabet, *aleph* is indicated by the symbol '. A single quotation mark curving in the opposite direction represents *ayin*. For scholars and linguists these oral and typographical comparisons are obviously inadequate—offering proof positive that it is literally impossible to effect exact reproduction in English of ancient Hebrew verbal symbols.

Words That Won't Stand Still

Rapid cultural changes have made it all but impossible for translators to frame a fixed version of one of the most quoted chapters in the Bible.

Several early versions used "charity" to render the complex pattern of ideas signified by the key word in the Greek original of I Corinthians 13. Almost before the ink was dry on pages spinkled with that word, "charity" had shifted in meaning to stand for almsgiving and benevolence to the poor. Hence many twentieth-century translators dropped that term and in its place used "love." This transition was barely accomplished before "love" came to be so strongly associated with lust and the Hollywood view of sex that many Bible readers think a new and different word will have to be found or invented to express Paul's original meaning.

Connotations of the term "bowels" have changed almost as radically. Translators of the King James Version have Paul affirming that "God is my record, how greatly I long after you all in the bowels of Jesus Christ" (Phil. 1:8). In Today's English Version, that ejaculation is rendered: "God knows that I tell the truth when I say that my deep feeling for you comes from the heart of Christ Jesus himself."

Though most vivid and abundant in English, instances in which words refuse to stand still can be found in practically all languages. A century ago the Van Dyke translation of the Arabic Bible was considered to be one of the finest works in existence. Now it is losing force because the Arabic language is changing so rapidly. In 1866 *dabbabat* (Gen. 1:25) meant "creeping thing"; to the average Arab reader today it means "armored tank."

Complicated Patterns of Speech

Bible translators working in "primitive" cultures have frequently found themselves dealing with languages more complex than any used by advanced nations. One language used in the Sudan, Africa, has fourteen vowels—more than twice the number in English.

In the Cakchiquel dialect of Guatemala any verb may have some 100,000 possible forms because of the variety of particles which may be added to its root. As if this were not enough of a complication, each of the fourteen vowels of Cakchiquel can be used in three lengths with two emphases on three different levels—making a total of 14x3x2x3 or 252 vowel possibilities.

James Evans' Printing Materials

James Evans, an early missionary to the Cree Indians of North America, probably used the crudest materials ever employed in publishing an edition of Scripture. Working hundreds of miles from costal centers and having no access to paper or printer's ink, he determined to do the best he could with what he found at hand.

A fiercely warlike tribe of Algonquian stock, the Crees ranged through much of the region east of the Great Lakes. They had no written language. Evans, who had no formal training in linguistics, devised a simple set of code symbols to designate major syllables in the Cree tongue. Instead of adapting letters of the English alphabet, he combined triangles, circles, and dots to form most of his patterns.

Then he built a crude printing press by hand and set out to impart the Word of God to a few tribesmen who had learned his system of symbols. Since he could not get ink, Evans mixed whale oil with soot. And because paper was unobtainable, he cut thin sheets from the inside of birch bark.

Scripture printed through Evans' labors failed to have any appreciable effect upon the Cree way of life. Warriors remained constantly on the warpath against white settlers and refused to settle their quarrels with the Sioux and Blackfeet. As a result by 1900 the once flourishing tribe was reduced to about fifteen thousand members, living chiefly in Manitoba, Canada. No copy of the Scripture so laboriously produced for their conversion has been preserved.

For the Benefit of Indians in Brooklyn

Though there isn't an Indian teepee in all Brooklyn, one of the most recent Bible translations into a North American language was made for the benefit of New Yorkers. So many Iroquois Indians lived in Brooklyn in 1942 that the American Bible Society issued the Gospel of Luke translated into their native tongue.

Officials of the society presented the first copy off the press to a parish in Brooklyn. In gratitude, a group of housewives and industrial workers pulled their tribal regalia out of closets and dressed as braves and squaws for a ceremonial visit to Bible House.

Seven Hundred Written Languages Produced

To an extent that is immeasurably greater than that of any other book or body of literature, the Bible has fostered world literacy. Since the time of Ulfilas in the fourth century, missionary-evangelists have been busy reducing spoken languages to writing in order that Scripture may be made available to persons in their native tongues. At least seven hundred written languages have been created in this fashion. Some of them serve only a handful of persons; others, such as the Chiluba tongue spoken in the Congo, claim several million adherents.

Most Confused Speech Patterns

There is a common but mistaken notion that Bible translators have experienced their greatest troubles in Africa, with its approximately eight hundred languages. Not so. Even the Dark Continent never offered the linguistic hodgepodge that still prevails in much of Latin America.

Experts say that in the southern part of Mexico alone, a translator trying to express to natives what Jesus said is confronted by as many diverse language families and types of structure as in the whole of Africa. Fifty-one different languages have won official recognition in the statistics of the Mexican government, and at least two hundred more are recognized by various South American nations. Bolivian Quechua has more than two million speakers, but many tongues and dialects are spoken by members of only one or two small tribes.

Scripture portions intended for use by members of such groups are often printed in their native language with the Spanish equivalent included in parallel columns or at the bottoms of pages.

Modern Work of Jewish Scholarship

In its earliest form Scripture was made up of only five books. Now grouped at the beginning of the Old Testament, this collection is often called the Pentateuch, from the Greek word for five. Ancient Jews knew it as the Torah—or Book of the Law.

A modern-language translation of the Torah, or "Five Books of Moses," was issued by the Jewish Translation Society of America in 1962. Scholars who prepared this new version of the first book that played the role of the modern Bible departed widely from now familiar versions.

For the convenience of readers who wish to make cross-references, the generally accepted chapter and verse numbers are noted. But they are not strictly followed in the translation since scholars who prepared it insisted that medieval Christians sometimes joined or separated the wrong paragraphs, sentences, or even parts of sentences.

But to the long-time Bible reader perhaps the most striking feature of this vivid Jewish work is the disappearance of "and" from many, many sentences. Hebrews used the particle *waw* to mean "and," but they also employed it to indicate "but," "yet," "when," "however," and other shades of meaning. Early English translators, by no means masters of the subtleties involved in the ancient text, almost always bypassed other connotations of *waw* in favor of the simple "and." That's why it appears so frequently and in such monotonous fashion in most English translations made prior to this century.

Traditions Folktales and Hocum

No Support for Racial Prejudice

A persistent and widespread legend makes a son of Noah the ancestor of all black men and the source of their oppression during most of recorded history. Not only is there no shred of evidence to support the view that this patriarch was the first Negro; Scripture nowhere includes a phrase such as "the curse of Ham."

As recounted in Genesis 9, the vivid story centers in a strange weakness and (to us) illogical retaliation on the part of Noah himself. After the deluge he "began to be an husbandman, and he planted a vineyard" (vs. 20). It was only a short time before he was able to produce enough wine to become drunk; in this state he staggered into his tent and collapsed—with his genital organs exposed.

His son Ham saw what had happened and told his two brothers. They took a garment and with eyes carefully averted from their father's shame walked backwards into the tent and covered him. When Noah sobered up and found what had happened, he showed no remorse for his own conduct. Instead he pronounced a curse upon the descendants of the son who had seen his nakedness: "Cursed be Canaan [Ham]; a servant of servants shall he be unto his brethren" (vs. 25).

Through a total lack of understanding about human origins and a grossly mistaken identification of the Canaanites (traditional descendants of Ham) with early members of the Negro race, generations of Bible readers accepted and spread the myth that through his servant Noah, God himself doomed black men to perpetual servitude.

The Twelve Tribes of Israel

Scripture gives considerable emphasis to the fact that there were precisely twelve tribes of Israel. Tradition stresses this mystical number even more than does Holy Writ. But in spite of the fact that the tribes are enumerated in Genesis 49 and there are treated as descendants of Jacob's sons, the actual number of functional units remained at twelve for only a brief period.

Quite early, the civil tribe of Levi was absorbed; only the name remained—attached to priests scattered among all the remaining tribes. The tribe of Simeon had a brief hour in the sun and then lost its identity through amalgamation with the tribe of Judah (Josh. 19:1-9). Reuben also grew weaker and is seldom mentioned after the time of the patriarchs. So references to the twelve tribes of Israel are likely to be poetic rather than historical.

In daily life and worship the concept of twelve tribes was kept alive by the fact that the breastplate, or official dress of the Jewish high priest, was adorned with a dozen precious stones engraved with names of the tribes (Exod. 28:15-21). Survival of the symbol is credited to the significance of the number twelve. This is the numerical basis for the lunar year and also establishes the number of signs in the Zodiac.

The religious significance of the number was so great that after the tribe of Levi disappeared, Ephraim and Manasseh (both descended from Joseph) were counted separately in order to maintain the fiction that Israel was composed of twelve blood groups descended from twelve sons of Jacob.

A similar development took place in the early Christian movement. Through the defection of Judas the ranks of the disciples were reduced to eleven, so an immediate replacement was found for Iscariot in order that the symbolic number might be maintained.

Special Role of Names

In his famous study of primitive cultures, *The Golden Bough,* Sir James G. Frazer stressed a fact already familiar to students of the Bible: among many peoples a mixture of traditions and folktales, compounded with awesome reverence for the power of words, serves to give semimagical qualities to a person's name.

Since the name of a person is the key to his spirit or essence, Hebrew patriarchs reasoned, to know one's name is to possess a degree of power over him. In a sense, the name was considered a substitute for the person himself, so it was thought imperative that the believer should know the secret name of his deity. (See Ps. 9:10; Isa. 52:6; Jer. 48:17.)

Just as some persons today try to guard themselves by having unlisted telephone numbers, so many members of ancient societies attempted to erect defensive barriers by having secret names, known only to their intimates. This practice was common in Egypt, but there is no biblical evidence that it was ever adopted by the Hebrews. As late as New Testament times, however, there was strong and virtually universal belief among Christians that supernatural power was linked with the name of Jesus. It was by invoking the name of their Master that disciples worked wonders (Mark 16:17), expelled demons (Luke 10:17), and performed miracles of healing (Acts 3:6; 4:12).

Secular scholars whose primary interests focus in science, mathematics, or philosophy now agree that there really is special potency in a name; until a thing or event is named, it cannot be a subject of discourse. Hence, for practical purposes nothing exists until it is named. Knowledge of a name really does confer a unique kind of power—far removed from magic, but nonetheless potent.

Molech Embroidered with Legends

After twenty centuries of circulation, an elaborate yarn concerning Moloch (Amos 5:26), or Molech as he is more often called in Scripture (Lev. 18:21; 20:2-5; I Kings 11:7; II Kings 23:10), can best be labeled "a lot of bull."

A title rather than a name, Molech was deliberately compounded by the Hebrews, who combined the consonants for "king" with the vowel sounds of "shame." This "king of shame" was a Canaanite deity to whom human sacrifice was made at a site not far from Jerusalem. Biblical writers do not describe rites connected with the worship of him but make numerous references to the practice of making one's children "pass through the fire."

As a result, in rabbinical tradition Molech was described as a bull-shaped, brazen image heated by a furnace underneath, into whose arms screaming children were tossed alive. This description from folklore caught the imagination of Christian artists. As a result, many medieval paintings, etchings, and woodcuts presented graphic views of the red-hot bull supposed to have been worshiped by Israel's foes.

Present-day findings give no hint concerning what beast or bird the images of Molech actually resembled. All evidence indicates that though children really were sacrificed, they were killed before public rites began. No one knows precisely what is meant by the reference to passing them through the fire.

Still the ancient legend retains great vitality. Jacques Boudet's elaborate pictorial history *Man and Beast,* issued in Paris in 1962, says of Molech that "screaming priests mutilating themselves with knives, chanting and sacred dances covered the shrieks of children flung living into the fire-reddened arms of the bull-headed god whose hollow, brass interior contained a raging furnace."

Seven Elevated to a Dominant Role

Though it was linked with both pagan religions and astrology, the number seven was accepted by the Hebrews as virtually sacred. Hence, of all numbers it plays the most important role in Scripture. Some authorities think seven came to be regarded as perfect because it represents the sun, moon, and five planets known to the ancients. Others believe it gained its predominance as a result of adding four (the favorite holy number in ancient Egypt) and three (a mystical symbol of completeness because it suggests beginning, middle, and end).

Before the time of Abraham, Egyptians used seven in both magic and medicine. It figured in many of their incantations and was associated with the goddess Isis. In ancient Mesopotamia seven was regarded as a holy number so early that the beginnings of reverence for it cannot be traced.

Hebrews who repudiated most or all other features of competing religious systems not only adopted seven as sacred; they elevated it to a dominant role in worship, thought, and everyday life. Seven days were required for the ordination of a priest or the consecration of an altar (Exod. 29:35-37). Sacrificial blood was sprinkled seven times (Lev. 4:6), and holy oil used in anointing was applied seven times (Lev. 8:11). All important Jewish religious festivals were linked with the number. Both Passover and Tabernacles are seven-day periods; the New Year, Day of Atonement, and Tabernacles occur in the seventh month of the Hebrew calendar.

Wedding festivals were celebrated for seven days (Judg. 14:12, 17). Both Solomon's prayer (I Kings 8:29-53) and the Lord's Prayer (Matt. 6:9-13) include precisely seven petitions. Jesus spoke seven times from the cross. The Revelation is full of symbolic references to seven. Contemporary persons who reject all views concerning "sacred," "lucky," and "perfect" numbers still find their lives ordered about the number seven as an axis, for it determined the length of the week as observed almost universally in the modern world.

Forged Scriptures of the Second Century

During the second century of the Christian era spurious Gospels and forged sets of holy writings abounded. Unsettled times helped set a climate in which such works could be produced. Slow communication made it difficult to check the authenticity of a document or letter. Most important of all, books destined to become a part of the New Testament were written or inscribed by hand in a great variety of styles. Lacking clear standards by which to make comparisons, any scroll that used the Christian vocabulary could readily be palmed off as sacred.

One popular fake was a letter reputed to have been written by an associate of Pontius Pilate, one Lentulus (not mentioned in the canonical Scriptures). Copies of this document were in great demand because it included a precise description of Jesus' appearance—a matter about which Gospel writers give virtually no details.

Another early forgery, actually a small anthology, consisted of letters said to have been written by Jesus himself and a royal correspondent. Abgar Uchomo, the latter, was ruler of the territory of Edessa. According to carefully prepared copies that were sold to believers for fancy prices, Abgar heard of the miracles performed by the man of Galilee and so wrote requesting Jesus to come heal him of a long-standing illness. Several letters supposed to have been exchanged between them were preserved and issued in multiple copies by scribes "eager to spread the good news of the Son of God." Actually, penmen burned the midnight oil over their parchments because they were in great commercial demand. A number of these bogus scriptures have survived.

Veneration for Relics

Polycarp, Bishop of Smyrna during the second century, incurred the wrath of many high-placed persons because of his vigorous attack upon heresy. As a result he was seized and burned at the stake. Faithful members of his flock collected his *reliquiae* ("remains") and went through a burial ceremony so that they could annually celebrate the anniversary of his martyrdom at his grave.

As a result of numerous similar incidents, the remains of bodies of saints (or portions of them) came to be venerated as avenues leading to miraculous benefits and divine grace. In time any object associated with a key figure of Christendom was jealously guarded as a wonder-working relic.

Veneration for relics, and the consequent search for the oldest of them all, took on frenzied proportions during the medieval period. Skulls, teeth, rings, and personal articles were especially sought after.

Inevitably, the whole of Christendom became obsessed with relics linked with the New Testament account of Jesus' own life. The chalice used in the Last Supper was transformed into the Holy Grail.

Discovery of "the true cross" came not once, but over and over. In the fourth century Cyril of Jerusalem caustically remarked that the whole world was filled with fragments of its wood. One thousand years later the search was still on; Sir John Mandeville, first modern author of a book of traveler's adventures, described a nail from the true cross used by an emperor to "make a brydille to his hors, to bere him in bataylle." By virtue of it he naturally "overcame his enemyes."

Most scholars doubt that any handed-down relic is genuine, yet thousands of them are still displayed—chiefly in Europe, Latin America, Asia, and the Near East—"for the edification of the pious."

The Unicorn in Holy Writ

Working in the third century B.C., translators of the Septuagint had limited knowledge of technical Hebrew words. They did their best with it, but a single word, *re'em,* threw them for such a loss that they helped spread and perpetuate a fantastic myth in the guise of scriptural truth.

Uncertain as to the size and nature of the animal known to Hebrews as the *re'em* but nowhere described, scholars settled on what they considered the nearest Greek equivalent: *monokeros.* Rendered into Latin several centuries later, the term became *unicornis.* Early French Bibles referred to it as *licorne;* Martin Luther called it *Einhorn;* and it entered English as *unicorn.* Translators of the King James Version made nine references to this fabulous beast.

In pre-Christian centuries, Greek naturalists described it as a white horse with a red head, blue eyes, and a single eighteen-inch horn on its forehead. Romans pondered the role of that fearful weapon and concluded that the horn was used to spear elephants.

Pursued by a hunter, a unicorn jumped off the nearest high cliff, managed to hit head first so that he landed on his horn and then bounded and rebounded so that he dashed off without injury. At least, that's the way the legend of the unicorn was usually told. A perennial favorite during the Middle Ages, it was strengthened by the frequent display of "horns of the unicorns"—really tusks of the narwhal (one of the smaller arctic whales).

Even in early times a few scientific students of nature challenged the existence of the unicorn, but many believers met objections by pointing out that the unicorn is frequently mentioned in the Bible. In his noted American translation of the Scriptures, J. M. P. Smith discarded "unicorn" in favor of "wild ox"; though followed in the Revised Standard Version and other modern translations, this translation of the word hasn't yet dislodged the unicorn from its established place in many popular translations.

Jacob's Potent Pillar

A relic made prominent by its alleged ties with Jacob is still a focus of controversy between Scotland and England. The famous Stone of Scone symbolizes Scottish independence, and was "kidnapped" at the midpoint of the twentieth century as an act of defiance against the British crown.

Old Scone, a parish of Perthshire, Scotland, was very early the capital of Pictavia, the kingdom of northern Picts. It was here that on the Mote Hill a Pictish king promulgated an edict establishing Christianity. Scone's abbey, founded in 1115 on the site of a much earlier monastery, was the place to which Kenneth of Scotland brought the Stone of Destiny on which Celtic kings were crowned, after he had seized it at Dunstaffnage Castle. In 1296 King Edward I took the ancient stone to Westminster Abbey and deposited it beneath England's coronation chair. It was from this closely guarded resting place that the stone was taken by twentieth-century Scottish independents and restored after a series of adventures and international detective work.

Long before the Stone of Scone became a focus of intrigue, it was revered as being the rock on which Jacob put his head at Bethel on the night when he dreamed of the ladder. From its biblical associations and the fact that Jacob's dream involved a divine promise of a vast dominion, the stone was considered to possess unique potency. In the light of such a view it was natural for monarchs to consider it vital that they sit upon "Jacob's pillow" during the ceremonies investing them with royal power.

Armageddon in Guildhall

Ezekiel's prophecy includes a stirring vision in which Jehovah does battle against a mighty foe—none other than Gog, chief prince of Meshech, who leads his forces from Magog ("the land of Gog"). This distinction between the king and the land he ruled is explicit in Ezek. 38:2.

In spite of it, John of Patmos erred in his interpretation or had a lapse of memory and treated Magog as a comrade in arms of Gog and a superhuman foe of Jehovah (Rev. 20:8). As a result of John's blunder, many medieval romances depicted Gog and Magog as evil giants.

One tale has the fearful pair captured and escorted to London in chains. At least as early as the fourteenth century huge wooden statues of Gog and Magog were erected in the capital city. Destroyed in the great fire of 1666, they were replaced half a century later by fourteen-foot effigies hand-carved by Richard Saunders and erected in the Guildhall. Few visitors who pause to stare at the two mighty participants in the Battle of Armageddon bother to check their Bibles in order to discover that the real Magog was a region and not a person.

The Fabulous Cockatrice

Precisely what the Hebrew word *tsepha'* means no one knows. Like many other terms from ancient natural history, it points to some creature—real or imaginary—so familiar to the earliest readers that no explanatory comments were considered necessary. Translators of early English Bibles were thus confronted with the riddle of trying to link the name with a beast known to them.

At various points in Scripture this name for an obscure animal is rendered as cockatrice (Isa. 11:8; 14:29; 59:5; Jer. 8:17); commentators striving for greater accuracy have wavered between such terms as adder, asp, viper, and even basilisk.

According to ancient legend, the creature whose name entered English as cockatrice is a kind of deadly serpent hatched from the egg of a cock (not a hen!). It was so fearful that it could kill at a distance by means of its breath or even a glance. Apparently it is this fearful beast to which the ancient naturalist, Pliny, refers in his famous *Natural History* under the name "basilisk."

By incorporating the name of the cockatrice (or the basilisk) into modern printed versions of Scripture, pioneer scholars helped perpetuate the notion that the mythical creature at one time actually existed. In the Revised Standard Version the vexatious Hebrew name is rendered "adder"—a form adopted even in the theologically conservative *Amplified Bible,* issued in 1965. George M. Lamsa, translating the Peshitta, prefers "asp." But virtually all analysts agree that regardless of what variety of serpent figured prominently in Isaiah's prophecies, it definitely was not the fabulous creature that in medieval times was thought to emerge from the egg of a rooster.

Phantom Dogs That Bring Bad News

James Howell's *English Proverbs,* issued in the seventeenth century, includes a number of folk sayings about doomsday. One of them declares that "when Gabriel blowes his horn, then this question will be decided." Colorful as this idea is, a careful look at the Bible gives no clue concerning the name of the spirit whose signal will announce the coming of Judgment Day.

In its original use Gabriel is a name meaning "man of God" or "hero." This title was applied to one of the seven archangels who functioned as divine messengers. Gabriel explained a vision to Daniel (Dan. 8:16) and visited Zacharias and Elisabeth to announce the coming of a son (Luke 1:5-20). But nowhere in Scripture is he described as the angel of death or the herald of Judgment Day.

Traditions about Gabriel are so deep-rooted that they have given rise to legends about his aides. Many parts of Northern Europe have seasonal waves of warnings called Gabriel's ratchets—eerie night sounds probably made by wild geese in flight. Farmers of rural England often hear the baying of Gabriel's hounds—phantom dogs said to be the souls of unbaptized children who are condemned to wander through the air until Doomsday, and meanwhile charged with the task of foretelling death by their baying on dark nights.

Evolution of the Cherub

Our word "cherub" comes straight from ancient Hebrew, with the spelling altered only a trifle in centuries of transmission. But the association of a cherub with an infant angel is relatively modern and quite without biblical foundation.

Both in the singular form and in the plural form, cherubim, there are numerous scriptural references. Practically all of them include descriptive details. A cherub might have two wings, but was more likely to have four. Instead of being an infant, he was a fearful creature who stood as much as fifteen feet high and had a wingspread of about the same distance. A typical cherub had arms as well as wings. In Ezekiel's vision each cherub had four faces—one of which was that of an ox (Ezek. 1:5-10).

Solomon decorated his temple with cherubim so huge that their wings spread from wall to wall of the most holy place (I Kings 6:23-27). Made of olive wood overlaid with gold, these and other cherubim are the chief images used in orthodox worship of Jehovah.

Whether Renaissance artists acted from sentimental reasons, a misunderstanding of biblical accounts, or other factors, cannot be known. But in their timeless masterpieces they began depicting cherubim as angelic babies. As a result, their concept became so firmly established in popular thought that the contradiction of the original verbal picture is seldom even noticed by readers of Scripture. The force of tradition is now so great that practically everyone pictures a cherub as an infant with wings.

Moses' Horns

Michelangelo's "Moses," one of the most famous of all existing works of the sculptor's art, shows the great lawgiver with horns sprouting from his head. Marble for the majestic statue reached Rome from Carrara about July, 1508, but the piece was not finished before 1513. Heavily bearded and draped, Moses sits grasping the tables of the

Law with one hand—an incarnation of majestic indignation at having found Aaron and the people engaged in the worship of a golden calf.

The horned figure is in keeping with ancient interpretations. To the Israelites, the horn of an ox (and sometimes even the horn of a ram or goat) was the supreme symbol of dignity and strength. Success was indicated by raising one's horn, failure by lowering it. God himself is termed "the horn of my salvation" at least twice (II Sam. 22:3; Ps. 18:2). Early Christian artists often gave horns to biblical figures in order to symbolize their power. At Vaison-la-Romaine, France, there is a rare sketch showing Christ himself with horns.

Widespread and notable though it was, the horn tradition was based on an error that grew out of ignorance. Far from adept in handling Hebrew, early translators rendering Exod. 34:29-35 mistook *qaran* for *qeren*. In the Latin Vulgate the descriptive term was rendered as *cornuta,* whose literal meaning is "horned." So through a blend of linguistic error and orally transmitted tradition, it was natural that medieval writers and artists should envision Moses as having horns. By depicting him so, Michelangelo therefore simply followed the tradition whose purpose was to show that the great prophet was spiritually "as powerful as a bull."

Biblical Ophir Found by Columbus!

Early translators of the English Bible were enamored with neat explanations for puzzling statements in Holy Writ. For this purpose, notes were often added in the margins or at the bottoms of columns. Uninformed readers tended to regard such comments as part of the original text of Scripture; even persons well versed in biblical lore frequently treated them as though they were on the same level of inspiration as the passages with which they dealt.

Marginal notes were abundant in the famous Geneva Bible. Many of them gave such vigorous support to then current interpretations of John Calvin's doctrines, particularly predestination, that for practical purposes this New Testament was a revision of the original.

Editors of the Bishops' Bible of 1568 threw out most of the marginal notes that supported Calvinistic doctrines, but they remained eager to link Scripture's veiled or little-understood references with current patterns of thought. As a result they included in their officially sponsored version of the Holy Book a memo supporting the notion that American Indians are descended from the lost tribes of Israel.

Ophir (or Opir) is repeatedly mentioned in Scripture as the source of abundant gold of high quality. This land yielded 3,000 talents of the precious metal that David left for completion of the temple (I Chron. 29:4). Phoenicians and Israelites are known to have brought an additional 450 talents of Ophir's gold to Solomon (II Chron. 8: 18). But neither Scripture, secular history, nor archaeology gives a satisfactory indication of where this land was located. It has been identified with regions of Arabia, India, and Central Africa, but no such identification is positive.

In their zeal for clarity, editors of the Bishops' Bible added a note at Ps. 45:9 (which mentions Ophir) indicating that "Ophir is thought to be the Ilande in the West Coast, of late founde by Christopher Colombo, from which at this day is brought most fine gold."

A Proverb Rooted in Tradition

Contrary to long-established opinion, the Bible nowhere says that man is divinely ordained to earn his living by the sweat of his brow. In fact, this precise phrase does not appear in Holy Writ. Gen. 3:19 is the probable origin; there Adam is told that "in the sweat of thy face shalt thou eat bread, till thou return unto the ground."

John Milton, noted for his habit of making slight alterations rather than quoting Scripture verbatim, urged his fellows: "Let us go forth and resolutely dare with sweat of brow to toil our little day." A century later Thomas Carlyle employed the vigorous figure of speech in a similar exhortation. But Henry David Thoreau turned it about-face. "It is not necessary that a man should earn his living by the sweat of his brow, unless he sweats easier than I do," he quipped in *Walden.*

James Ussher's Chronology of the World

James Ussher, born in Dublin on January 4, 1581, holds a record for creating confusion in the minds of Bible readers. Active in both politics and the church, he was appointed a bishop by King James I in 1620. Later he became an archbishop. As one of his many projects he set out to harmonize and systematize all time references in the Old Testament. His finished chronology was admired as a work of great piety and scholarship.

In 1701, partly in order to promote the sales of new editions, some publishers of the King James Version began including his scheme of dates in center columns and marginal notes. As a result, generations of readers jumped to the logical conclusion that these dates must have been part of the original text of Scripture.

Ussher's work was a major factor contributing to the conflict between science and religion. Findings of geologists and astronomers concerning the antiquity of our planet seemed like pure heresy to generations of persons who had grown up on the Irish archbishop's chronology. According to it, the world was created in 4004 B.C.—at ten o'clock in the morning.

Absalom's Story Altered

Practically all readers of the Bible's historical books will stake their reputations on the proposition that Absalom, third son of King David, died as a result of having his hair caught in the limbs of a tree. Maybe so, but there is no scriptural foundation for this verdict.

As the ancient account actually reads, "Absalom rode upon a mule, and the mule went under the thick boughs of a great oak, and his head caught hold of the oak, and he was taken up between the heaven and the earth; and the mule that was under him went away" (II Sam. 18:9). Hebrew words for "head" and "hair" are quite specific; scholars who differ on other issues agree that the term used here means the former and not the latter.

But the popular conception that credits the fatal accident to Absalom's long hair was widespread in earlier centuries as well as our own. A London wigmaker once took advantage of it and had a special sign painted for his shop. It showed Absalom dangling from the branches of a tree by his hair and promised potential customers:

> If Absalom hadn't worn his own hair,
> He'd ne'er been found a hanging there.

Benjamin Franklin's Practical Jokes

The Complete Works of Benjamin Franklin includes two minor gems concocted by the sage of Philadelphia as practical jokes upon his friends. But persons not acquainted with their background have sometimes seen reprints, taken them seriously, and wondered why their own Bibles are incomplete.

Using biblical language, Franklin wrote "A Parable on Brotherly Love." Then he printed it in the style customarily used for Scripture and circulated it as a hitherto-lost story. Reuben, son of Jacob, is the central character. He buys a fine new ax that excites the envy and admiration of his brothers, who one by one make unsuccessful attempts to borrow it. About the time he has completed the cycle by refusing all overtures, Reuben drops his ax into a river and loses it. Meanwhile some of his brothers have managed to get new ones of their own. Reuben approaches them with his head hanging low and requests permission to borrow one of their implements. Simeon flatly refuses. Levi haggles but reluctantly gives in. But Judah learns of his brother's plight and, in spite of having received a harsh "no" to his own request, spontaneously offers to lend his ax.

In another instance Franklin went a step farther. He not only imitated the literary style and physical appearance of Scripture, but actually bound a story about tolerance into a copy of his Bible as Genesis 51. Though he had in mind nothing more than a mild prank, he executed it so well that it backfired. Copies of "the lost chapter of Genesis" are still circulating and from time to time stir controversy when stoutly defended as authentic.

The Death Warrant of Jesus

Many unanswered questions center about a hoax perpetrated in the name of piety and circulated practically everywhere the Bible is read. In 1810 the commissioner of arts of the French Army, superintending excavations in the ancient city of Aquila (a famous summer resort in central Italy), reported the discovery of an antique marble vase. Inside the vase was a copper plate with an elaborate inscription. Translated, it reads:

> Sentence rendered by Pontius Pilate, acting Governor of Lower Galilee, stating that Jesus of Nazareth shall suffer death on the cross.
>
> In the year seventeen of the Emperor Tiberius Caesar, and the 27th day of March, the city of the Holy Jerusalem—Annas and Caiaphas being priests, sacrifactors of the people of God—Pontius Pilate, Governor of Lower Galilee, sitting in the presidential chair of the praetory, condemns Jesus of Nazareth to die on the cross between two thieves.

Additional paragraphs spell out the charges against Jesus, specify that he shall be led to the place of execution by Quilius Cornelius, and forbid any person rich or poor to oppose the execution of the sentence. Signatures of four witnesses are attached: Daniel Robani, a Pharisee; Joannus Robani; Raphael Robani; and Capet, a citizen.

This death warrant of Jesus, ostensibly supplementing the Gospel account, is unquestionably fraudulent. But the identity of the person who went to the trouble of making the elaborate engraving which included a postscript: "A similar plate is sent to each tribe"—is not known. It could have been the work of the man who claimed to have discovered it. Or it could have been a genuine archaeological find of a hoax skillfully made much earlier and buried for safekeeping in time of war or pestilence.

Legendary Origin of American Indians

Though there is no evidence to support it, the legend that American Indians are descended from the lost tribes of Israel has persisted for nearly four hundred years.

Diego Duran's monumental history of the New World, written about 1575, was the first book to advance the theory; however, the theory had circulated orally at least two or three generations earlier. According to Duran, the natives of the West Indies definitely are "the ten tribes of Israel that Shalmaneser, king of the Assyrians, made prisoners and carried to Assyria."

Dozens of amateur and professional historians have since written articles and books offering proof of the fantastic theory. Even William Penn gave the weight of his name to it.

Far the most ambitious study of the subject was financed by the Irish eccentric Edward K. Kingsborough. His subsidized nine-volume work on the *Antiquities of Mexico,* published at two-year intervals beginning in 1830, cost him more than £100,000. Though he died in debtor's prison as a result of riding his hobby horse, Kingsborough's attempt to identify the ancient Mexicans with the ten lost tribes satisfied few but himself. Not only is there no linguistic, archaeological, or historical evidence that any American Indians are of Hebrew ancestry; the Bible itself nowhere advances a theory that ten of the traditional twelve tribes suddenly vanished. Even the phrase "lost tribes" does not appear in Scripture.

Paintings Repaired and Retouched

Numerous wealthy patrons of the arts have concentrated on collecting biblical subject matter. Some Victorian collectors accumulated entire galleries filled with interpretations of scriptural events. So there is a degree of plausibility in an account relayed by William S. Walsh in his *Handy-Book of Literary Curiosities.* In 1865 an artist repaired and retouched the paintings in the collection of an English lord, he says. According to Walsh some of the services for which a bill was rendered were:

Filling up the chink in the Red Sea and repairing the damages of Pharaoh's host.

Cleaning six of the apostles and adding an entirely new Judas Iscariot.

Painting a pair of new hands for Daniel in the lion's den and a set of teeth for the lioness.

Making a pair of ears for Balaam and a new tongue for the ass.
Painting twenty-one new steps to Jacob's ladder.
Giving a blush to the cheeks of Eve on presenting the apple to Adam.
Painting a shoulder of mutton and a shin of beef in the mouths of the two ravens feeding Elijah.
Repairing Solomon's nose and making a new nail for his middle finger.
Making an exact representation of Noah in the character of a general reviewing his troops preparatory to their march, with the dove dressed as an aide-de-camp.

Though Walsh offered his list tongue in cheek, the practice of restoring and repainting was actually widespread, and still is. A classic case is that of Giotto's murals. Twentieth-century detective work has shown that many of his figures were repainted and radically altered, while the "St. Louis of France" long attributed to him is an outright forgery. Long after Giotto's death, some dignitary who wanted the artist's work changed to suit his own wishes had the figure of St. Louis added to an existing mural.

Proverbs 32:1

If it must be assigned a place in Scripture, "God helps those who help themselves" logically belongs at Prov. 32:1. Long-standing tradition to the contrary, there is no biblical maxim even close to the centuries-old formula exhorting action as a prelude to the receipt of divine bounty. (In all versions and translations the book of Proverbs ends with chapter 31, verse 31.)

Fragment 223 of the works of Aeschylus, Greek tragic dramatist of the fifth century B.C., promises that "God loves to help him who strives to help himself." From this earliest of known uses until the present time, the maxim has been employed by hack writers and world-famous figures alike. Sophocles and Benjamin Franklin, Cervantes and La Fontaine used the basic idea with language modified a trifle. By 1698 Algernon Sidney quoted it as "an old proverb," and since then it has entered most major languages of the world. But the person who seeks it in Holy Writ is doomed to disappointment.

Isaiah's "Foreknowledge" of the Auto

A widespread legend asserts that the prophet Isaiah had foreknowledge of the automobile. Persons who accept this point of view cite as proof of their position the fact that in a single passage, just six verses long, the ancient seer mentions half a dozen components of the modern car.

His list begins with "round tires like the moon" and continues with "chains." Next he refers to mufflers, then to rings and glasses. Finally he alludes to hoods, already mentioned under the earlier English name of bonnets. If you doubt the accuracy of this list, check it in your own Bible: Isa. 3:18-23.

There's only one serious difficulty with the argument that Isaiah's great spiritual and psychic power made him anticipate the work of modern inventors by many centuries. A look at the list of "automobile parts," seen in context, reveals that he was talking about clothing and jewelry worn by fashionable Israelite women 2,500 years ago.

The Gospel According to Joseph

According to a manuscript account of the life and message of Jesus, all four Gospel writers are indebted to a single man. Largely unknown to readers of the Bible, this historian was Joseph of Jerusalem. In the preface to his work, he made a careful note to the effect that "fearing that this writing may be modified and destroyed by some of our opposers, I have left four copies to our excellent brothers: Matthew of Capernaum, Mark of Jerusalem, Luke of Antioch, and John of Thesda." His detailed account was written, he said, shortly before "the Holy City [Jerusalem] was destroyed by the Roman Emperor Titus" (A.D. 70).

But Joseph's work was not made public until 1927. That year a clerk on the payroll of the city of Cerignola, Italy, gave scholars a look at a parchment he said he had stumbled upon eight years earlier. Fearing government confiscation, Luigi Moccia had kept quiet about his find and even when he revealed it was careful to stress factors that supported his claim of legal ownership.

It took only a glance from qualified experts to see that the Gospel According to Joseph of Jerusalem was a crude forgery. Even the order in which the writer named his literary heirs is a dead giveaway; the present sequence of the Gospels was not fixed until long after the time of Titus. Some authorities ventured to guess that the newly discovered work was medieval in origin. Most assigned it to modern times, on the basis of the kind of parchment on which it was written and the rather garbled form of Greek that was used.

A few zealots disagreed with both verdicts. Privately printed in

Italian by a pastor then living in Schenectady, New York, the document was favorably reviewed by John R. van Der Veer of Union College. So far, however, ardent proponents of the Gospel According to Joseph of Jerusalem have received little support for their proposal that it be included in future versions of the New Testament.

Versions and Translations of the Book

Earliest Translation into Greek

A bit of fiction framed with pious motives and tinged with a romantic glow named the first of all formal translations of Scripture: the Septuagint. This Greek-language version of the Torah, or Book of the Law that makes up the first five books of the modern Bible, was prepared at the ancient Egyptian city of Alexandria.

Long a center of learning and culture, the city named for Alexander the Great became a haven for Jews who had left Palestine. In their self-chosen exile they tried to live according to the biblical code. They erected a fine synagogue and observed all the Jewish festivals. But the pervasive Greek influence could not be escaped. Within a few generations most of these people were no longer able to read the Torah in Hebrew. So in the third century B.C. a few competent scholars, versatile in both languages, rendered their Scriptures into a vernacular form of Greek. Their work is still considered a monumental achievement, remarkably accurate as well as expressive.

Small wonder, therefore, that in later generations those who used this translation began to weave legends about it. Late in the second century B.C. Aristeas of Alexandria gathered some of these stories and put them into writing. According to his account, the Egyptian prince Ptolemy Philadelphus had a library of 200,000 volumes. But it had no Greek-language version of the Hebrew Scriptures. So the ruler shut seventy-two scholars (six men from each of the twelve tribes of Israel) in a monastery on the island of Phares. Each man translated separately without checking the work of his comrades. But when all had finished after seventy-two days, their copies proved to be identical.

Aristeas' readers began to talk about the work of the Seventy—Latin, *septuaginta*—and the artificial number designating the translators became attached to their version of the Book of the Law—later expanded to include the entire Old Testament.

Scripture in the Syrian Language

The translation of the oldest part of the Hebrew Scriptures into Syriac was launched at least as early as the second century A.D. This was made necessary by the fact that substantial numbers of Jews in Syria no longer knew Hebrew and were unacquainted with the then dominant language of western civilization, Greek.

But like most other languages, ancient and modern, Syriac had more than one form. Words and grammatical forms that scholars could take in stride were a source of confusion to poorly trained leaders of rural synagogues. To make matters worse, the earliest portions of Scripture in Syriac were accompanied by copious notes that pointed out alternative readings for doubtful passages.

No later than the third century, individual translators and groups of Syrians began work on a simple version in their native language. From their word for "straight, sincere, or true," it was called the Peshitta. Eventually it became the sole officially recognized version for use in the Syriac Church, independent from both the Greek Orthodox and Roman Catholic Churches.

Until recent times there was no satisfactory English translation of the Peshitta. This defect was remedied by an Assyrian who lived in biblical lands until after World War I. Working with Syriac manuscripts from the Ambrosia Library of Milan, Italy, and the Morgan Library of New York City, plus one from the British Museum, George M. Lamsa first translated the Gospels. Later he rendered the rest of the New Testament and Psalms into English; then in 1957 he published an English version of the entire Peshitta.

The manuscript from the British Museum has the distinction of being the oldest dated biblical manuscript in existence—produced by Syrian scribes in A.D. 442.

A Heretic Forces Adoption of an Official List

Debate over precisely which inspired writings should be included in the New Testament began in the first quarter of the second century. Though formal councils of the church tried to settle the question for all time, and thought they succeeded, it is still a point of contention in the twentieth century.

From the Greek word *kanon* (reed used in measuring) books measured and found to be inspired by the Holy Spirit are said to be canonical. Many scholars think the first attempt at fixing a list, or canon, of writings containing the full message of Jesus was made by a famous heretic, Marcion. About A.D. 150 he considered all available materials and concluded that Luke, Romans 1–2, and Paul's letters to the Corinthians, Galatians, Ephesians, and Colossians, contained the Good News unadulterated by ideas foreign to Jesus' message.

The circulation of Marcion's private list probably forced church authorities to take formal action. Before A.D. 200 a number of church councils had selected as authoritative those books that now make up the New Testament. The contents of the Bible were formally fixed at thirty-nine books for the Old Testament and twenty-seven for the New Testament by the Synod of Rome in 382. Reformation leaders caused the Council of Trent to give additional attention to the matter; in 1546 it endorsed the ancient list and stressed that no traditional book should be omitted and no others should be added. Martin Luther translated and printed the New Testament in the form inherited from the past, but he called the letter of James "an epistle of straw" and questioned that the Revelation of John could possibly be the work of the Holy Spirit.

As late as 1966 a Lutheran church historian tried to revive the debate. Stressing the great value of such ancient writings as the Gospel of Peter and the Epistle of Barnabas, Robert L. Wilken suggested by implication that they should be treated as being on a par with canonical books. Regardless of the merit or lack of it in his suggestion, the possibility that it will be accepted is remote.

Jerome and the Latin Vulgate

Though it was not well received at first, the Vulgate Bible in Latin eventually became so significant among Roman Catholics that printers were ordered to retain its words, phrases, and even punctuation unaltered "from now on."

Beginning in the second century, a series of translations were made that employed Old Latin. By A.D. 382 it was obvious that these works were inferior in scholarship and employed many words no longer commonly used and understood. Pope Damasus I gave a formal commission to the learned scholar Jerome to study the existing translations and standardize them.

At first Jerome revised an Old Latin version of the book of Psalms, correcting it by referring to the Septuagint. Then he made a far more sweeping revision which he completed in 387. Still not satisfied, he worked another ten years rendering the rest of the Old Testament directly from Hebrew into common or "vulgar" Latin. His translation into forceful contemporary Latin was as accurate as it could be made with the resources available. But great numbers of priests clung stubbornly to Old Latin. "So great is the force of established usage that even recognized errors please the majority," complained Jerome, "for they prefer to have their copies pretty rather than correct."

Over a period of about four hundred years, Jerome's work gradually displaced all competitors. But it was not until the thirteenth century that Latin *vulgata* (or "common") gave it the title it has held ever since. Three hundred years later the Council of Trent formally endorsed the text of the Vulgate, modified only slightly from Jerome's final version, and ordered that it should be retained without alteration for all time. Until publication of the Jerusalem Bible in 1966 every existing complete English-language version of the Old Testament produced by Catholics was based on the Vulgate in the form established by the Council of Trent in 1546.

Scripture for the Anglo-Saxons

Slaves launched a chain reaction that led to the first translation of the Bible into a tongue spoken in Britain.

As described by the eighth-century scholar generally known as the Venerable Bede, slave dealers of Rome had a bargain day late in the sixth century. They had a number of blond-haired captives on their hands, and because of their fierce appearance no one wanted them. Publicly exhibited and offered at prices well below the prevailing market, they drew the attention of Gregory, a monk in high favor with both church authorities and the general public. He inquired about them and was told that they were Angles from distant Britain. "Not Angles—but Angels," he quipped.

On behalf of the "angels" he petitioned the pope to let him organize a band of missionaries who would bear the faith to the bleak island where fair-haired men were found. His request was rejected. But when he himself became pope in 590, Gregory the Great remembered the incident of the slaves. From St. Andrew's monastery in Rome he chose the monk Augustine to head a band of forty missionaries appointed to England. Augustine later became the first Archbishop of Canterbury. As a result of labors by him and his men, part of the Bible was translated into an Anglo-Saxon dialect before the beginning of the seventh century.

Fifteenth-Century Comic Strip

Contrary to popular belief, presentation of the biblical story in comic-strip format is not a modern invention but antedates the Reformation. Well before any European began experiments aimed at printing with moveable type, a Bible heavily illustrated with woodcuts was published under the formal title *Biblia Pauperum* or "Bible of the Poor." The printing of it has been attributed to Laurens Koster, of Harlem, Germany, who probably worked sometime in the decade after 1410.

His Bible of the Poor is a picture book with brief explanatory captions or Scripture texts in Latin. Leading events in the drama of salvation, some from the Old and some from the New Testament, are included. Frequently there are three scenes on a page: one from the New Testament in the middle, flanked by Old Testament scenes dealing with the same or a similar emphasis.

Koster seems to have produced this earliest of all printed picture books in response to requests from mendicant friars. They worked among the common people, many of whom were poor only in learning, not worldly goods. Because Scripture was a sealed book to the illiterate masses of the period, the illustrated Bible of the Poor was the only interpretation of Holy Writ that many persons ever saw. Manuscript versions of it were in circulation before the thirteenth century, but it took the genius of a German printer to work out techniques for mechanical production by means of woodcuts.

Complete block books are very rare; one of the few in the United States is in Harvard University's Houghton Library. Printed in Germany about 1465, it is a vivid pictorial treatment of the Revelation —whose seven-headed monster has much in common with beasts shown in present-day horror comic books.

John Wycliffe's Translation

John Wycliffe, one of the most fiercely abused men in the entire saga of Bible translation, took all attacks in stride and died in his bed after suffering a stroke while hearing mass in his own church at Lutterworth, England.

He was unable to work from Hebrew and Greek versions but was determined that England's common people should have the Scripture in their own tongue. A fervent man said to be perpetually hungry because he was afraid he would take food from the poor by filling his own stomach, Wycliffe, if he did not do all the work, at least led the way in the preparation of the first English-language edition of the entire Bible.

Henry Knighton, a learned historian and ecclesiastical leader of his day, accused him of casting evangelical pearls before swine by rendering the eternal word into so barbaric a language as English. In a letter to the Catholic pontiff Baldassare Cossa, written about 1412, Archbishop Thomas Arundel referred to the Bible translator as "that miserable, pestilential John Wycliffe of damnable memory, son of the old serpent, forerunner and disciple of Antichrist." An anonymous pamphlet called him "the Devells Instrument, Hereticks Idoll, Hypocrites Mirrous, Hatreds Sower, Lyes Forger" and charged that at his death, "stricken by the horrible judgment of God, he breathed forth his wicked soule to the dark mansion of the black devell."

Despite the hatred he stirred up, Wycliffe's translation—a very poor work in terms of scholarship but monumental in its emphasis upon rendering Scripture into common speech—made a tremendous impact.

William Tyndale's New Testament

Numerous printings of William Tyndale's translation of the New Testament in English brought the total number produced to an astonishingly high level for the sixteenth century: at least eighteen thousand copies, published in more than forty editions. The opposition of church authorities was so great that they practically eliminated the hated translation. Yet the vocabulary and literary style of its translator helped shape the subsequent development of the English language.

Looking back from the perspective of centuries, C. S. Lewis concluded that Tyndale was "the best prose writer of his age." He was the first man of letters to use the word "beautiful." He polished many existing idiomatic phrases and coined new terms like scapegoat, long-suffering, and peacemaker. In a unique and distinctive fashion, he made words sing.

Forbidden to publish in England, he fled to Germany in search of a printer. Authorities sent him scurrying from Hamburg to Wittenberg, back to Hamburg and then to Cologne and Worms, where he succeeded in getting completed copies off the press. Smuggled back to England with the help of merchants, they were circulating in illegal channels by April, 1526. Persons in high places as well as low places read Tyndale; Anne Boleyn, wife of King Henry VIII, kept a copy in her room.

After denouncing the rebel who had dared to translate the New Testament into "our English language," the Bishop of London burned a copy in a public ceremony. Cardinal Wolsey agreed that "no burnt offering could be more pleasing to Almighty God." He seized all the copies he could find and through an agent bought others before they could be circulated. Authorities were so zealous and efficient that only two complete copies of the octavo edition are known to exist today; one of them is badly damaged.

But Tyndale's picturesque expressions and unique rhythmic style were picked up by later translators. Some authorities hold that he contributed at least 90 percent of the English used in the King James Version, and 80 percent of that in the Revised Standard Version.

Two Versions of the Lord's Prayer

The Lord's Prayer (Matt. 6:9-13) is the most widely used petition in Christendom. In this modern day, however, several large groups of Christians cling to the language of William Tyndale's pioneer translation. This odd situation arose as a result of early work in translation, has existed for centuries, and may continue long into the future.

William Tyndale rendered verse 12: "And forgeve us oure treaspases, even as we forgeve oure trespacers." Within a few years editors of the Great Bible (1539) pondered the problem of meanings expressed in the Greek original and the connotations of current English terms and altered the verse to read: "And forgeve us our dettes, as we for geve oure detters." Instead of being an innovation, this change represented a return to the vocabulary of John Wycliffe (who spelled the key word "dettis" since the modern form "debts" had not yet taken shape).

Every important English version of the New Testament since the Great Bible has followed its usage. It is *debts* rather than *trespasses* which are stressed in the Lord's Prayer as it appears in the Geneva Bible (1560), the Bishops' Bible (1568), the Rheims New Testament (1582), the King James Version (1611), the English Revised Version (1881), the Revised Standard Version (1946), and many others.

But church officials who compiled the English *Book of Common Prayer* for publication in 1549 turned to Tyndale's language for the Lord's Prayer. Officially sanctioned by both houses of the English parliament, the prayer book was for practical purposes "frozen" so that the language couldn't be changed. Episcopalians and Methodists borrowed from it in framing their own rituals. So in spite of the fact that the King James Version has made "forgive us our debts" proverbial throughout the English-speaking world, members of communions descended from the Church of England persist in beseeching "forgive us our trespasses."

Miles Coverdale's Pioneer Work

Miles Coverdale succeeded in producing the first complete Bible printed in English. Yet he had to overcome so many obstacles that no one knows positively where this epoch-making version was originally printed.

Coverdale had little knowledge of ancient languages. Still, he was humiliated and grieved that his native land lagged behind Germany, France, and Spain. In order to correct a situation in which "yet other nacyons be more plenteously prouyded for with ye scripture in theyre mother tongue, then we," he sought assistance in high places.

There is a possibility that he got unofficial encouragement from Thomas Cromwell, then serving as Chancellor of the Exchequer under King Henry VIII. Whether that is the case or not, he did arrange for unbound sheets to be printed somewhere in Europe. They are known to have been completed on October 4, 1535, but scholars disagree concerning the place of publication. Much evidence points to Zurich, Switzerland. But there are strong arguments in favor of both Marburg and Cologne, Germany. Unless new information is discovered, the debate isn't likely to be resolved.

This much is certain, though. The original title page of the first printed English Bible labeled it as "the holy Scripture of the Olde and New Testament, faithfully and truly translated out of Douche and Latyn." Before printed sheets were bound in England, a new title page was substituted so that the finished work was formally dedicated to the king of England by "his humble subjecte and dayle oratour, Myles Coverdale." Title page notwithstanding, this first edition of the Coverdale Bible was issued without a license. It was not until publication of the second edition in 1537 that the king, through his officers, actually granted permission for the translation to be printed.

John Rogers and Matthew's Bible

Since a Bible version of 1537 is famous under the title Matthew's Bible, it seems that it might have been dedicated to the writer of the First Gospel. But that was not the case. The title grew out of a pseudonym adopted by the translator with the futile hope that this strategem would save his neck.

John Rogers, a Cambridge graduate who became a Lutheran pastor and served for ten years in Wittenberg, took up work on Tyndale's unpublished manuscripts. Using these plus the Tyndale New Testament and the Coverdale Bible, Rogers edited a new edition that was issued from a European press (probably Antwerp) in 1537. Royal sanction was granted as a result of Archbishop Cranmer's interest and Thomas Cromwell's request. Rogers had already inserted on the title page the announcement that it was "set forth with the King's most gracious license." But as a precaution in case of official reprisal, he printed the name Thomas Matthew after the dedication.

Some scholars have suggested that Thomas Matthew may have been a London fish dealer who gave financial support to Rogers. Most, however, think the name is fictional.

In any case, Rogers made the mistake of returning to England during the reign of King Edward VI. He was associated with St. Paul's cathedral for a period. Mary Tudor, often called "Bloody Mary," gained the throne in 1553 and promptly set out to restore Catholicism. Bible-publisher Rogers was arrested, condemned as a heretic, and burned at the stake before the eyes of his wife and eleven children. He was the first of three hundred Protestant martyrs to die between February, 1555, and November, 1558. Though Rogers' name is all but forgotten today and no one reads Matthew's Bible, its blending of Tyndale's New Testament and Coverdale's Old Testament makes it a forerunner of such notable modern works as the Smith-Goodspeed American translation.

The Great Bible of 1539

Thomas Cromwell, vicar-general of King Henry VIII, was the leading figure behind the publication of the Great Bible. Though famous in the history of the English Scriptures, this version gained its title not because of literary excellence but because of its size.

Two Bibles were already available in England in printed form (Coverdale's and Matthew's). Since neither was authorized for public use although they could be read privately, the high-ranking government official set out to correct the situation. He was so successful that he gained the sanction of both king and church to produce "a monumental volume."

Coverdale drew up plans for a Bible so big and beautiful that no printer in England was able to meet his specifications. He made a contract with a Paris house. But before work could be completed, officers of the Roman Catholic Inquisition interfered. Type, skilled printers, paper, and even a printing press were smuggled out of Paris and taken to London. There the new Bible appeared in 1539, pages measuring nine by fifteen inches in size.

Unbound, the huge volume sold for ten to thirteen shillings—about three weeks' wages of a skilled craftsman. Its sale was encouraged by the fact that it bore the inscription "Appointed to be read in Churches." Bishops encouraged each parish in the kingdom to secure a copy and set it up in the church.

But it had several strikes against it. Black-letter type, difficult to read even in the sixteenth century, was used in printing it. Verses weren't numbered, and high cost made it almost prohibitive for private use. Hence, the first (and strictly speaking the only fully) authorized edition of the English Bible never gained wide acceptance.

Tremendous Impact of the Geneva Bible

Pilgrim Fathers who came to the New World on the *Mayflower* conducted daily worship services on the long voyage—using a Bible whose first edition couldn't be printed in England. Though the King James Version was available when the *Mayflower* sailed from Southampton on August 5, 1620, most of the 120 refugees aboard preferred the then familiar Geneva Bible.

Issued in 1560, it was named for the place of publication—Geneva, Switzerland. During the reign of England's "Bloody Mary," many Protestants fled to the city dominated by the influence of John Calvin. With the help of colleagues, William Wittingham published there the Scripture version that was destined to be the most influential English-language work of the sixteenth century.

During the life of Queen Elizabeth, more than ninety editions of the Geneva Bible were published—compared with about forty for all other English versions combined. It became the authorized version for the Scottish kirk and long after the Mayflower reached Plymouth was almost universally used in the Massachusetts and Virginia settlements.

Studded with marginal notes and subtitles introduced to break the monotony of long chapters, it was in every sense a scholarly Bible. But it clearly reflected the puritanical views of those who prepared it; inserted above the account of the death of John the Baptist is a heading which labels it: "The Inconvenience of Dancing."

The Bishops' Bible

Marginal notes in the Geneva Bible gave it a decidedly Calvinistic tone. Largely to combat its "pernicious influence," prelates of the Church of England determined to replace it with a version of their own.

Archbishop Matthew Parker took the leading role in the undertaking. Unlike earlier translators and editors, he drew up a set of formal principles to guide the work. Most of his rules were simple and sensible. The language of the Great Bible was to be followed except in cases where it departed widely from the true sense of the original text; all the latest findings of biblical scholarship were to be employed; and editorial notes fostering controversy or supporting particular doctrines were to be avoided.

Some of the less important principles established proved unworkable, though. Parker wanted the "offensive" language of the New Testament toned down so that it would be suitable to use in the most refined parlor circles. And he suggested that the publisher "bestowe his thickest paper in the New Testament"—on the theory that these pages would be turned much more often and would wear out quicker if paper of uniform thickness was used throughout the volume.

Because eight bishops of the Anglican Church were key figures in the revision, the completed work that included a portrait of Queen Elizabeth came to be known as the Bishops' Bible. It had the sanction of both the throne and the church, and so quickly displaced the Great Bible for church use. But ordinary folk clung to the Geneva Bible so stubbornly that few copies of the new work were sold for private use. In the end popular feeling prevailed over ecclesiastical pressure, for the Geneva Bible continued to be published for forty years after the last edition of the Bishops' Bible was issued.

The Rheims-Douai Version

Religious quarrels divided England at the time Elizabeth, daughter of Henry VIII and Anne Boleyn, gained the nation's throne in 1558. Reversing the policies of Queen Mary, the new monarch supported the Protestant position. "Good Queen Bess" made things so uncomfortable for her Catholic subjects that many of them were driven into exile.

Considerable numbers of these English Catholics formed little colonies in France and Flanders. One such group undertook the task of preparing an English Bible that would be acceptable to officials and members of their faith. They succeeded in getting the New Testament off the press of John Fogny in 1582. From the city in which it originated, it was called the Rheims New Testament. It took more than twenty-five years to complete a companion version of the Old Testament, issued at Douai in 1609/10.

Jesuits who sparked the undertaking were hopeful that it would be a major weapon in their proposed "religious reconquest of the British isles." But their conservative views concerning translation so handicapped them that the Rheims-Douai Version was almost from the time of publication regarded as inferior. Much of the difficulty grew out of the fact that translators felt themselves required to adhere not simply to the meaning, but even to the form of the Latin text of the Vulgate. This resulted in a stiff and sometimes awkward literary style, with little power and no originality. Notoriously inept passages that resulted include: "Our Lord exinanited himself" (Phil. 2:7) and "My chalice which inebriateth me, how goodly it is" (Ps. 23:5). Words like "scenopegia" and "parasceve" were sprinkled through the text.

The Rheims-Douai Version was seldom reprinted and has had little influence upon English and American speech. One critic holds that this Roman Catholic Bible became best known through seventeenth-century Protestant booklets written in attack of it!

A Bible Named for King James

By all odds the most influential English-language Bible ever produced is dedicated to a many-sided monarch. He ruled Scotland as James VI, then added England to his domain at the death of Queen Elizabeth, and ruled that country as James I. He fought Presbyterians for years, persecuted Puritans until they were forced to flee to the New World, asserted the divine right of kings, and alternated between plotting with Rome and thinking up new ways to make Catholics uncomfortable. James even made the *Book of Sports* required reading from the pulpit.

But the group of canny scholars who prepared the version of 1611 dedicated it "to the Most High and Mighty Prince, James, by the Grace of God, King of Great Britain, France, and Ireland, Defender of the Faith." Some contemporary scholars doubt that this princely defender of the faith ever formally sanctioned the dedication to him. Whether he did or not, hosts of persons honor this royal rogue by use of the Bible that bears his name.

First printed in London by Robert Barker it was an instant success; fourteen editions appeared within three years. By 1650 it had become *the* Bible of the English-speaking world. Dozens of other versions and translations now compete with it, but the King James Version continues to outsell them all. Of the thirty million or so Bibles printed annually in the United States, more than half perpetuate the memory of James I.

Appearance and Spelling Altered

Some persons sincerely oppose all attempts to render Scripture into contemporary language and format, insisting that only the King James Version represents the true Word of God. Still, present-day readers inevitably stumble over the words of the hallowed version in its original form.

Gothic type was used in the first printing in 1611. There are no records to indicate that the Church of England ever officially endorsed a change to Roman type, but the Cambridge Bible of 1638 (issued by

Cambridge University Press and accepted as standard for generations) employed type that looks modern by comparison with that used a quarter of a century earlier. Even so, in this edition it is frequently difficult to determine whether a letter is an *s* or an *f*.

In addition to switching from Gothic to Roman type and later redesigning Roman letters, publishers have gradually made many changes in spelling. As a result, a copy of the King James Version published today is radically different from one issued in 1611 or even in 1638.

Here is a facsimile of the Lord's Prayer as reported in Luke—photographed from a copy of the original King James Version.

ND it came to paſſe, that as he was praying in a certaine place, when hee ceaſed, one of his diſciples ſaid vnto him, Lord, teach vs to pray, as Iohn alſo taught his diſciples.

2 And hee ſaid vnto them, When ye pray, ſay, * Our Father which art in heauen, Halowed be thy Name, Thy kingdome come, Thy will be done as in heauen, ſo in earth.

3 Giue vs || day by day our dayly bread.

4 And forgiue vs our ſinnes: for we alſo forgiue euery one that is indebted to vs. And lead vs not into temptation, but deliuer vs from euill.

* Matth. 6. 9.

|| *Or, for the day.*

Thomas Jefferson's Bible

Many notable persons have set out to edit Scripture with the purpose of producing private versions. Of them all, none was more zealous than Thomas Jefferson.

While serving as President of the United States, he devoted many hours to the task of selecting verses and portions of verses from the Gospels in order to form a connected account of "The Life and Morals of Jesus of Nazareth." He originally hoped to publish this condensed and edited version of the Gospel story as a book whose simple form would make it especially useful among the American Indians.

This plan never materialized. So the scholar-president used scissors and paste to fill a blank book with his selected passages in four parallel columns that employed Greek, Latin, French, and English. When he finished, he had the book bound in red morocco with gilt lettering, but it was not published until long after his death. In 1902, Congress voted funds with which to publish 9,000 copies (3,000 for use of the Senate and 6,000 for use of the House) of Jefferson's *The Life and Morals of Jesus of Nazareth.* This book is so rare and expensive that in 1964 a photographic reprint of the President's original paste-up job was issued. The paperback volume now sold at newsstands under the title *The Jefferson Bible* offers a faithful reproduction of the English text as arranged by Jefferson, but gives no hint that his original version made it possible for him to read "His own Testament" in four languages.

The English Revised Version

Few translations of Scripture have received as enthusiastic a reception as the English Revised Version—and no other important one has died so quickly.

As a result of an 1870 resolution by the Church of England Convocation, scholars set out to revise the King James Version. By 1881 the New Testament was finished; issued by the express authority of the church, it constituted an official or "authorized" version.

Public response was immediate and enthusiastic. Within a few days of publication two million copies were sold in England. Two Chicago newspapers issued special sections in which the entire New Testament, as rendered by the English revisers, was printed.

But initial enthusiasm quickly gave way to criticism that the new work was too dependent upon the language of the King James and earlier versions. By the time the Old Testament appeared in 1885, comparatively few persons were sufficiently interested to secure it.

The impact of the English Revised Version was precisely opposite to that of the King James. Published in comparatively small printings and generally received with little enthusiasm, within fifty years the King James Version had won first place in the English-speaking world. Published in huge printings and hailed as a definitive work, the version of 1881-85 was quickly pushed aside and within fifty years was virtually unknown to members of the general public.

Language Changes Since 1611

In all history few languages have changed as much as English has in the last four centuries. It was already in a period of rapid transition at the time the King James Version was issued, and the process of change has continued ever since at an accelerated rate. As a result, scholars list great numbers of words in the Bible whose meanings have been radically altered since 1611.

A few samples are listed here, giving the King James term followed by its present-day equivalent: advertise—advise (Num. 24:14); amazement—terror (I Pet. 3:6); let—hinder (Rom. 1:13); gender—breed (Lev. 19:19); allow—approve (Luke 11:48); communicate unto—share with (Gal. 6:6); damned—condemned (Mark 16:16); compass—circle (Prov. 8:27); by and by—immediately (Matt. 13:21); careful—anxious (Luke 10:41); goodman—my husband (Prov. 7:19); governor—pilot (Jas. 3:4); take no thought—be not anxious (Matt. 6:25); wist—knew (Exod. 16:15); vanity—falsehood (Ps. 12:2). Most of these and other archaic words appear not once, but over and over in the version that to generations of readers was *the* Bible.

A comparatively brief list of archaic and obsolete words from the King James Version, compiled by the American Bible Society, runs to about six hundred words and phrases. It does not include such shifts of meaning as that in "host" as used in the Christmas story (Luke 2:13). Clearly a military word in 1611, it now simply suggests a large number.

Surprising Reception of the RSV

The limitations of existing English-language versions were clearly recognized before World War I. Scholars talked hopefully of a major revision that would have both official standing and popular acceptance, but war and the great financial depression created ever-increasing delays. Serious work on revision was begun in 1937.

By agreement the objective was revision of the American Standard Version of 1901 in the light of the King James Version. But in spite of the fact that this goal was continually emphasized, the resulting work was for practical purposes a new translation and not simply a revision.

Preliminary work on the New Testament was completed in August, 1943, with publication following on February 11, 1946. Contemporary language and modern typography helped it gain quick acceptance with many groups of American Protestants. On September 30, 1952, the Old Testament was published.

When first officially projected in 1936, the RSV was not considered likely to be a financial success. Thomas Nelson & Sons agreed to finance production in return for a ten-year exclusive license to print and sell the new Bible. They invested $3,000,000 in preparation and printing plates and then spent $500,000 on their 1952 advertising campaign.

Results exceeded even the most optimistic forecasts. One year Nelson's bought the entire North American catch of seals in order to secure leather with which to bind pulpit editions of the RSV. Even so, they didn't have enough covering material and were forced to begin using the hides of water buffalo from India.

At the expiration of Nelson's ten-year exclusive license, numerous other publishers were permitted to issue their own editions of the RSV. More than a score of major denominations, plus many smaller ones, now use the text of the RSV exclusively in Sunday school lesson materials.

The New English Bible

More than any other influence, World War II led to publication of a New Testament that set records for best sellers—religious and secular.

Early in 1946 a group of Presbyterians near Glasglow asked the Church of Scotland to take the lead in publishing Scripture "in the language of the present day." Their request grew out of wartime surveys which showed that the majority of persons in Britain no longer really understood the King James Version and as a result had lost interest in the Bible.

Presbyterians succeeded in enlisting the support of British Methodists, Anglicans, Baptists, and Congregationalists. With added backing from the Society of Friends plus church bodies in Wales and Ireland, a joint committee for a new translation was set up.

Though the New Testament in the Revised Standard Version was still brand-new and had been well received, committee members adopted far more radical guidelines than those used for the American venture. They stressed the fact that "the New Testament was originally written in the 'common' language of the time." They concentrated upon producing a translation that would communicate with youth and non-churchmen. Instead of using individual words as the bases for translation, the sentence was treated as central. This led to a free literary style; all attempts at "literal" translation in word-for-word fashion were abandoned.

Released on March 14, 1961, the New Testament set publishing records; 3,965,000 hardbound copies were distributed during the first year. Though sponsored by numerous church bodies, this translation does not have official authorization such as that given to the Revised Standard Version.

The Jerusalem Bible

Jerusalem has no close rival for the place of first importance among biblical cities, yet it wasn't until this century that a major edition of Scripture was published there. Practically all previous translations and versions important to the western world came from printing presses of Europe and America. This tradition was shattered in 1948-55 when the Jerusalem Bible was issued by scholars in the capital city of the Judeo-Christian world.

More than fifty years ago Père Marie-Joseph Lagrange, a French Dominican priest, established a small school of biblical studies in Jerusalem. Scholars didn't regard it as important because it was too remote from great libraries and universities. But during the past half century more major biblical manuscripts have been found than during any comparable period in history. Many were discovered in the Holy Land, and this factor helped make Lagrange's L'Ecole Biblique de Jérusalem a world center for translation and the exchange of information.

Beginning in 1948, scholars associated with the school issued a new French translation of the Bible—published not in a handsome leather-bound edition but in forty-three paper volumes. In 1956 their work was issued in France in one-volume form. From its place of origin it was naturally called *La Bible de Jérusalem.*

Acclaimed by Catholic and Protestant scholars alike, the Jerusalem Bible was issued in an English version in 1966. Scholars who prepared it tried hard for both accuracy and literary power. Among notables who served as editors was J. R. R. Tolkien, author of *The Lord of the Rings.* Though *La Bible de Jérusalem* was constantly used as a guide, the actual work of translation was based upon the original Hebrew and Greek rather than the French. As a result, the Jerusalem Bible is the first complete English translation from the original languages ever made by Roman Catholic scholars.

Good News for Modern Man

In spite of the rising costs of both materials and labor, the cheapest brand-new translation of all time was issued in 1966. Entitled *Good News for Modern Man,* the six-hundred-page paperback volume employs twentieth-century vernacular. Issued by the American Bible Society in connection with its 150th anniversary celebration, the New Testament sold for twenty-five cents a copy. This compares with an estimated cost of at least five hundred dollars for a parchment scroll New Testament during centuries in which these were made.

Though designed for use overseas, *Good News for Modern Man* has had its most spectacular success in the United States.

Soon after the close of World War II, Bible Society workers began searching for an effective way to communicate scriptural truths to persons who use English as a second language. After a period of study and experiment, the Gospel According to Mark was published in a carefully devised vocabulary and style that Bible distributors came to call "today's English." Technical words are avoided and simple line drawings enhance the eye appeal of the text. The impact of Mark's Gospel in "today's English" was so great that the entire New Testament was prepared in a similar style, and was titled Today's English Version of the New Testament.

Current words and active verbs as well as contractions such as "can't," "don't," and "isn't" are used. Obscure or ambiguous terms are avoided while weights, measures, dimensions, and currencies are given modern equivalents or substitutes. For example, in Today's English Version readers learn that the Mount of Olives was about half a mile from Jerusalem—rather than "a sabbath day's journey" (Acts 1:12).

Popular response to the new translation was so great that the first printing of 250,000 copies was exhausted within a week. By the time an additional 100,000 copies could be rushed through the presses, there were back orders for 160,000. More than 4,000,000 copies were produced within a year.

No Stopping Place in Translation

Some Bible readers regard a particular version or translation as "right" and all others as "wrong" or inferior, but most translators agree that no translation suitable for use "from now on" will ever issue from the press.

Two major factors support this point of view.

In the first place, language is fluid and not static. Especially in the case of English, the rate of change is accelerating. Under the impact of the mass media of communication such as television, radio, and newspapers, new words are adopted rapidly. At the same time, old ones are discarded or take on fresh shades of meaning. Paying tribute to the majestic language of the King James Version while stressing the fact that it is rapidly becoming incomprehensible, Alexander Jones of Christ College, Liverpool, has called it "a beautiful mummy embalmed in Elizabethan English."

Hundreds of words that were current just three centuries ago are obsolete, archaic, or so radically altered that earlier connotations are known only to scholars and specialists. This means that a version of Scripture ideally suited for readers at the midpoint of the twentieth century will sound strange and perhaps clumsy to readers in the twenty-first century.

At the same time, the progress of archaeology and research into ways of the past is constantly throwing new light upon words and ideas employed by writers of Scripture. The shades of meaning in first-century Greek are now known far more accurately than they were during the Elizabethan era. Manuscripts older than any previously known to scholars are being found in increasing numbers; some of them yield words and phrases that have been "lost" through scribal changes incorporated in manuscripts previously considered our oldest and most accurate ones.

As a result of these two sets of factors, it is practically certain that as long as men revere the Bible as a living and not a dead book it will be issued in new and contemporary translations suited to the needs of fresh generations of readers.

Some Notable Discoveries

Hilkiah Discovers the Law

The discovery of ancient documents is usually linked with the work of archaeologists, but about twenty-six centuries before the Dead Sea Scrolls created an intellectual storm throughout Christendom, a Jewish high priest made an "archaeological find" that transformed the kingdom of Judah.

Hilkiah, chief officer of the temple of Jerusalem, was given an important commission in the eighteenth year of the reign of the boy king Josiah. He was instructed to make an audit showing the value of the silver held in the temple treasury so that it could be used for much-needed repairs on the building. In the process of searching nooks and crannies to be sure he found all the precious metal on the premises, the high priest came across a scroll, or "Book of the Law," that no one knew existed.

Records do not indicate the details of the actual discovery. There is some evidence that early Hebrews had a custom comparable to that of storing mementos and historic papers in the cornerstones of modern buildings. Hilkiah may have opened a forgotten niche in the foundation of the temple or simply found the scroll under a pile of rubbish in a corner. But once he had it in his hands, he recognized its importance. He first showed it to Shaphan the scribe. This official, in turn, took it to Josiah and read it to him. As a result the king called a solemn public assembly and required his subjects to listen to the laws in the long-lost document. Then he instituted sweeping reforms that temporarily ended pagan practices on the part of the Israelites. (II Kings 22:3–23:25.)

Precisely how long the book was lost or who was responsible for placing a copy in the temple we do not know. But it is generally agreed that the scroll found by Hilkiah forms the core of Deuteronomy.

The Codex Sinaiticus

One of the world's most important manuscripts of the Bible was discovered in a pile of trash.

Count Constantine Tischendorf, a German-born scholar, was responsible for the find. Using Cairo as his headquarters, in 1844 he began a systematic search for old manuscripts. Working out from the city, he visited monasteries and churches. None of them proved fruitful, but from conversation there he learned that the ancient monastery of St.

Catherine was reputed to have many old rolls containing Scripture and devotional works.

Tischendorf rode camelback for ten days through the desert and finally reached Mt. Sinai. At the foot of it was the famous monastery, said to be the oldest in the Coptic branch of Christendom. In the sprawling establishment there were twenty-two chapels—in addition to kitchens, sleeping rooms, and a library. Though the librarian was cordial, he confessed he knew nothing about old parchments, but he vaguely remembered having heard someone say that the monastery had a New Testament that had belonged to the Roman Emperor Theodosius.

After days of searching, the European scholar found 129 parchment leaves 15 by 13½ inches with four columns to a page, written in what to his trained eye was obviously very early Greek. Some of the vellum sheets were salvaged and found to date from the fourth century. Tischendorf succeeded in getting 43 of the 129 sheets; after two more trips to Mt. Sinai, in 1859 he persuaded the monks to give a fourth-century New Testament to the Czar of Russia. As G. S. Wegener tells the story, years later it developed that the 346 leaves of the now priceless Codex Sinaiticus were discovered when monks were gathering rubbish to use as fuel for their ovens. The Codex Sinaiticus was produced shortly before or after the Codex Vaticanus and is thus one of the two oldest complete Bibles in existence.

Sennacherib's Prism

Scientific archaeology had not been born in 1854, but in that year the British Foreign Office launched an expedition at the request of the British Museum. It was headed by J. E. Taylor, an amateur in every sense of the word. He was not particularly interested in biblical relics or inscriptions produced thousands of years earlier; he simply had a job to do. With a group of untrained men he set out to search southern Mesopotamia. His goal was the discovery of ancient monuments.

Though he had not been instructed to dig, he explored the surface layers of a huge red mound now known as Tell al Muqayyar. Situated near the biblical city of Ur, it was built before the pyramids. Even to Taylor's untrained eye it was obvious that the bricks and broken tiles which helped form the mound were extremely old. But weeks of digging and exploring uncovered no splendid monuments and not a single precious stone or object made of gold.

Taylor found nothing more interesting than a quantity of little prisms made of baked clay and covered with inscriptions that he could not decipher. He shipped many of them to London, but scholars who took a look at them were not impressed. During this period there was feverish interest in treasures from the tombs of ancient kings and even statues and household objects from antiquity, but few persons placed any value upon clay prisms. As a result, those uncovered by Taylor were pushed on a storage shelf and forgotten.

Years later, after linguists had learned to decipher ancient cuneiform writing, someone came across the prisms recovered at Tell al Muqayyar. One of them contained a detailed account of events in the reign of Sennacherib, king of Assyria from 705 to 681 B.C. Now generally called "the Taylor prism of Sennacherib," the priceless relic rediscovered on a shelf in the British Museum confirms and amplifies details of the biblical account in II Kings 18–19 and Isaiah 36–37.

A Milestone in the Study of Ancient Literature

Application to the Bible of historical and literary modes of study was not made by high-ranking churchman or professional students of religion. This radical innovation, by which sections of Scripture came to be examined in the same fashion as secular writings, was made by a physician rather than a priest or a pastor.

Born at Sauve, France, in 1684, Jean Astruc studied medicine at the then famous university of Montpellier. The critical examination of writings from classical Greece and Rome was just beginning; earlier it had been a bylaw of scholarship that "what Aristotle says is so"—even if what the ancient scholar reported was flatly contradicted by casual observation.

Astruc was made professor of anatomy at Toulouse, where he served for seven years before returning to Montpellier as professor of medicine. Later he was appointed superintendent of the mineral waters for the health resorts in the region of Languedoc. In 1729 he became first physician to the king of Poland. Two years later he was named professor of medicine at the University of Paris, where he was frequently consulted concerning the health of King Louis XV.

An ardent student of Scripture, he applied to his Bible some of the principles he had earlier used for the study of ancient works on medicine and physic. Centuries earlier, commentators had noticed that there are two separate accounts of the creation in the book of Genesis. Astruc took the revolutionary step of trying to separate the material on the basis of literary style. Though he didn't succeed very well by modern standards, he arrived at the conclusion that Moses couldn't have written the whole of Genesis. His book on this problem, published in 1753, marks a milestone not only in the study of Scripture but also in the attempt to develop scientific methods for the interpretation of documents from dead cultures.

The Moabite Stone

A world-famous inscription, used by scholars in the early phase of modern detective work by which much knowledge of the ancient Hebrews has been obtained, exists only as a reconstruction. Portions of its message are known only through a copy executed less than a century ago.

Universally known as the Moabite Stone because it told the story of Israel's victory over Moabite armies, the relic was about three feet high. Since kings and rulers of that epoch usually had commemorative stones made soon after the events they describe, the Moabite Stone is presumed to date from the ninth century B.C.

An otherwise forgotten German missionary, F. A. Klein, made the find. Scientific archaeology had hardly been launched in 1868. Still, he sensed that there was something special about the slab of black volcanic rock that he found in the sand near the village of Dibon, east of the Jordan River. Klein tried to buy the piece from local bedouins but was not adept at haggling and failed to seal the purchase.

But he made a sketch of the site and published a report describing the thirty-four lines of writing on the stone.

Charles Clermont-Ganneau, a noted Hebrew scholar of the era, used Klein's directions to locate the stone. Though he couldn't gain possession of it, he used a putty-like substance to make a complete impression. A bit later the French government provided him with funds to purchase it; but when he returned to bargain with tribesmen of the area, he found that they had used gunpowder to blow it into many small pieces with the hope of getting more money by selling the fragments one at a time.

Two large chunks and eighteen smaller pieces were eventually found, but it proved impossible to secure and assemble all the fragments. Clermont-Ganneau's "squeeze" copy provided a basis for combining the original fragments and plaster restorations. Scholars of the world later traveled to the Louvre in Paris to study it.

The Moabite Stone substantiates and amplifies the biblical record of I Kings 16 and II Kings 3:4-27. In addition it is of special significance because it reveals a great deal about the influence of Phoenician writing upon the development of early Hebrew script.

Tunnel Building Commemorated

Tunnel building was among the earliest large-scale building enterprises carried out by man. Natural caves and tunnels, it is thought, suggested the idea of putting dwellings and tombs underground; eventually conduits for drainage, water supply, and other needs were built. Still, nineteenth-century experts considered it a radical innovation to design and execute tunnels in such fashion that two crews started simultaneously—one at each end—and dug until they met in the middle.

Actually, this sophisticated building technique was used in Bible times. Late in the eighth century B.C. Hezekiah, king of Judah, became alarmed about the possibilities of an Assyrian invasion. He felt Jerusalem's walls were strong enough to repel the enemy, but the city didn't have a suitable water supply to withstand a long siege. So Hebrew engineers designed an S-shaped tunnel to convey water 1,760 feet from the spring of Gihon into the city. It terminated near the spot where the famous pool of Siloam was later located. Cutting into solid rock and working from both ends toward the middle, crews were practically "on target" when they met in the middle.

About 1880, archaeologists discovered a commemorative inscription twenty feet from the Siloam entrance. It represents one of the few known examples of Hebrew script written in eighth century B.C. style and the earliest record of tunnel building from both ends toward the middle. "While the excavators were still lifting up their picks," it says, "and while there were yet three cubits to excavate there was heard the voice of one calling to another. On the day they completed the boring through, the stonecutters struck pick against pick; and water flowed from the spring to the pool, a distance of a hundred cubits. And a hundred cubits was the height of the rock above the heads of the stonecutters."

Cairo's Abandoned Treasures

Virtually all peoples have devised some equivalent of the nineteenth-century attic and the twentieth-century storage room. Even buildings dedicated to study and worship need places to put things not good enough to use but too good (or too sacred) to discard. As a result, many an early Jewish synagogue was equipped with a storage bin, or *genizah*. Hundreds of them were searched without success in the nineteenth-century heyday of enthusiasm for ancient manuscripts of the Bible. A single bin in Cairo, crammed with discarded scrolls and documents, gave new understanding of the Hebrew language and hence of the Old Testament.

As early as 1864 Jacob Saphir knew that the Cairo synagogue—formerly a Christian church—included an especially large genizah. His records indicate that he got permission to look through it but didn't see anything that particularly interested him. Since the room had been walled up long ago and was never used, it remained untouched for another quarter century.

Then it became necessary to renovate the building. In the process, rabbis opened the genizah and found it full of old documents—by this time in considerable demand as souvenirs for tourists. Some of their ancient "junk" entered the market with the result that Solomon Schechter of Cambridge University became interested. He succeeded in buying the entire contents of the storage room, with no idea of what it might contain.

So many ancient manuscripts were secured that it took a decade to make the first tentative catalog of them. Today they fill more than 150 display cases in the Cambridge Library. Secular documents predominate over religious, and there are Mohammedan ones in addition to Jewish and Christian. Only one portion of Scripture—Ecclesiasticus—is complete. But in conjunction with other dust-covered writings it gave scholars the key to the development of Hebrew "punctuation" by which vowel sounds are added to words originally made up entirely of consonants.

A Lost Speech of Moses?

A controversial document was placed on the market about the middle of the nineteenth century by a Polish Jew who lived in Jerusalem. After becoming a convert to Christianity, M. W. Shapira made a name for himself as a dealer in antiquities as well as an expert on ancient documents and curios. One of his important customers was the British Museum; he also sold some rare and fine items to the Berlin Museum.

About 1882 he announced to potential customers that he had the greatest find of his career. This was a scroll preserved by having been embalmed somewhat like a mummy, which he said had come to him from a band of bedouins. They, in turn, had found it in a cave near a wadi (dry river bed) about whose location they remained politely vague.

Shapira had made a careful examination of the manuscript. He estimated its age at approximately three thousand years—which meant that it was written shortly after the death of Moses. It included much of the book of Deuteronomy and preserved a hitherto unknown public speech by Moses.

Since there are clear indications in Scripture that Moses actually spoke and wrote messages not included in the text, the story was not implausible. So eager institutional heads investigated the possibility of raising funds to cover the purchase price: one million pounds.

Though other prospective purchasers were competing, a tentative agreement was reached with the British Museum. Charles Clermont-Ganneau, the most renowned authority then living, was asked by the prospective purchasers to examine the find. He concluded it to be a forgery—largely on the basis of doubt that the parchment could be as old as represented, plus the fact that Shapira had earlier sold some ancient pots that proved to be fake. Officials of the British Museum not only refused to pay for the scroll; they also asked for the arrest of Shapira. He got word of this development and shot himself. In the hubbub that followed, museum workers failed to catalog the scroll and have never been able to trace it. After World War II one scholar announced the discovery of new evidence supporting the view that the Shapira scroll actually did preserve a lost speech of Moses, but unless the manuscript that the museum acquired for nothing is identified and checked by present-day techniques, the mystery concerning its authenticity will never be solved.

Deissmann Identifies New Testament Greek

For centuries experts recognized that the Greek of the New Testament varied widely from that employed by classical writers and so considered it framed especially for works of piety. Many went so far as to hold that its purity stemmed from dictation by the Holy Spirit.

Just before the beginning of this century a young German pastor —later noted as a scholar—looked over a collection of archaeological finds dating from about two thousand years earlier. Adolf Deissmann insisted that these household records and commercial papers were written in the language employed by Gospel writers, so he proposed that "New Testament Greek" was actually the tongue of the common man rather than the trained scribe.

His suggestion was rejected as nonsense by a generation of experts, but it later proved to be correct. Tremendous bodies of evidence, uncovered in recent decades, support the view that in their original form most or all documents in the New Testament were written in the vernacular rather than the learned form of Greek. In order to distinguish it from literary Greek it came to be called *koine dialektos* ("the common speech"), now usually abbreviated in English to Koine. In the first century A.D. this was the language of commerce, politics, personal correspondence, and street-corner talk throughout most of the eastern portion of the Roman Empire. Discovery of this basic factor has greatly fostered the production of English-language translations rendered into everyday rather than academic speech.

Papyri from the Island of Elephantine

Few episodes of the Old Testament are so precisely dated as events described in the book of Ezra. Sacrificial worship in the temple interrupted by war and captivity was resumed by the Hebrews in the seventh month (Ezra 3:1-7) of a year identified from secular records of the period as 538 B.C. Because the scriptural text deals with so remote a period, a letter incorporated in it has given scholars no end of trouble.

According to the biblical account, a diplomatic letter was addressed to Artaxerxes, king of Persia, by a group of Hebrew leaders. There is specific reference to the fact that the message was not written in Hebrew. Translators of the King James Version made an informed guess and translated the key passage as reporting that "the writing of the letter was written in the Syrian tongue" (Ezra 4:7). Growing knowledge of ancient languages led to the recognition that the tongue here mentioned is not Syrian but Aramaic.

This created a problem, for linguists considered Aramaic (which may have been the language spoken by Jesus) as a comparatively late formation. Experts dismissed the reference in Ezra as founded on tradition, since they didn't think Aramaic was used in that epoch.

All this changed in 1903 through the chance discovery of the Elephantine papyri. Scholars who were primarily interested in Egyptian history were working at the site of an ancient military colony on the island of Elephantine near present-day Aswan. In addition to relics from the land of the Nile, they uncovered a group of letters dating from the end of the fifth century B.C. Penned by Jews who were living on the island, they proved to be written in Aramaic rather than Hebrew. This discovery gave dramatic confirmation to the report that the letter quoted in Ezra 4:11-16 employed a language already well established and widely used both in commerce and diplomacy and proved, once more, that the biblical record is astonishingly accurate.

The Chalice of Antioch

Far the most controversial drinking vessel known to man, the "cup" used by Jesus and his disciples for the Last Supper (Matt. 26:27; Mark

14:23; Luke 22:17) is not described in the Gospels. Nor is there a hint as to what was done with it when the ritualistic meal was finished.

Very early there arose a legend according to which Joseph of Arimathea took the cup from the table after the Last Supper and used it to catch some of Jesus' blood at the Crucifixion. After his death it was reputed to have been taken to England and handed down from generation to generation of his descendants.

It was this cup, by then revered as the Holy Grail, which figured in many stories about King Arthur and his knights of the Round Table. Having disappeared due to the sinfulness of its guardians, the story ran, the Holy Grail could be recovered only by a pure and spotless seeker. According to one tradition, Sir Galahad found the Holy Grail at Glastonbury and took it to the mysterious city of Serras in the East, where it again vanished.

Archaeologists became tremendously excited about 1910 when Arabs digging a well near Antioch turned up a magnificent silver chalice. Decorated with grapevines in which appear various small birds, animals, and insects, the Chalice of Antioch also bears two representations of a youthful and beardless Jesus. For a time it was seriously proposed that this exquisite piece of craftsmanship was in fact the Holy Grail. More recent investigations support the view that it was made no earlier than the late fourth century, but was perhaps fashioned as a symbolic reminder of the potent and fabulous cup which itself may have been unadorned clay.

Jewelry from Ur of the Chaldees

Until comparatively recent times many persons considered Ur to be just another in a long list of obscure settlements mentioned in the Bible and beyond identification. Not so. Abraham's journey from Ur (Gen. 11:31) represents an early example of turning one's back upon a highly developed urban culture in order to seek a new life in frontier land.

Located close to the mouth of the great Euphrates River in lower Mesopotamia (present-day Iraq), Ur was a major metropolis by the time her most influential dynasty of kings began reigning about 2700 B.C. Much earlier than that, Queen Shubad was given a funeral that indicates the size and wealth of the city. Buried with her about 5,000 years ago were twenty-nine finger rings plus garters of lapis lazuli and a string of golden beads. She wore a thick black wig and a jeweled cap of gold with silver fillets, held in place by a delicate gold-tooth comb.

But the most remarkable piece of jewelry created in Abraham's city centuries before he was born was Queen Shubad's personal diadem. Made entirely of gold, it consisted of elaborate rosettes, flowerets, and palmettes which formed a background for tiny stags, antelopes, and bearded bulls. Many of the pieces buried with Shubad were discovered by Sir Leonard Woolley in a series of archaeological expeditions and are now housed in the British Museum and the Museum of the University of Pennyslvania.

"We Have Found the Flood!"

The tangled account in Scripture has given ammunition to many skeptics, yet experts now think there really was a great deluge (Gen. 6:5–9:17).

Two separate traditions enter into the biblical story. This is made clear by the fact that at one point the rain is said to have fallen for forty days (Gen. 7:12), while at another (Gen. 7:24) the waters continue to rise for 150 days. The entire body of evidence collected by geophysicists strongly argues against the fact that there ever was a period when all the earth was covered by flood waters many feet deep. Hence scholars for many years were inclined to dismiss the whole story as an ancient myth.

This point of view was seriously challenged by the discovery that Mesopotamian literature also includes reports of a universal deluge. One of the longest and best-preserved accounts is included in the famous Gilgamesh Epic, whose discovery and translation marked a major landmark in the history of archaeology.

On the basis of evidence from Scripture plus the Gilgamesh Epic and other ancient documents, British archaeologist Sir Leonard Woolley concluded that there really was a deluge of such proportions that it virtually wiped out the whole of the ancient civilization that was concentrated in the Near East.

At Ur of the Chaldees he dug for months, trying to find the oldest and lowest layer of debris in a group of big mounds. At the 2800 B.C. level he reached the bottom of a tomb; below it were bits of broken pottery that dated from about 3000 B.C. Evidently this marked the beginning of Ur as an inhabited place. Still digging, the archaeologist found a deposit of clay ten feet thick—and beneath that clay were traces of a Stone Age settlement. Only an enormous flood could have deposited so thick a layer of sediment. In 1929 Woolley triumphantly announced to the world: "We have found the flood!" Most scholars think it probable that his discovery does pinpoint the region whose inundation is recorded in the story of Noah and the flood.

Oldest Known Fragment of the New Testament

Though it hasn't settled the question to the satisfaction of Bible scholars, a fragment of papyrus found in 1935 has helped to reopen the question of whether or not the Gospel of John was written by the apostle of that name.

Scholars of the late nineteenth century were practically unanimous in regarding John as the latest of the four Gospels. Largely on the basis of evidence about Greek literary style, it came to be taken for granted that this account of Jesus' life and message was committed to writing no earlier than the middle of the second century. Even taking into account the possibility that the brother of James may have lived to be a very old man, such a date challenges the arguments in favor of apostolic authorship. Had John written about A.D. 150, he would have been at least 140 years old.

Scholarly evidence to the contrary, many Christians clung stubbornly to the conviction that only John the apostle could have written so tender and perceptive an account as that which bears his name, so the gap between supporters and challengers of this view grew wider with passing years.

All this changed as a result of a chance discovery. A tiny bit of frayed papyrus, now known as Papyrus Bodmer II, was uncovered in Egypt. It took only a short time to determine that the characters scrawled on it conveyed part of the eighteenth chapter of John.

In itself, that was not especially noteworthy; there are thousands of New Testament fragments in existence, some of which date from the days of the late Roman Empire. But painstaking study demonstrated that Papyrus Bodmer II was produced shortly before or during the reign of the emperor Trajan, who sat on the throne from A.D. 98 to 117. Generally conceded to be the oldest existing manuscript of any portion of the New Testament, it has helped persuade some contemporary experts that John may be the earliest of the Gospels—and could have been dictated by the apostle himself in his extreme old age.

King Solomon's Mines Rediscovered

Modern technology requires vast amounts of copper, whose properties are such that for many uses no substitute is suitable. For centuries it had been assumed that copper used long ago in the Holy Land was imported. But a Bible expert began to ponder.

Scripture mentions brass many times, remembered Nelson Glueck of Hebrew Union College. Brass is not a pure metal, but an alloy compounded of copper and other ingredients. Tracing Old Testament references one by one, the scholar stopped at Deut. 8:9, where the region promised to the chosen people by Jehovah is described as "a land whose stones are iron, and out of whose hills thou mayest dig brass." If those ancient words were accurate and not merely poetic, there *had* to be copper within a short distance of Jerusalem.

Glueck had color photos made from high-flying planes. These indicated the presence of small quantities of copper on some ridges. Exploring downward from them in three archaeological campaigns from 1938 to 1940, he uncovered the remains of equipment used in copper smelters a few miles south of the Sea of Galilee in the Wadi el Arabah. From these he traced unworked veins of the metal. Contrary to suggestions by writers of biblical novels, the fabulous mines of King Solomon yielded copper—not gold, silver, or gems.

In 1957 acute shortages of copper led to the reopening of King Solomon's copper mines, discovered as a result of detective work in Scripture.

Chance Finding of First Dead Sea Scroll

The Dead Sea Scrolls constitute one of the most important biblical archaeological finds of all times. Their intrinsic value is less than that of treasures found in royal tombs of Near Eastern lands, but their significance for the study of the Bible and the background from which it came is without par. The central characters in the drama that set off a chain reaction were not scholars or professional students of antiquity—they were a goat and a boy.

In company with older herdsmen Mohammed adh-Dhib was following a route that took the men and their animals along a path close to the cliff that rims the west side of the Dead Sea. One spring morning a sturdy goat strayed away from the rest of the flock. Fifteen-year-old Mohammed followed him, chased him without success, and then threw a stone to distract his attention.

As he later told the story, the boy lost sight of the stone and surmised that it must have fallen into a cave. Caves sometimes contain treasure; this one looked as though it hadn't been disturbed in a long time. Mohammed pushed and scrambled his way through a cleft, entered a chamber, and searched it. To his disappointment it contained nothing more than clay jars that seemed to be stuffed with old leather, but Mohammed reported his adventure to the leader of his band. He decided to take a look for himself, and with the hope that the jars might bring a few copper coins took some of them with him to Bethlehem.

The jars proved practically worthless, but the old rolls of leather they contained were destined to become world famous as the first of the Dead Sea Scrolls, presumably hidden in sealed jars during a time when Jews were in open conflict with Roman occupation troops. Monks believed to have called themselves *chasidim* or "holy ones" established a community that once probably had four thousand inhabitants. They built numerous sturdy buildings—but were no match for Roman soldiers. Qumran monastery is believed to have been destroyed about the time Jerusalem was laid waste in the aftermath of the siege of the year A.D. 70.

Documents Written Before the Time of Moses

Ugarit was in ancient times an important city. Located on the north Syrian coast about fifty miles southwest of Antioch, it was the capital of the surrounding region. Destroyed by an earthquake and rebuilt, it was later captured and razed by invaders from the sea. Since the twelfth century B.C. the site has been unoccupied.

Excavations by Claude F. A. Schaeffer from 1929 to 1937 yielded several hundred clay tablets. Unlike most found earlier the Ras Shamra tablets, as they came to be called, were religious texts rather than commercial documents. Written in a cuneiform script, they employed twenty-nine letters of which only three were vowels. Scribes probably produced them in the period shortly after 1400 B.C.

When deciphered, these "lost Canaanite texts" shed new light upon both the Hebrew language and the religious backgrounds of the Old Testament. Literary relics buried under the debris of Ugarit for three thousand years revealed that the chief deity in the Canaanite pantheon was El. Though it seldom appears in English translations, this name was frequently applied to Jehovah in books that became part of our Old Testament.

Strong tensions between Canaanite and Israelite religious systems are stressed in Scripture; discovery of the Ras Shamra tablets shows that the conflict was real and not theoretical or imaginary. As a result, some instances of "wanton cruelty" on the part of the chosen people are better understood. The extermination of the inhabitants of Canaanite cities (notably Ai and Jericho) was a policy forced by the tension between Israelites and Canaanites. Religiously as well as politically, competition was so keen that it was a case of "destroy Jehovah's foes and their gods—or see Israel perish and all homage to her God cease."

Bibliography and Index

Bibliography

The works listed below were particularly important in the preparation of this volume. Most of them are current books still in print; others are available from libraries. Numerous other books that were consulted concerning one or two topics are so specialized that they are not listed here. Extensive use was made of the American Bible Society *Record* for the years 1900-1966 and other publications of the Society.

Albright, William F. *The Archaeology of Palestine.* Rev. ed. Baltimore: Penguin Books, 1960.

Auclair, Marcelle. *Christ's Image.* [Christian art.] Trans. Lionel Izod. New York: Tudor, 1961.

Bouquet, Alan C. *Everyday Life in New Testament Times.* New York: Charles Scribner's Sons, 1954.

Brewer, E. Cobham. *Dictionary of Phrase & Fable.* 8th Rev. ed. by John Freeman. New York: Harper & Row, 1964.

De Vaux, Roland. *Ancient Israel.* Trans. John McHugh. New York: McGraw-Hill, 1961.

Emmrich, Kurt. (Peter Bamm, pseud.) *The Kingdoms of Christ.* Trans. Christopher Holme. New York: McGraw-Hill, 1960.

Freedman, David N., and Campbell, Edward F., eds. *The Biblical Archaeologist Reader.* Vol. II. Anchor Books ed. New York: Doubleday, 1964.

———, and Wright, G. Ernest, eds. *The Biblical Archaeologist Reader.* Anchor Books ed. New York: Doubleday, 1961.

Fulghum, W. B., Jr. *A Dictionary of Biblical Allusions in English Literature.* New York: Holt, Rinehart & Winston, 1965.

Grant, Michael. *The World of Rome.* New York: World, 1960.

Gray, John. *Archaeology and the Old Testament World.* London: Thomas Nelson & Sons, 1962.

Greenblatt, Robert B. *Search the Scriptures.* [A physician's view of many biblical incidents.] Philadelphia: J. B. Lippincott, 1963.

Greenslade, S. L., ed. *The West from the Reformation to the Present Day.* (*The Cambridge History of the Bible,* Vol. II.) Cambridge: Cambridge University Press, 1963.

Harrison, R. K. *The Archaeology of the Old Testament.* London: English University Press, 1963.

Illustrated World of the Bible Library. 5 vols. Trans. Merton Dagut. New York: McGraw-Hill, 1961.

The Interpreter's Dictionary of the Bible. 4 vols. Nashville: Abingdon, 1962.

Jones, Clifford M. *New Testament Illustrations*. Cambridge: Cambridge University Press, 1966.

Keller, Werner. *The Bible as History*. Trans. William Neil. New York: William Morrow, 1956.

———. *The Bible as History in Pictures*. Trans. William Neil. New York: William Morrow, 1964.

Kenyon, Kathleen M. *Archaeology in the Holy Land*. New York: Frederick A. Praeger, 1960.

Knowlson, T. Sharper. *The Origins of Popular Superstitions and Customs*. London: T. Werner Laurie, 1934.

Kraeling, Emil G. *Rand McNally Bible Atlas*. New York: Rand McNally, 1956..

———. *The Four Gospels*. (*The Clarified New Testament*, Vol. I.) New York: McGraw-Hill, 1962.

Lowrie, Walter. *Art in the Early Church*. 2nd rev. ed. Torchbooks ed. New York: Harper & Row, 1965.

Margolis, Max L., and Marx, Alexander. *A History of the Jewish People*. Philadelphia: Jewish Publication Society of America, 1927.

McKenzie, John L. *Dictionary of the Bible*. Milwaukee: Bruce, 1965.

Miller, Madeleine S., and Miller, J. Lane. *Encyclopedia of Bible Life*. Rev. ed. New York: Harper & Row, 1955.

———. *Harper's Bible Dictionary*. 7th ed. New York: Harper & Row, 1961.

Nelson, Lawrence E. *Our Roving Bible*. Apex ed. Nashville: Abingdon, 1945.

Newton, Eric, and Neil, William. *2,000 Years of Christian Art*. New York: Harper & Row, 1966.

Plumb, J. H. *The Horizon Book of the Renaissance*. New York: American Heritage, 1961.

Reumann, John. *Four Centuries of the English Bible*. Philadelphia: Fortress, 1961.

———. *The Romance of Bible Scripts and Scholars*. Englewood Cliffs, N. J.: Prentice-Hall, 1965.

Wegener, Gunther S. *6,000 Years of the Bible*. Trans. Margaret Shenfield. New York: Harper & Row, 1963.

White, Andrew D. *A History of the Warfare of Science with Theology in Christendom*. 2 vols. Gloucester, Mass.: Peter Smith, 1965.

Wright, G. Ernest. *Biblical Archaeology*. Rev. ed. Philadelphia: Westminster, 1963.

Yadin, Yigael. *The Art of Warfare in Biblical Lands*. Trans. M. Pearlman. 2 vols. New York: McGraw-Hill, 1963.

Index